This book is dedicated to my Parents,
Teachers and Students

About the Book:

This book brings into picture the holistic approach of gaining knowledge relating to the long volatile war against the insurgency activities of Northeast India since its beginning and today's developmental aspects and Governmental policies and success in bringing it down. This book is purely based on profuse research articles, current events and historical data.

About the Author:

Rajat Paul is an educator, Blogger, and knowledge-based content creator. Presently employed with Assam Financial Corporation, Govt of Assam. Ex-employed with Assam State Warehousing Corporation, Govt of Assam and Army Public School, Jorhat. With 5+ Years of teaching experience in competitive exams (online youtube and offline) after completing M.COM (Hons) from Calcutta University, B.COM (Hons) from Gauhati Commerce College, Certified Financial Planner (Inter), and other certification courses from various institutions he kept on writing many articles on his blogging platform and various newspapers focusing on Social Issues, Internal Security of Northeast India and so on.

Awards: 1. Best content writer of 2020's Assam Tourism Development Corporation competition. 2. Assam Book of Record winner.

Administrator of Facebook Page: Northeast India (Sharing of Daily News and Important General Knowledge).

I wish everyone all the very best and suggestions are welcomed at my e-mail I'd which is rajatpaul304@gmail.com.

Follow My YouTube Channel : North East India for more updates.

Contents

1. Scenario

When we talk about unrest, militancy, insurgency, and separatism in India eventually either we are talking about Jammu and Kashmir or the Seven Northeastern states. Yes, here we will discuss and highlight the issues that led to the militancy and insurgency in the northeast since independence and how successful the government of India has been in solving it. We will also discuss all the militant organizations and India's counter operations and most importantly the reasons that led the people of North-east to hold arms and ask for separation instead of joining the Union of India.

For centuries, western and central India witnessed the thunderous march of many armies. Some were led by plunderers who returned with the loot, and some by more ambitious warlords who stayed back to establish their dynastic rule. All through this, the northeastern region had remained by and large unaffected. Emperors in Delhi rarely set their eyes beyond the Gangetic plains and even the rulers in Patliptura did not find reasons enough to venture far into the east. Similarly, it was only their commercial interests in tea and oil that led the British into Assam. They too let the myriad tribal societies in the east continue with their old ways. Following the Japanese invasion, some arterial road infrastructural facilities were created to sustain campaigning in Burma. By and large, however, the region remained undeveloped.

Ever since Independence, the people of the northeastern states have been restive. This is because these states, though they are rich in natural resources, have experienced little industrial or economic growth. Unemployment has caused frustration among the youth. Demographic changes threatened the continuation of the special ethnic identity of these people as also their culture and traditions. To crown it all, this jungle-covered mountainous terrain having porous borders with many neighboring countries, provides an ideal setting for the growth of insurgency. Not surprisingly, therefore, for the past four decades, the formations and the units of Eastern Command have remained heavily committed. Some facets of this gnawing threat from within, highlight the complexities of the Command's task at hand.

The insurgency in Nagaland was the first one to begin and it set the tone for the others that followed.

In February 1947, it was formally announced that the British rule in India was to come to an end. Soon thereafter, the Naga National Council (NNC) set down their demands for an interim Naga Government for ten years. The matter could not be resolved despite many rounds of talks. Consequently, on 14 August 1947, Mr Z Phizo, who was then the most powerful spokesman of the Nagas, declared independence. He was arrested and was jailed for two years. Incidentally, he had been arrested earlier also for collaborating with the Japanese and had been released only in 1946. Be that as it may, despite the government's efforts to solve this vexed problem, the Naga secessionist demand for an independent state continued. By 1953, the hostile elements had become bold enough to attack policemen and to snatch away their weapons. By 1955, the Konyaks, a warring tribe, began resorting to attacking Assam Rifles personnel. In 1956, an infantry battalion was deployed in the area and it did well to quickly suppress the hostiles. With that commenced Eastern Command's unending and ever-increasing involvement in CI operations. Soon Phizo announced the formation of his 'government' and also started raising an armed wing. Initial cadres were armed with anything from muzzleloaders to assorted weapons left behind by the retreating British and Japanese armies in Burma.

The growing activities of the hostiles led to the deployment of a brigade in Nagaland. The grouping of villages was attempted in 1957, as had been done in Malaya before, but it did not persist. Years rolled by as the moderates held a series of parleys with the Centre while the underground Nagas stuck to their hostile ways. There was no let up even when Nagaland came into being as a separate state in 1963. The insurgents stepped up their activities when troops from Nagaland were pulled out during the Sino-Indian conflict of 1962. The 8 Mountain Division was raised in 1963 to combat insurgency in Nagaland. The Counter Insurgency and Jungle Warfare (CIJW) School was established at Vairangte, Mizoram to impart pre-induction training to all the incoming units. Towards the end of the 1960s, 8 Mountain Division had well over thirty battalions under command, including those of the Assam Rifles and the other Central Police Organisations. They had notched up a series of spectacular successes as some of the gang leaders − self-styled 'Generals' − and their gangs were intercepted. Thinning out of the troops for the 1971 operations gave a breather to the insurgents once again.

Hardliners shunned the Shillong Accord of 1975 and the triumvirate of Swu, Khaplang, and Muivah formed the National Socialist Council of Nagaland (NSCN). It soon became the most powerful underground organization in the northeast. Between 1980-86, over 300 security personnel are estimated to have lost their lives due to the NSCN 's militant activities. As a result, in February 1985, Headquarters 3 Corps was raised to ensure a more coordinated employment of all troops combating insurgency. Consequently, the formations of 3 Corps launched large-scale operations, in conjunction with units of the Myanmar Army, to gain the upper hand over the NSCN. By then, some cracks had begun to appear amongst the NSCN's top leadership and the ensuing inter-gang rivalry in 1988 left the organization disjointed for a while. However, the pulling out of troops of the 8 Mountain Division for employment in Jammu and Kashmir gave them time to regroup yet again.

Thus, there have been many ups and downs during the long-drawn-out insurgency in Nagaland. The quantum of deployment of troops has increased steadily over the years. Army units have carried out endless cordon and searches of villages, interceptions, and raids to maintain a strike rate higher than the insurgent's ability to recoup. More importantly, formations and units of the Eastern Command have initiated many steps to win the hearts and minds of the people. The insurgencies in Mizoram and Tripura have also run a similar course. The undercurrents of frustration among the youth in the Mizo Hill Districts were akin to the ones in Nagaland. By the mid-1950s, the signs of discontentment and uneasiness were visible. Besides, the ongoing activities in Nagaland had not escaped the attention of the Mizos. Matters came to a head, when, towards the end-1950s, relief measures for the famine hit Mizos failed to ease their plight. A voluntary organization sprung up to lend a helping hand. Soon, however, under the leadership of La Denga, the organization came to be known as the Mizo National Front (MNF) and went on to raise the demand for an independent state. With easy access to the Chittagong hill tracts in East Pakistan, their hostile activities grew. Lal Denga was arrested in 1963 but was released almost immediately. By 1966, the MNF was in full cry and had raided several armories and treasuries and a few far-flung police posts in the southern parts of Mizoram. These incidents led to the Army's deployment and the launching of combing operations that forced the rebels to disperse and flee. The grouping of villages was undertaken with greater care and strictness. Soon, matters quietened and the Mizo Hill district was given the status of a Union Territory.

In January 1975, the hostiles raised their head once again and, in a daring act, killed three senior police officers. The Army launched relentless operations yet again and by the year-end, had broken the cohesion of MNF hostiles for good. Consequent to a series of talks in 1976, Lal Denga gave up his demand for an independent state. The princely state of Manipur had formally merged with India in October 1949. As is usual, a small section of the people was against such a merger. Their leader, Irabot, died in 1951 and Manipur remained quiet for a decade and a half.

However, trouble started in a different form in the mid-1960s when the frustrated and unemployed Meiteis objected to settlers coming to their state from elsewhere. Some of them decided to resort to violence and found their way to East Pakistan to seek help. That, however, came to an end with the liberation of Bangladesh. Thereafter, all the splinter groups in Manipur came together again to form the Peoples Liberation Army (PLA) and commenced their efforts afresh to seek support from other underground outfits. Some of their emissaries even trekked to Lhasa to seek Chinese assistance. The end-1970s saw numerous killings, extortion, and encounters as PLA members increased their hostile acts. The Army was called out and was soon gaining ground. Acting on a tip-off, Second Lieutenant Pithawalla raided a hideout in July 1981 to kill seven top leaders and also to capture Bisheshwar, the PLA chief, with his trusted associates. This young and spirited officer earned a well-deserved Ashok Chakra (AC) – the highest peacetime award for gallantry. The hostile organisation had barely regrouped when in April 1982, the new PLA chief and eight of his associates were eliminated. However, quite contrary to the assessment of the Army and other intelligence agencies, the PLA was to emerge yet again.

For two good reasons, a scan of insurgency in Assam is merited. Firstly, being the entry point for the entire northeastern region, happenings in Assam have wider ramifications. Secondly, unlike other insurgencies of this region, the one in Assam also has an urban touch and a degree of technical sophistication.

For long the people of Assam have harboured the feeling of being exploited. They also strongly resent the 'foreigners' since these outsiders have gradually taken over the control of the civil administration and business in the state. In the 1970s, there were a series of agitations and the All Assam Student's Union (AASU) emerged as a forceful party. In April 1979, a secessionist organization came into being. It raised its banner at Rang Ghar in Sibsagar where Ahom kings used to witness tusker fights. Misguided cadres, acting against the 'exploiters', soon acquired a Robin Hood image. They had swanky motorcycles, moved about in urban centers, and frequently made long-distance calls to remain in contact. They knew the power of the media and they had learned to use improvised explosive devices (IEDs).

The signing of the Assam Accord in 1985 did nothing to curb hostile acts. Soon they are indulging in weapon snatching, kidnapping, and killings. In November 1990, Assam was declared a disturbed area and the Army was called out.

The situation soon came back to near normal and the Army returned to the barracks in May 1991. However, misguided cadres were soon back to their errant ways. More outfits jumped into the fray. The Army was called out yet again in September 1991. In the next four months, it delivered severe body blows to insurgency in Assam. The army operations were then suspended as insurgents agreed to come to the negotiating table. As it turned out, under the pretense of the peace talks, the insurgent's leadership was, buying time to recast its future course.

In the northeast, there are over 15 underground political organizations. Only four or five out of these are active. Some of these are beset by gang rivalry. Internecine quarrelling among themselves continue for the control of tribes, geographical areas and for overall say in the affairs of Nagaland. Manipur faces similar factional fights which have claimed many lives. The entire situation has been further complicated by recent trends in ethnic strife.

Kuki-Naga clashes have been going on since 1991. In Assam, many violent acts of ethnic cleansing have been committed.

The complexities of insurgency in the northeastern states notwithstanding, for over forty years, Eastern Command and its formations have dealt with a vitiated internal security situation with a firm yet patient and understanding hand. Restrained and the minimum necessary forces were always resorted to, that too when it was unavoidable. Successive commanders at all levels have always sought to reduce the Army's presence and primacy so that other organs of the state attend to the root causes of the insurgency. All through these years, the troops have operated under trying conditions – no rules apply to the hostiles – to adhere to the stipulated regulations and not to violate human rights. Many officers and men have laid down their lives to bring peace to these troubled states. Above all, it is commendable that not once in the last four decades have the officers and men of the Eastern Command ever been faulted for their apolitical stance and absolute impartiality. Indeed, they also deserve to be commended for much else that they have done for the people of the region.

2. The States
A. Arunachal Pradesh:

Arunachal Pradesh means Land of the Dawn-Lit Mountains, also known as the Orchid State of India or the Paradise of the Botanists. The state's mountain ranges, in the extreme East of India, are described as "the place where the sun rises" in historical Indian texts and named the Aruna Mountains, which inspired the name of the state.

Major rivers of Arunachal Pradesh include the Kameng, Subansiri, Siang (Brahmaputra), Dibang, Lohit and Noa Dihing rivers. Subsurface flows and summer snow melt contribute to the volume of water. Mountains until the Siang river are classified as the Eastern Himalayas. Those between the Siang and Noa Dihing are classified as the Mishmi Hills that may be part of the Hengduan Mountains. Mountains south of the Noa Dihing in the Tirap and Longding districts are part of the Patkai Range.

The majority of residents of Arunachal Pradesh belong to the five Tani tribes (Nyishi, Adi, Galo, Apatani, Tagin) supposedly descended from Abotani, and the history of the Tani people is found in the ancient libraries of Tibet as the Tani people traded swords and other metals to Tibetans in exchange for meat and wool. Tibetans referred to the Tani people as the Lhobhas; lho means south and bha means people. Apart from these groups, other Tibeto-Burman groups Mishmis, Chutias, Nocte, Tangsa, and Wancho also occupied different regions of the state. Tawang Monastery in Arunachal Pradesh is the largest monastery in India and the second-largest in the world after the Potala Palace in Lhasa, Tibet. It is one of the few monasteries of Tibetan Buddhism that have remained protected from Mao's Cultural Revolution without any damage. The sixth Dalai Lama 'Tsangyang Gyatso' was born in Tawang.

During the medieval period, Northwestern parts of this area came under the control of the Monpa kingdom of Monyul, which flourished between 500 BCE and 600 CE. The Monpa and Sherdukpen keep historical records of the existence of local chiefdoms in the northwest as well. The remaining parts of the state, especially the foothills and the plains, were under the control of the Chutia Kings of Assam. Recent excavations of ruins of Hindu temples, such as the 14th-century

Malinithan at the foot of the Siang hills in West Siang, indicate they were built during the Chutia reign. Another notable heritage site, Bhismaknagar (built in the 8th century), has led to suggestions that the Chutia people had an advanced culture and administration. The third heritage site, the 400-year-old Tawang Monastery in the extreme northwest of the state, provides some historical evidence of the Buddhist tribal people because the sixth Dalai Lama 'Tsangyang Gyatso' was born in Tawang.

In 1912–13, the British Indian government made agreements with the indigenous peoples of the Himalayas of northeastern India to establish the North-East Frontier Agency from five tracts of frontier lands. In a nutshell, from 1913–1914, the representatives of the de facto independent state of Tibet and Britain met in India to define the borders of 'Outer Tibet' (concerning China). British administrator Sir Henry McMahon drew the 550 miles (890 km) McMahon Line as the border between British India and Tibet, placing Tawang and other areas within British India. The Tibetan and British representatives devised the Simla Accord including the McMahon Line, but the Chinese representatives did not concur. The Simla Accord denies other benefits to China while it declines to assent to the Accord.

The Chinese position was that Tibet was not independent of China and could not sign treaties, so the Accord was invalid, like the Anglo-Chinese (1906) and Anglo-Russian (1907) conventions. British records show that the condition for the Tibetan government to accept the new border was that China must accept the Simla Convention. As Britain was not able to get an acceptance from China, Tibetans considered the MacMahon line invalid. During that time that China did not exercise power in Tibet, the line had no serious challenges. In 1935, a Deputy Secretary in the Foreign Department, Olaf Caroe, "discovered" that the McMahon Line was not drawn on official maps. The Survey of India published a map showing the McMahon Line as the official boundary in 1937. In 1938, two decades after the Simla Conference, the British finally published the Simla Accord as a bilateral accord and the Survey of India published a detailed map showing the McMahon Line as a border of India. In 1944, Britain established administrations in the area, from Dirang Dzong in the west to Walong in the east.

India became independent in 1947 and the People's Republic of China (PRC) was established in 1949. The new Chinese government still considered the McMahon Line invalid. In November 1950, the PRC was poised to take over Tibet by force, and India supported Tibet. Journalist Sudha Ramachandran argued that China claimed Tawang on behalf of Tibetans, though Tibetans did not claim Tawang was in Tibet. What is now Arunachal Pradesh was established as the North-East Frontier Agency (NEFA) in 1954 and Sino-Indian relations were cordial until 1960. The resurgence of the border disagreement was a factor leading to the Sino-Indian War in 1962, during which China captured most of Arunachal Pradesh. However, China soon declared victory, withdrew back to the McMahon Line, and returned Indian prisoners of war in 1963. The war resulted in the termination of barter trade with Tibet, although since 2007 the Indian government has shown signs of wanting to resume barter trade. The North-East Frontier Agency was renamed Arunachal Pradesh by Sri Bibhabasu Das Shastri, the Director of Research, and K.A.A. Raja, the Chief Commissioner of Arunachal Pradesh on 20 January 1972, and it became a union territory. Arunachal Pradesh became a state on 20 February 1987.

In 2003, the Dalai Lama said that Arunachal was part of Tibet. In January 2007, the Dalai Lama said that both Britain and Tibet had recognized the McMahon Line in 1914. In 2008, he said that "Arunachal Pradesh was a part of India under the agreement signed by Tibetan and British representatives". According to the Dalai Lama, "In 1962 during the India-China war, the People's Liberation Army (PLA) occupied all these areas (Arunachal Pradesh) but they announced a unilateral ceasefire and withdrew, accepting the current international boundary". In recent years, China has occasionally asserted its claims on Tawang. India has rebutted these claims and informed the Chinese government that Tawang is an integral part of India. India reiterated this to China when the two prime ministers met in Thailand in October 2009. A report that the Chinese Army had briefly invaded Arunachal Pradesh in 2016 was denied by India's Minister of State for Home Affairs, Kiren Rijiju. In April 2017, China strongly objected to a visit to Tawang by the Dalai Lama, as it had to an earlier visit by the US ambassador to India. China had objected to the Dalai Lama's previous visits to the area. This adamantly shows how China is nurturing the insurgency movement in Arunachal Pradesh broadly in northeast India.

Insurgency: Northeast India covers an area of 255,083 sq. km. It shares 98 percent of its boundary with four countries. It is connected to the rest of India by 28 km. Vide Siliguri Corridor. It comprises seven states which possess a distinct culture, and historical traditions and are in different stages of political and economic development. Physiographically, the Northeast comprises three distinct regions – Assam Valley, Purvanchal Region (which includes Nagaland, Tripura, Mizo Hills, and Cachar Hills), and Meghalaya and Mikir Region. The complete area is inhabited by 213 different tribes speaking 325 different dialects.

Arunachal Pradesh – which spreads over 83,743 square kilometers with a population of about 1.3 million – is a logistical hub for militants from adjacent states of Manipur, Assam, and Nagaland.

Arunachal Pradesh has faced threats from insurgent groups, notably the National Socialist Council of Nagaland (NSCN), who are believed to have base camps in the districts of Tirap, Changlang, and Longding. These groups seek to decrease the influence of the Indian government in the region and merge part of Arunachal Pradesh into Nagaland. The militants use the state to cross over to the loosely governed Sagaing region of the Naga Self-Administered Zone (NSAZ) in Myanmar, where at least 2,500 Indian militants are based. The Tirap, Changlang, and Longding Districts of the state share 520 kilometers of the 1,643 Kilometers long porous border with Myanmar. According to security agencies, these Districts along with Nagaland's Mon and Tuensang Districts have become the nerve centre of militant activity in the region. As of January 31, 2018, in the last ten years, these five Districts accounted for about 313 fatalities. Fatalities from five bordering districts of India (Source: SATP)

District	Civilian	Security Forces	Terrorists	Total
Mon	6	13	110	129
Tirap	1	11	73	85
Tuesang	18	0	43	61
Changlang	5	3	26	34
Longding	0	0	4	4
Total	30	27	256	313

The three districts of Arunachal host militant groups such as NSCN-K, a reformation faction of NSCN (NSCN-R); the ULFA-I; the Saigora faction of National Democratic Front of Bodoland (NDFB-S); and CorCom. According to a Union Ministry of Home Affairs (UMHA) report, 'several armed modules of ULFA-I either individually or jointly with CorCom are active in several locations in Longding, Tirap and

Changlang Districts.' The notification also adds that the Assam-Arunachal interstate boundary continues to be used as hideouts and corridors for movement by militant groups.

NSCN-K, which abrogated the ceasefire agreement with the Indian Government in 2015, has been the predominant organization in Arunachal Pradesh. With a plethora of groups present in the region, the possibility of one militant group attempting to gain dominance in the area remains likely, which may result in a spike in factional clashes. According to an intelligence official, NSCN-IM, which currently conducts peace talks with the Indian Government and is also a rival to NSCN-K, has attempted to gain dominance and destabilize NSCN-K by propping up local proxy militant groups such as the Eastern Naga National Government (ENNG).

Arunachal Pradesh Police records from 2016 indicate that there were at least 80 cases of extortion and about 103 incidents of abduction. In 2017, the number of abduction cases stood at 106 and extortion at 75. A majority of these incidents are perpetrated by militant groups as a means to generate funds. Moreover, Arunachal Pradesh is located adjacent to the 'Golden Triangle', one of the primary opium-producing regions in the world comprised of Myanmar, Laos, and Thailand. According to a 2016 report, NSCN-R has reportedly been recruiting drug addicts across the opium belt of Arunachal Pradesh to broaden its extortion racket. Apart from Longding, Tirap, and Changlang, Lohit and Anjaw Districts are notorious for opium cultivation. According to the Narcotics Control Bureau (NCB), Arunachal topped the list of states in illegal poppy production for opium during 2014-15. NCB officials also claim that illegal poppy farms are guarded by armed militia who are known to work with insurgents.

The Indian army is present along the Tibetan border to thwart any Chinese incursion. Under the Foreigners (Protected Areas) Order 1958 (India), Inner Line Permits (ILPs) are required to enter Arunachal Pradesh through any of its checkgates on the border with Assam. China renamed six places in Arunachal Pradesh in 2017 and these new names have started to appear on Chinese maps.

When the Constitution was framed, a sub-committee headed by Gopinath Bordoloi was appointed to examine and recommend the constitutional arrangements that would fulfill the aspirations of the tribal population of the Northeast and thus set at rest fears about the possible loss of their unique identity. Recommendations of the Bordoloi sub-committee were extensively debated and incorporated with some amendments into the Constitution as the Sixth Schedule which protected not only the tribal laws, customs, and land rights; but also gave sufficient autonomy to the tribes to administer themselves with minimum outside interference. However, as events unfolded, hopes were belied. Tribal insurgencies erupted in Nagaland, Mizoram, Manipur, Assam, and Tripura at different points in time. The Mizo insurgency was resolved through a political settlement. The Naga insurgency, the oldest in the Northeast, has been in a state of suspended animation for more than a decade through various ceasefires negotiated from time to time since 1997 but a solution is yet to be found.

Militancy:
On February 1, 2018, Indian Security Forces (SFs) killed two militants of the independent faction of the United Liberation Front (ULFA-I) and People's Liberation Army (PLA) at Shankapani in Changlang District of Arunachal Pradesh. Only a week earlier, on January 24, 2018, an Indian Army trooper of the 11 Grenadiers regiment was killed in a joint ambush by the Coordination Committee (CorCom) of Manipur and ULFA-I, at Namsai District along the Assam-Arunachal Pradesh border. This was the first SF fatality in more than a year. The last in-state SF fatality was recorded in December 3, 2016, when two SFs were killed and eight wounded in Nginu village in Tirap District in a joint operation by the Khaplang faction of National Socialist Council of Nagaland (NSCN-K), ULFA-I and Kanglei Yawol Kanna Lup (KYKL). The highest militancy-related fatality in Arunachal was recorded in 2001 with 63 fatalities, however between 2007-17 only three years recorded more than ten insurgency-related fatalities.

Year	Civilians	Security Forces	Terrorists	Total
2000	7	3	24	34
2001	40	12	11	63
2002	7	4	21	32
2003	7	1	31	39
2004	6	2	35	43
2005	3	1	15	19
2006	0	0	4	4
2007	2	3	16	21
2008	0	0	2	2

2009	0	0	9	9
2010	0	0	0	0
2011	0	0	41	41
2012	0	0	4	4
2013	0	0	4	4
2014	3	0	6	9
2015	2	4	4	10
2016	0	2	7	9
2017	0	0	6	6
2018	0	1	2	3
Total	77	33	242	352

*Militancy fatalities between 2000-18 (Source : SATP)

External Factors

After Sheikh Hasina became the Prime Minister of Bangladesh in 2014, Dhaka cracked down on Indian insurgents based in the country, resulting in militant groups relocating to Myanmar's Sagaing region. With this development, the 'center of gravity' for the insurgent movement shifted to Myanmar. Union Minister for Home Hansraj Ahir stated that between 2015 and March 31, 2017, the Indo-Myanmar border witnessed a steady rise in insurgent activities, resulting in the death of 18 security personnel and 32 insurgents, as well as the arrest of 337 militants.

Other Indian militant groups such as PLA and ULFA-I have shifted their bases to Shan State in Myanmar bordering China's Yunnan province. Chinese intelligence has reportedly renewed relations with some militant leaders. ULFA has established links with Beijing's proxy in Myanmar the United Wa State Army (UWSA). Additionally, Chinese intelligence officers arguably favored the constitution of UNFLWESA, a conglomerate of various groups. In 2017, ULFA-I issued a statement against the visit of the Dalai Lama to Arunachal Pradesh.

Impact

The insurgents of both Nagaland and Assam are using Arunachal Pradesh as a transit route to Myanmar, and also for setting up camps and indulging in extortion. Most importantly, an indigenous insurgent outfit, the East India Liberation Tiger Force

(EILTF) has arisen in the State with the active support of the NSCN.

It was assumed that only two districts in the State, namely Tirap and Changlang were affected by the factional warfare between the Khaplang and Isak-Muivah factions of the NSCN. These two districts have been traditional strongholds of the NSCN-K, because of their proximity to the headquarters of the Khaplang faction in Myanmar. However, forays made by the NSCN-IM into the area have led to several internecine clashes. Recent events established that the United Liberation Front of Asom (ULFA) and the National Democratic Front of Bodoland (NDFB) have made incursions into the area. The thick forest areas of Tirap and Changlang suit the insurgents. A base in the area facilitates the movement of recruits on their way to Myanmar for training. Further, outfits like ULFA can monitor their operations in the entire Upper Assam tea belts and industrial locations from these bases.

It was believed that the insurgents would not venture into the interior districts of Arunachal Pradesh. However, recent developments have revealed that two more districts – Lohit and East Kameng , are becoming the haunts of the insurgents. Their foray into these interior districts underlines their long-term interests in the region.

The impact of insurgency on the State has been serious. According to intelligence sources, every government employee and businessman in Tirap is forced to pay nearly twenty-five percent of his gross income as a tax for the Republic of Nagalim. In the districts of Tirap and Changlang, branches of the State Bank of India have been shut down after they were served with extortion notes by the NSCN-K. In 2001, the operations of Oil India Limited in Changlang district were brought to a halt after the NSCN-IM demanded an amount of Rs. 60 lakhs (US$ 125,000). The oil major had to pull out 130 of its technical staff from the area.

B. Assam:

The problem of militancy in Assam has its origin in the large-scale migration of refugees from East Pakistan – what is now Bangladesh – since India's Partition in 1947. A continuous flow of illegal migrants across the borders has disturbed the local demography and brought much of India's Northeast to the knife-edge of violence. In July 1979, the All Assam Students Union (AASU) and the All Assam Gana Sangram Parishad (AAGSP) launched a mass movement for the detection of illegal immigrants, their deletion from the voters' list, and their deportation to Bangladesh. The agitators demanded that the process of detection should cover all migrants who had entered India since 1951. The Central government agreed to the policy of deportation but insisted on a 'cut-off' date of 1971 for the identification of illegal aliens. Irrespective of the cut-off date, it is a fact that a minute fraction of the illegal migrants have actually faced deportation and the processes of identification have, even now, barely begun. However, talks between the Central government and the AASU-AAGSP agitators broke down on this point, and the agitation gathered momentum towards the end of November 1979, when the entire State administration was brought to a halt as government employees joined the movement. In December 1979, Assam was brought under the President's rule.

Note: Insurgency began in Assam with the birth of the United Liberation Front of Asom (ULFA) in 1979. On 7 April 1979, six radical Assamese youths met at the Rang Ghar, the famous amphitheater of the Ahom royalty, and formed the ULFA, vowing to fight against the —colonial Indian Government with the ultimate aim of achieving a —sovereign, socialist Assam. They agreed that the Indian state has been —exploiting Assam's rich tea, oil, and forest resources without benefiting the people of Assam. The late 80s witnessed ULFA's influence in Assam reaching new heights. Rebels of the outfit killed, kidnapped, and threatened tea planters and businessmen in the State to procure funds to purchase weapons and to send its cadres for advanced training in Myanmar, Afghanistan, and other places. A reign of terror prevailed as ULFA assassinated and threatened businessmen and industrialists across the State. In 1990, the governance in Assam broke down which led to the declaration of President's rule in the State with a subsequent ban on the ULFA.

The anti-foreigner agitation soon took a violent turn and began to display secessionist tendencies. A militant organization, the United Liberation Front of Asom (ULFA), was established on April 7, 1979, under the leadership of Paresh Barua. While secession from India was the declared goal, the organization adopted an anti-foreigner plank since this was the popular issue gripping the masses in Assam. Pushing its objective of secession to the background, the ULFA operated within the AASU-AAGSP's agitation.

On March 28, 1980, the army was deployed in the State to restore law and order. The entire State, with the exception of Cachar and the North Cachar Hills districts, was declared a disturbed area and was brought under the Assam Disturbed Areas Act, 1955, and the Armed Forces (Special Powers) Act, 1958, on April 6, 1980.

Several rounds of talks were held between the Central government and the leaders of the Assam agitation over the period 1980-83, but they failed to make any headway. Despite a call for a boycott by the agitators, the Central government decided to hold elections to the State Legislature in February 1983. On February 18, over 600 Bangladeshi settlers, including women and children, were massacred in Nellie, Nagaon district. Nevertheless, elections were held. The Congress (I) under Hiteshwar Saikia, came to power, and, while the agitation continued, a measure of order was restored in the State.

Talks between the Centre and the leaders of the agitation were resumed when the Rajiv Gandhi government came to power in Delhi, and on August 15, 1985, the Assam Accord was signed. According to the terms of the Accord, all foreigners who entered Assam on or after March 25, 1971, were to be detected and deported.

After the Accord, a new regional party, the Asom Gana Parishad (AGP) was created, bringing together many of the prominent leaders of the agitation. Elections to the State Legislature were held in December 1985, and the AGP was swept to power, with Prafulla Kumar Mahanta as the Chief Minister.

At this stage, the ULFA emphasized its basic objective i.e., to 'liberate Assam from Indian colonial rule' and to form a 'sovereign, socialist Assam' through an armed struggle. As the Assam Accord and the subsequent political settlement were inimical to this objective, the

ULFA continued with its violent activities even after the AGP assumed power in the State. By 1986, the ULFA had established contacts with agents of Pakistan's Inter-Services Intelligence (ISI), as well as with militants from the National Socialist Council of Nagaland (NSCN) and the Kachin Independence Army (KIA). Its strength then was estimated at 3,000 militants with access to some 2,000 weapons of various makes. The ULFA created terror in the State, disrupting communications and hitting various economic targets, kidnapping prominent businessmen for ransom, and killing government officials. Its activities escalated, reaching unprecedented heights in 1990. As the AGP government lost control of the situation, the State was, once again, brought under the President's rule on November 28, 1990, and the ULFA was banned under the Unlawful Activities (Prevention) Act, of 1967. The army had been re-inducted in the State and Operation Bajrang was conducted between September 1990 and April 1991. 209 hardcore militants were arrested during this operation and a large quantity of arms, along with Rs. 48 million in cash – the proceeds of extortion – were also recovered.

Operation Bajrang succeeded in restoring a measure of normalcy in Assam, and elections were held in June 1991 for the State Legislature. The Congress (I) defeated the AGP and Hiteshwar Saikia was, once again, sworn in as Chief Minister on July 1. ULFA resumed its violent campaign almost at once, and the army launched Operation Rhino in September 1991. Over the succeeding four months, 2,578 hardcore militants were nabbed, along with large quantities of arms and Rs. 780,000 in cash. The army also destroyed 15 ULFA camps. However, in January 1992, the Saikia government suspended army operations and announced an amnesty for all militants who were willing to surrender. By March 1992, some 4,000 ULFA militants had surrendered to the authorities.

The ULFA, however, proved extremely resilient and restored its strength and activities, acquiring new military hardware and establishing a chain of training camps across the border in Myanmar, and later in Bhutan. In April-May 1995, the Indian and Myanmarese armed forces jointly launched Operation Golden Bird along their border. 50 militants were killed during this operation and huge quantities of arms and ammunition were recovered.

The AGP returned to power in the State Legislature elections of May 1996. Counter-insurgency operations continued, and on January 20, 1997, a Unified Command structure was set up to coordinate the functioning of the various forces carrying out operations against the terrorists. Since then, continuous military and para-military operations have considerably weakened the ULFA, driving its senior leadership into exile. A disturbing trend, however, is the widening network of extortion, criminal, and quasi-legal operations that this leadership-in-exile now commands in Assam, which not only fuels and finances militancy but, more significantly, has had an extremely corrosive impact on democratic institutions and structures in the State and a deeply corrupting influence on increasingly collusive government officials and political leaders. With this, there has also been a continuous process of 'compensation' among the rank and file of the ULFA cadres, as increasing numbers of criminals join in the extortionary and other illegal activities of the organization.

The emergence of a Bodo insurgency in the State has become another major problem. The Bodos, a major tribe of plainsmen, are one of the earliest settlers in Assam. They have been demanding better social, political, and economic conditions since independence. There has been a long history of tensions between the Bodos and the Assamese. The former feel that they have been neglected and exploited by the latter. The All Bodo Students Union (ABSU) was formed in 1967 to represent the Bodo cause. In the early 1980s, the ABSU emerged as a potent force under the leadership of Upendranath Brahma.

A militant organization, the Bodo Security Force (BSF) came into being in 1989 under the leadership of Ranjan Daimari. The BSF, later renamed the National Democratic Front of Bodoland (NDFB), resorted to terrorism in order to secure an 'independent Bodo nation' north of the river Brahmaputra. A very large proportion of violent activities in the State, including killings, explosions, arson, and attacks on police stations, have been carried out by the NDFB. This is an organized and well-trained militant group with a strength of about 900. It has established a 'working arrangement' with the NSCN – Isak-Muivah (NSCN-IM).

Another terrorist group, the Bodo Liberation Tiger Force (BLTF), headed by Prem Singh Brahma, has been fighting for a separate State of Bodoland within the Indian Union.

An accord was signed on February 20, 1993, between the Government of India, the Government of Assam, and Bodo leaders, creating the Bodoland Autonomous Council (BAC) within Assam. However, since Bodo villages are not contiguous, the demarcation of the jurisdiction of the BAC has remained a problem. Both the NDFB and the BLTF have condemned the Bodo Accord, and have, since the mid-1990s, been engaged in a campaign of violence directed against other ethnic groups within 'Bodo areas'. Large-scale attacks were carried out against Santhal tribals in May 1996, displacing tens of thousands of people. A second wave of attacks in May 1998 displaced another couple of thousand Santhals. The Santhals and other non-Bodo communities have also begun to arm themselves and fight back. This has resulted in significant displacement of the Bodo population from areas where they are a minority.

These trends in retaliatory violence are not restricted to the Bodos. Muslim migrants in Assam have also shown signs of incipient militancy. The Muslim United Liberation Front of Assam has been constituted. A demand for a separate State bringing together the five border districts in Assam, which now have a Muslim majority, has been already voiced.

The recent history of the fissionary trend in which every tribal, linguistic, religious or cultural sub-group demands separation from the others, compounded by the rhetoric of ethnic sub-nationalism, radical demographic shifts and a long history of poor governance, make this State, perhaps more than any other region in the country, a potential source of increasing mass strife over the coming decades.

Tribal Insurgencies In Assam

On April, 2023; After the government signed a peace settlement with the Dimasa National Liberation Army (DNLA), both Union Home Minister Amit Shah and Assam Chief Minister Himanta Biswa Sarma declared that it marked the end of the tribal insurgency in Assam.
This was a significant claim for a state which — even after Nagaland, Mizoram, Meghalaya, and Arunachal Pradesh were carved out of it — has seen insurgency by various tribal militant groups, particularly from the 1980s onwards. The core demand of most of these groups has been

greater political autonomy, primarily through separate statehood demands.

The creation of Autonomous District Councils (ADCs) in the hill districts of Assam was a step towards integrating the tribes into the Indian mainstream. However, the poor performance of the ADCs generated disillusionment among the tribal elites who demanded separate states. The Union government tried to resolve the issue through periodic peace deals with the agitators and militant groups, which provided incremental autonomy to the ADCs in Assam. These pacts however did not address the interests of the smaller tribes and non-tribals who reside in the Council areas.

Located in the strategic northeastern corner of India, it is part of a region that shares a highly porous and sensitive frontier with China in the North, Myanmar in the East, Bangladesh in the Southwest, and Bhutan to the Northwest. Spread over 2,62,179 sq. km, the strategic importance of Northeast India can be determined from the fact that it shares a 4,500 km-long international border with four South Asian neighbors but is connected to the Indian mainland by only a tenuous 22 km-long land corridor passing through Siliguri in the eastern state of West Bengal.

Ethnicity: The northeastern region is also an ethnic minefield, as it comprises of around 160 Scheduled Tribes, besides an estimated 400 other tribal or sub-tribal communities and groups.

Tribes in Assam: There are 15 recognized tribes in the autonomous districts of Karbi Anglong and North Cachar Hills and 14 recognized tribes in the rest of the state. Of these, the major tribes are Bodo (35% of the state's tribal population), Mishing (17.52%), Karbi (11.1%), Rabha (7.6%), Sonowal Kachari (6.5%), Lalung (5.2%), Garo (4.2%), and Dimasa (3.2%). Of these, the most sustained and violent movement for autonomy has been carried out by Bodo groups, but there have also been Karbi and Dimasa groups that waged militant operations over the decades. The peace process has been a long one and the claim of ending insurgency in tribal areas comes after a string of peace settlements with different groups in recent years.

Turbulence in India's Northeast is, therefore, not caused just by armed separatist groups representing different ethnic communities fighting the central or the local governments or their symbols to press for either total independence or autonomy, but also by the recurring battles for territorial supremacy among the different ethnic groups themselves.

Bodo: While the first organized demand for a separate Bodo state emerged in the 1960s, it revived and gained strength through the All Bodo Students' Union (ABSU) after the signing of the Assam Accord in 1985.

The first Bodo Accord was signed with the ABSU in 1993 and paved the way for the Bodoland Autonomous Council. But this fell through when the ABSU withdrew from it and revived the demand for a separate state.

The second Accord in 2003 with the Bodo Liberation Tigers subsequently led to the formation of the Bodo Territorial Council (BTC), with jurisdiction over the Bodo Territorial Autonomous District (BTAD).

The third Bodo Accord of 2020 was essentially a truce with four factions of the militant National Democratic Front of Bodoland (NDFB). It extended provisions already in effect through the previous accords by providing more legislative, administrative, executive, and financial powers to the BTC; the power to alter the area of the BTAD; and the notification of the Bodo language as an associate official language in the state.

The Memorandum of Settlement (MoS) was signed on 27 January 2020 between the union and the state governments with four Bodo insurgent groups—the National Democratic Front of Bodoland-Progressive (NDFB-P), the NDFB-Ranjan Diamary (NDFB-RD), NDFB-Dhirendra Boro (NDFB-DB) and the NDFB-Saoraigwra (NDFB-S), as well as the United Bodo People's Organization (UBPO) and the All Bodo Students Union (ABSU). Subsequent to the agreement, the NDFB factions disbanded in March 2020.

Karbi: In 2021, a settlement was arrived at with five militant groups of Karbi Anglong that was said to have brought the Karbi insurgency to an end. The insurgency by Karbi groups, too, revolved around the demand for an autonomous state and had taken off in the 1980s. In 2011, the United People's Democratic Solidarity signed a tripartite settlement with the Union and Assam governments that provided for greater autonomy and special packages for the Karbi Anglong Autonomous Council. The 2021 settlement further granted more autonomy and provided a special development package of Rs 1,000 crore over five years. The MoS was signed on 4 September 2021 with various Karbi insurgent groups active in the Karbi Anglong district of Assam. Following the agreement, around 1,000 cadres surrendered.

Dimasa: The DNLA, with which a tripartite agreement was reached, was the newest group to take up arms in the Dima Hasao district. The settlement signed with the DNLA now has similar provisions along the lines of the settlement arrived at with the five Karbi Anglong groups two years ago.

The MoS was signed on 23 April 2023 with the Dimasa militant group called the Dimasa National Liberation Army and its political wing—the Dimasa Peoples' Supreme Council (DNLA/ DPSC), to end the insurgency in Dima Hasao District of Assam. The DNLA was disbanded and 181 cadres surrendered.6 Like the Adivasi groups, the Assam government had signed a Suspension of Operation (SoO) agreement with the DNLA/DPSC on 28 October 2021, which agreed to shun violence and achieve their objectives 'through peaceful dialogue'.

Adivasi Tea Tribe: The MoS was signed on 15 September 2022 with the representatives of eight Adivasi (tea tribe) militant groups. In fact, these Adivasi militant groups had surrendered in January 2012 and were engaged in peace talks with the government since October 2016. The agreement saw the surrender of 1,182 militants belonging to the eight Adivasi insurgent groups.

ASSAM ACCORD

Assam Accord was a Memorandum of Settlement (MoS) signed between representatives of the Government of India and the leaders of the Assam Movement.
It was signed in the presence of the then-Prime Minister Rajiv Gandhi in New Delhi on 15 August 1985.
It followed a six-year agitation that started in 1979. Led by the All Assam Students' Union (AASU), the protestors demanded the identification and deportation of all illegal foreigners – predominantly Bangladeshi immigrants.
The leaders of the Assam Movement agreed to accept all migrants who had entered into Assam prior to 1 January 1966.
The Government of India acknowledged the political, social, cultural, and economic concerns of the Assamese people and agreed to revise the electoral database based on that date.

Further, the government agreed to identify and deport any refugees and migrants after March 25, 1971.

The Karbi-Dimasa Movement
During the time of India's independence, the tribal elites of undivided Assam had raised apprehensions regarding joining the Indian Union. They argued that if the tribal communities joined the Union, their land rights and socio-cultural identity would be jeopardized. To assuage these fears of the tribes, the political leadership in New Delhi promised decentralized self-governance in the form of Autonomous District Councils (ADC) to the tribals so that they could safeguard their culture and tradition.

Accordingly, five ADCs were established under the Sixth Schedule of the Constitution in the hill districts of undivided Assam. Two of these ADCs were established in the tribal-dominated United Mikir and North Cachar Hills districts in November 1951 and April 1952 respectively. These were known as the Mikir Hills District Council and the North Cachar Hills District Council.10 In 1970, the district was bifurcated into two separate districts named the 'Mikir Hills' district and the 'North Cachar Hills' district. In October 1976, the Mikir Hills District was renamed as Karbi Anglong, and the Council was named Karbi Anglong District Council.

The dissatisfaction with the ADCs among the educated tribal elites soon became apparent when within two years of their establishment, demands for autonomous states were raised before the States Reorganization Committee in 1954. Interestingly, leaders from the Mikir and Cachar Hills did not put forward any such demand either in the 1950s or in the 1960s when clamor for separate states intensified following the imposition of the Assamese language as the official language in undivided Assam. It was only after separate states and union territories were formed in the region in 1972 that the leaders of the two hill districts started their demands for a separate state in 1973. While the demand for a separate state was not accepted, the union government made provisions for increasing developmental funds for the two districts.

This arrangement suited the leaders for some time, but they again revived their demand for an autonomous state under Article 244 (A) of the Constitution11 in 1980. The demand for an autonomous state was in response to the call of the All Assam Student Union (AASU) and All Assam Gana Sangram Parishad (AAGSP) during the Assam Agitation to revoke all privileges extended to the Scheduled Castes and Tribes of the state.12 This demand for a separate state got a fillip in 1986 with the formation of the Autonomous State Demand Committee (ASDC) and the Karbi Anglong North Cachar Hills Autonomous State Demand Committee (KANCHASDCOM) following the installation of the Asom Gana Parishad (AGP) led government in the state. The ASDC along with several Karbi and Dimasa students' organisations intensified their agitation. The agitation gradually turned violent with the involvement of militant organizations such as the Karbi National Volunteers (KNV) and the Dimasa National Security Force (DNSF).

Significantly, the return of the Congress government in Assam opened up avenues for dialogue with the ASDC and other organizations and on 1 April 1995, a tripartite Memorandum of Understanding (MoU) was signed between the union and the state governments and the ASDC and other organizations. The government did not accept the demand for a separate state but provided more autonomy to the Councils by transferring 30 subjects from the State List. Further, the government upgraded both the District Councils as Autonomous Councils. Thus, the Karbi Anglong Autonomous Council and North Cachar Hills Autonomous Councils came into being.

The agreement, however, was not acceptable to KANCHASDCOM as well as a section of the youths, who were frustrated by the denial of a separate state. Inspired by other militant organizations in the region, they took to the path of violence and formed militant groups such as the United People's Democratic Solidarity (UPDS) in Karbi Anglong and the Dima Halam Daogah (DHD) Nunisa & Jewel Garlossa factions in the North Cachar Hills. After a decade and a half of mindless violence, these militant organizations eventually surrendered.

Following their surrender, the government signed two MoUs—one with the UPDS on 25 January 2011 and the other with the DHD (both factions) on 8 October 2012. The MoUs upgraded the Autonomous Councils into Territorial Councils and provided a special economic package for the socio-economic and educational development of these areas. These MoUs could not bring peace because disgruntled factions and groups emerged and restarted the demand for a separate state. For example, in the North Cachar Hills, in spite of signing the peace agreement, the Nunisa faction of the DHD as well as the Student Unions and Civil Society Organisations reiterated their resolve to get the separate state of Dimaraji.

In Karbi Anglong, several militant organizations such as the Karbi Longri North Cachar Hills Liberation Front (KLNLF), the Karbi People's Liberation Tigers (KPLT), People's Democratic Council of Karbi Longri (PDCK), and the United People's Liberation Army (UPLA) continued their violent 'struggle' for a separate state. However, in 2021, all these groups either surrendered before the Assam government or suspended their armed operations, thus, paving the way for negotiations and peace agreements.

The Bodoland movement
While the hill tribes of Assam were given the opportunity of self-governance through the ADCs, the plains tribes such as the Bodos did not get such an opportunity even though the demand for a separate homeland for the Bodos was articulated in the pre-independence period. Post-independence, it was in 1967 that the first demand for an autonomous homeland for the Bodos was articulated by the Plains Tribal Council of Assam (PTCA) and the All Bodo Students' Union (ABSU). This demand was reiterated following the reorganization of the Northeast in 1973. However, while the PTCA demanded a Union Territory for the Plains Tribes, the ABSU demanded a separate state for the Bodos.

In the initial years, the demand for the Bodo homeland was relatively peaceful, but the movement acquired an aggressive and violent tenor by the mid-1980s. The Bodos, who had supported the AASU and AGSP during the Assam agitation, had hoped that their demand for a separate homeland would be fulfilled after the signing of the Assam Accord. But when the AGP came to power in 1985, it did not acquiesce to the demands of a separate Bodoland. Consequently, the Bodos relaunched their agitation in March 1987 with the slogan of 'divide Assam 50-50'.
The Bodoland movement was led by the Bodo People's Action Committee (BPAC) and the ABSU and supported by militant organizations such as the Bodo Security Force (BSF) and the United Tribal Nationalist Liberation Front (UTNLF).

The violent agitation by the Bodos in the late 1980s and early 1980s was brought to an end with the signing of the Bodo Agreement in

February 1993. While the demand for a separate Bodoland was not accepted, the Union government facilitated the creation of a territorially defined self-governing Council—the Bodo Autonomous Council (BAC). However, a section of disgruntled Bodo youths rejected the peace agreement and formed two militant organizations viz. the National Democratic Front of Bodoland (NDFB) and the Bodo Liberation Tigers (BLT) to 'achieve a separate homeland for the Bodos'.

After a period of six years in 1999, the BLT decided to give up insurgency and enter into a peace dialogue with the government. Peace negotiations between the Union government and the BLT started only after the militant organisation gave up its demand for a separate Bodoland in 2001.19 The negotiations culminated into the signing of a tripartite MoS in February 2003 between the Union government, the Assam government and the BLT. The agreement enabled the establishment of an autonomous self-governing body called the Bodoland Territorial Council (BTC) under the Sixth Schedule.
This arrangement, again, did not go down well with the NDFB who continued with their demand for a sovereign 'Boroland'. Over the next two decades or so, the Bodo Territorial Areas District (BTAD) witnessed numerous cycles of violence as the NDFB continued to target not only innocent civilians but also ex-cadres of the BLT. The NDFB also witnessed a series of splits with one faction surrendering to the state government while the breakaway ones continued with their violent activities. It was the sustained counterinsurgency operations by the Indian army and the loss of bases in Bangladesh and Myanmar that forced all the factions of the NDFB to lay down their arms and come to the negotiating table led to the signing of the MoS in January 2020.

United Liberation Front of Assam (ULFA)
History: The United Liberation Front of Assam, one of the militant organizations operating in the northeast region, was established in 1979 when anti-foreigner agitation launched by the All Assam Students' Union reached its peak in the state. The front was formed by Paresh Baruah along with associates including Rajiv Raj Konwar alies Arabinda Rajkhowa, Golap Baruah alies Anup Chetia, Samiran Gogoi alies Pradip Gogoi and Bhadreshwar Gohain on 7 April 1979, at the Rang Ghar pavilion of the Ahom Kings located in Sibsagar to establish a Sovereign, Socialist Assam through an armed struggle.

The front remained dormant till 1986, except for recruiting its cadres between late 1983 to early 1984. Soon after establishing contacts with the Kachin Independence Army (KIA) and the Nationalist Socialist Council of Nagaland (NSCN) in the year 1986 for training and procuring arms, ULFA went on a fund-raising spree through a train of extortion from a circle of traders, businessmen, tea gardens, both Indian and foreign-owned, and others. It also set up camps in Tinsukia and Dibrugarh districts of the state. In view of ULFA's increasing militant activities in the state, New Delhi imposed President's Rule on November 7. The entire State of Assam was declared a "disturbed area. ULFA was banned under the Unlawful Activities (Prevention) Act, of 1967 and the Indian army launched Operation Bajrang.

From the early 1990s, the front embarked on a more aggressive campaign to further its goal by targeting security forces, blasting rail links, killing political opponents, and weakening basic infrastructures. In July 1991, ULFA militants abducted 14 people, including an engineer, and a national of (the erstwhile) Soviet Union, and demanded a huge amount of money as ransom. Throughout the 1990s, the front resorted to many terrorist activities.

Strength: According to the Indian Army sources, the total strength of ULFA is around 3,000, while various other sources put the figure ranging from 4,000 to 6,000. A military wing of the ULFA, the Sanjukta Mukti Fouj (SMF) was formed on 16 March 1996. SMF has three full-fledged battalions: the 7th, 8th, and the 709th. The remaining battalions exist only on paper at best they have the strengths of a company or so.

The command structure of the ULFA comprises Arvinda Rajkhowa as the Commander-in-Chief, Paresh Baruah as the Chairman and Pradeep Gogoi as the Vice-Chairman of the front. Vice-Chairman Pradip Gogoi was arrested on April 8, 1998, and has been in judicial custody in Guwahati ever since. ULFA General Secretary, Anup Chetia is also presently under detention at the high-security Dhaka Central Jail after his arrest in Dhaka (Bangladesh) on December 7, 1997. Chittaranjan Barua, Sasadhar Chaudhary, and Matinga hold Finance, Foreign, and Publicity secretaries respectively.

ULFA has a three-tier organizational structure namely (i) Central Unit, (ii) District Units, and (iii) Anachalik Units. The ULFA has a civil and military wing. The civil wing is headed by Paresh Baruah and the military wing of the front is led by Arvinda Rajkhawa. The district units are led by district Presidents/district Commanders respectively. A district is further divided into Anchals which comprise a number of villages headed by an Anchalik President. For operational purposes, ULFA has divided the entire Assam into four zones. Each zone is further divided into four regions.

Training Camps: In 1986, ULFA first established contacts with the then-unified National Socialist Council of Nagaland (NSCN) and the Kachin Independent Army (KIA) of Myanmar for training camps and arms.

Subsequently, the front shifted to Bangladesh its training camps. ULFA's training camps have been functioning since in the Bangladeshi soil since 1989.

But its main training camps are located in Sandrup Jongkhar, a district in Southern Bhutan that borders with Assam's Nalbari district. According to Bhutan, ULFA has six major camps between Lhamoizingkha and Daifam.

On May 17, 2003, Bhutanese King Jighme Singhye Wangchuk called upon the people to volunteer for the formation of a militia force to counter Indian militant groups ULFA, NDBF, and the KLO on its soil. Media reports say that the 81st National Assembly of Bhutan adopted a resolution for the last attempt to persuade ULFA, NBFD, and the KLO to close down their camps within this year peacefully failing which terrorists would face military action.

The funding for the front comes from three sources:
Extortion: The front's main source of income comes from extortion from businessmen, politicians, government employees, industrialists and tea companies. It also indulges in bank robberies and other criminal activities to finance its activities.

Drug Trafficking: It is reported that the front is also involved in drug smuggling. As far back as 1988, one ULFA leader was caught with seven kilograms of Burmese heroin. Drug money had been used to purchase arms at the rate of 50,000 for automatic rifles, Rs.40,000 for pistols, and Rs.45,000 for wireless sets.

There is no proper source for ULFA's annual budget but according to an accomplished journalist and security analyst from Guwahati, Mr. Jaideep Saikia's calculations, the ULFA's budget for the year 2001 was a whooping Rs.31 crore plus.

Activities: After lying low for some time during the year 2002, ULFA has begun resuming its terrorist violence. Events of the first three months of the year 2003 indicate that no respite for the people in Assam from ULFA's terrorist activities. It initiated a series of attacks on vital public installations and civilian targets towards the latter part of the last year, and which continue into the present year, in what appeared to be a concerted bid to reestablish the fact that it is still a force to be reckoned with in Assam. The major attacks in the first quarter of the year included:

21 January 2003: ULFA carried out an attack on a security force (SF) camp in the Dibrugarh district, though there were no casualties.

7 March 2003: ULFA attacked a police commando barrack in Bongaigaon town. No fatalities were reported in this incident.

8 March 2003: ULFA militants triggered an explosion at a five million-litre petrol reservoir at Digboi refinery in the Tinsukia district by throwing mortar bombs, causing property loss estimated at approximately Rs 200 million. On the same day, ULFA cadres also separately damaged a gas pipeline at Kathalguri in Tinsukia. In another incident, ULFA killed two persons at a migrant's settlement and injured six more while escaping after an attack on the Darrangiri police outpost in Goalpara district.

16 March 2003: On ULFA's Army Day, six civilians were killed and approximately 55 others injured in an Improvised Explosive Device (IED) blast under a passenger bus on National Highway No.7 in the Goalpara district. The series of attacks also reinforces the group's consistent rejection of any plausible peace process.

Casualties: The front lost many of its cadres in the past decade. From 1992 to 2001, 855 cadres of the front were killed by the Indian security forces.

Popular Support: ULFA draws its main support from the upper Assam districts of Lakhimpur, Jorhat, Sibsagar, Tinsukia, Dibrugarh, Karbi Anglong, Golaghat and Sonitpur. Many of the ULFA leaders are from these districts. A large number of ULFA cadres have been recruited from the upper Assam districts. In the West, its activities and presence are low. The western districts of Assam are dominated by Bodo militants. In the districts of Kokrajhar, Barpeta, and Darrang ethnic Bodo rebels such as NDFB and Bodo Security Force (BSF) militants have control over the areas. In the Southern parts of Assam, ULFA has also a low presence. The front cannot take up any activities in lower Assam districts due to a lack of support base. In July ULFA went on a recruitment drive from these districts, however, it received a poor response from the youths and they showed their unwillingness to join the front.

The front is losing its support because of hostile terrorist activities. Kidnapping, liquidation of common people, and assassination of political opponents have caused much disenchantment among the Assamese people and their support base is beginning to dwindle in the state. The popular mood among the people of Assam is towards a negotiated settlement. Public meetings were held all over the state to issue appeals to the front to rejoin the mainstream. The pressure exerted by the military operations and the built-up public opinion took its toll on the militants' morale. A section of ULFA cadres laid down their weapons en masse before the state government in March 1992.

On ULFA raising day (April 7, 2000) common people came out of their homes, and peace rallies were held all over the state for the first time. Even newspapers carried editorials condemning the ULFA for its violence, claiming that the people were totally against its ideology. The Director General, BSF while speaking to the IAS officers course at IIC, New Delhi on October 16, 2000, stated that the ULFA has really broken up because now people are not with them.

Another setback to the ULFA came in the form of the rejection by the people of Assam of the outfit's demand for a plebiscite in Assam on the issue of sovereignty under the supervision of the UN observers. As much as 70 percent of the state's 1.4 crore voters defied the ULFA's call for the 1999 Lok Sabha poll boycott and exercise their franchise. The organization today seeks meaning in methods and motives other than the ideologies by which it came into existence on April 7, 1979. The banned outfit is looking out for soft targets to spread its terror. A rather dismal picture of an organization that was formed to bring Aikya, Biplap, and Mukti to the Assamese people.

Areas of Operation: ULFA organisational structure is divided into four command zones and the districts under each are: Lakhimpur, Jorhat, Sibsagar, Tinsukia, Dibrugarh, Bokajan of Kabri, Anglong, Golaghat, Part of Sonitpur, Dhubri, Kokrajhar, Bongaigaon, Goalpara, Barpeta, Nalbari, South Kamrup Darrang, Karbi, Anglong, Nagaon, Moirigaon, Dhemaji, Part of Sonitpur, North Kamrup, Hailakandi, NC Hills, Cachar Hills, Karimganj.

Internal Linkages: ULFA maintains close strategic links with the National Democratic Front Bodoland (NDFB). Presently, NDFB works in tandem with the ULFA. Both outfits have also set up camps in Bhutan after were driven into the Bhutanese foothills by a major Indian military offensive in 1990-1991. Sometime in 1999, the ULFA and NDFB formed a coordination committee to launch a united struggle. It has joined hands with the Muslim United Liberation Tigers of Assam (MULTA) to carry out joint operations in the areas dominated by immigrants.

External Linkages: The front maintains close relations with many militant organizations of the northeast and other groups from Myanmar. The Kachin Independent Army has traditionally been providing support to all the undergrounds in the Northeast. As per LT. Gen. V.K. Nayyer, ex-Governor of Manipur, there have been confirmed reports of KIA and NSCN providing training and weapons to ULFA. But it came under pressure of joint military operations of the Indian and Myanmarese Army in April-May 1995. The ULFA and the NSCN (K) along with a foreign Army, and the Northeast Students' Organisation (NESO) have formed an umbrella organization that calls itself the United Liberation Front of Seven Sisters with the aim of carrying out violent activities in the Northeast.

In 1989, The Indo-Burma Revolutionary Front (IBRF) was set up, which included NSCN-K, ULFA, UNLF, United Liberation Front of Bodoland, Kuki National Front (KNF) (all from India) and Chin National Front (Myanmar). It is also reported that the front has a close nexus with the Liberation Tigers of Tamil Elam. The LTTE is reported to have trained various ULFA cadres in explosives handling. The External Affairs Ministry confirmed that several top leaders of the outfit including its chairman, and commander-in-chief have procured foreign passports through fraudulent means.

ULFA also established a strategic alliance with the United Liberation Front (UNLF) of Manipur in August 2002. Reports hold ULFA and NDFB procure arms from UNLF. The link between ULFA and UNLF became visible when the latter in a statement on July 17, 2002, indicated that the killing of three security forces in Assam's Cachar district by Manipur People's Army's armed wing of UNLF was carried out at ULFA's behest. Reports indicate that ULFA, the Manipur People's Liberation Front (MPLF) a conglomerate of three militant groups United Liberation Front (UNLF), People's Liberation Army (PLA), and People's Revolutionary Party of Kangleipak (PREPAK) active in Manipur, and the Tripura People's Democratic Front (TPDF), a front outfit of all the Tripura Tiger Force (ATTF), operating in Tripura under a common platform have launched a 'Coordinated Regional Military Offensive for liberation of the Region from Indian colonial occupation,' code name Operation Freedom.

ULFA and other militant groups from the Northeast maintain links with the militants of Kashmir and Punjab. It is also in touch with many other organizations engaged in struggles in Andhra Pradesh, Bihar, and other states of India.

The ULFA chairman attended the annual session of the UN Working Group on Indigenous Population in Geneva in 1997. In the same year, a four-member delegation of the ULFA including the chairman Arabinda Rajkhowa, general secretary Anup Chetia, and the foreign secretary Sasha Choudhury went to Geneva and tried to enter the Unrepresented Nations Peoples Organisation (UNPO). But the permanent representative of India in the United Nations Smt Arundhuti Ghosh objected to the presence of the ULFA leaders in the meeting and raised the issue of the killing of social worker Sanjoy Ghosh by the ULFA. Finding themselves in a tight corner, the ULFA leaders were forced to leave Geneva. Its attempt to enter the Unrepresented Nations and People's Organization was blocked by the Government of India.

Of late, ULFA has spread its tentacles in West Bengal's northern districts. It has established a strategic alliance with the Kamtapur Liberation Organization (KLO). Security forces believe that it was the ULFA that propped up and got the KLO formed in December 1995. The ULFA's alliance with the KLO gives it access to certain KLO-controlled corridors that provide the rebels from Assam a bridge linking their bases in Bhutan with hideouts in Bangladesh.

Publications and Website: Swadhinata (Freedom) is the mouthpiece of the front. ULFA and three Northeast insurgents launched websites www.geocities.com/CapitalHill/Congress/7434/ulfa.htm in October 1999.

SULFA: Surrendered ULFA cadres are known as SULFA. The former Chief Minister of Assam Hiteswar Saikia played a major role in splitting the front. Saikhia bestowed blue-eyed status on the surrendered boys, granting them all kinds of favors. Very soon the term syndicate, referring to its mafia-style mode of operations, became synonymous with the SULFA, coined by the local media, took on a pejorative connotation.

Many of the surrendered ULFA have joined the security forces and are working in the state and central forces. The combined onslaught of the SULFA and the security forces took their toll on an already-weaken ULFA. The SULFA has become an effective fighting machine and served as an important tool for counter insurgency in the state of Assam.

Surrender and Rehabilitation: A Published on Sept 25, 2023: A total of 5,202 militants have been arrested in the last 12 years from various parts of Assam, but only one of them has been convicted so far, according to official records. The Assam Police arrested 5,202 cadres of ULFA and other extremist groups, comprising people from the Bodo, Garo, Rabha, Karbi, Adivasi, and Muslim communities, from 2011 to September 4, 2023.

A Published on December 11, 2022, IANS, Assam Police have arrested a member of the Liberation Tigers of Tribals (LTT) terror outfit in Cachar district. Superintendent of Police Numal Mahato said that Seiminthang alias Alex Gangte, was arrested and one 9mm pistol along with ammunition was found in his possession. The cadre originally hails from Jinam Ghat area in the Dima Hasao district.

Organization	Cadres Rehabilitated
NDFB	4205
Karbi	1926
Adivasi	1182
NLFB	301
ADF	88
NSLA	83
RNLF	28
URPF	29
ULFA-I (sporadic surrender)	124
UGPO	127
TLA	74
KNLA	38
DNLA (sporadic surrender)	11
DNLA (Mios)	181
NLFB (Bodo)	164
Others	164

A Published on Nov 16, 2023: A total of 8,756 former militants of various outfits were rehabilitated across Assam over the last two years, Chief Minister Himanta Biswa Sarma said. Out of them, the highest number of cadres (4,203) belonged to the National Democratic Front of Boroland (NDFB), followed by 1,926 members of various Karbi militant organisa-tions and 1,182 people from a number of Adivasi extremist groups.

Kamtapur Liberation Organisation (KLO)

Origin: The origin of the Kamtapur Liberation Organisation (KLO) can be traced to the attempts of certain members of the Rajbongshi community belonging to the All Kamtapur Students' Union (AKSU) to organize an armed struggle for a separate Kamtapur State. For this purpose, they approached the United Liberation Front of Asom (ULFA). ULFA reportedly agreed to train them in order to gain a foothold outside Assam, in the other geographically contiguous Indian States, to use them as transit routes. ULFA's line of thinking was that it would not only facilitate the movement of its cadres to their base camps in Bhutan but also provide a safe haven for the injured or sick cadres.
The KLO came into existence on December 28, 1995. At the time of its formation, its cadre strength was an estimated 60. However, subsequently, it is said to be operating with approximately 300 'active cadres'.

Objectives: The objective of the KLO is to carve out a separate Kamtapur State comprising six districts— Cooch Behar, Darjeeling, Jalpaiguri, North and South Dinajpur and Malda—of West Bengal and four contiguous districts of Assam— Kokrajhar, Bongaigaon, Dhubri and Goalpara. At its inception, the KLO was an over-ground organization and was formed to address problems such as large-scale unemployment, land alienation, perceived neglect of the

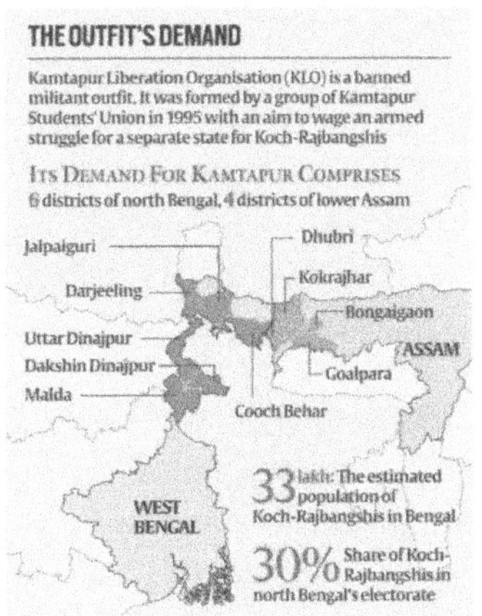

Kamtapuri language and identity, and grievances of economic deprivation. Soon, its strategy transformed into waging an armed struggle.

Leadership and organisation: Tamir Das alias Jibon Singha is the chairman of the KLO. He was arrested in October 1999. However, he regained control over the outfit after he was released by the Assam Police in a bid to make the other KLO cadres surrender.

Milton Burman alias Mihir Das is the second in command of the outfit. Tom Adhikary alias Joydeb Roy is the outfit's 'crack squad' chief. Both of them were arrested by the RBA during the December 2003 operations.

Bharati Das, Chairperson of the Women's Wing, was arrested from Jalpaiguri district in West Bengal on August 7, 2002. The outfit's operations chief, Suresh Roy, surrendered on January 24, 2002. Some of the other prominent KLO insurgents who could be in positions of decision-making are Hiten Roy, Ravi Rajbongshi, Rahul Roy and Kajal Roy.

Area of Operation: The KLO is active in the following areas of West Bengal and Assam.
West Bengal—six districts of North Bengal (South Dinajpur, North Dinajpur, Coochbehar, Jalpaiguri, Malda, Darjeeling)
Assam—four districts of lower Assam (Kokrajhar, Bongaigaon, Dhubri, Goalpara)
However, the outfit is most active in Alipurduar in Jalpaiguri and the Siliguri subdivision of Darjeeling.

The KLO maintains a string of camps in Bhutan. Several of its camps are located across the Wangchu River, close to the Chuka district in Bhutan. According to Lyonpo Thinley Gyamtsho, the Bhutanese Home Minister, two of its camps are in the Bhangtar and Lhamoizingkha areas of Bhutan.

Linkages: The KLO is alleged to be the armed underground wing of Kamtapur People's Party (KPP). Available evidence suggests that it maintains close linkages with the ULFA. Soon after its formation, its members were imparted arms training during 1996-97 in Samdrup Jhankar in Bhutan, and also subsequently at Gelengphu and Kalaikhola. The KLO's headquarters is situated near that of ULFA's at Samdrup Jhankar. Reports even suggest that the KLO is the brainchild of Raju Baruah, ULFA's 'deputy commander'.

As mentioned already, the ULFA wants to use West Bengal as a transit point to cross over to Bhutan, and then into Bangladesh. Also, this area provides a safe haven for injured and battle-weary ULFA cadres. The outfit is also reportedly linked to the National Democratic Front of Bodoland (NDFB). Media reports suggest that the KLO, ULFA and the NDFB have formed an umbrella organisation to coordinate their activities. Moreover, the KLO is also said to have linkages with the Maoist insurgents of Nepal. An August 2001-report indicated that, a meeting of NDFB, KLO, ULFA and the Maoists was held at Birganj, near the Indo-Nepal border, to discuss a joint strategy to carry out subversive activities against India.

Besides these linkages, the Tiwa National Revolutionary Front (TNRF), an insurgent outfit based in the Nagaon district of Assam, also has a working relationship with the KLO. In addition, the National Socialist Council of Nagaland-Isak-Muivah (NSCN-IM), too, reportedly maintains links with the KLO.
Reports also suggest that Pakistan's Inter-Services Intelligence (ISI) is assisting terrorist groups, including the KLO, to commit subversion along the Siliguri Corridor of West Bengal.

C. Nagaland:

Nagaland is one of the most beautiful state covered and surrounded by hills and mountains in northeast India which has many nicknames to it, likewise, Switzerland of the East, Land of Festivals, Falcon Capital of the World. This is the 4th smallest state in India after Goa, Sikkim and Tripura. Also it is a landlocked state in the north-eastern region of India bordered by Arunachal Pradesh to the north, Assam to the west, Manipur to the south, and the Sagaing Region of Myanmar (Burma) to the east. Its capital city is Kohima and its largest city is basically a twin city named Chumoukedima–Dimapur. Nagaland is one of the three states in India with English as one and only official language as of 2023.

The Nagas are an indigenous community residing in the northeastern part of India and the neighbouring areas of Myanmar. It is widely believed that they are Indo-Mongoloids who migrated to India around the 10th century BC.

Nagaland is formed by bringing together 16 to 17 different tribes therefore the Government of Nagaland has their Motto and Emblem as: Unity.

The Nagas comprise some 17 major tribes and over 20 sub-tribes. Some of the major tribes include Ao, Angami, Sema, Lotha, Tangkhul, Konyak, Rengma, and Mao. Each tribe and sub-tribe speaks a different language, though each of these belongs to the Tibeto-Burmese group of languages.

History of Nagas: Nagas under British rule: The Nagas came under foreign rule for the first time when the British occupied their land in the 19th century.
Nagas during World War II: During World War II, the Nagas assisted the British forces.
The Naga National Council (NNC) was founded in 1946 and signed a Nine-Point Agreement with the Assam Governor, granting Nagas control over their territory.
Naga independence was declared on 14th August 1947.
In the 1950s, the NNC took up arms and resorted to violence over Naga's sovereignty.
The NNC formed the underground Naga Federal Government (NFG) and its military wing, the Naga Federal Army (NFA), in 1952.
Following the Shillong Accord (1975) the NNC split into NSCN, which further split into NSCN (IM) and NSCN (Khaplang) in 1988.

Naga groups are primarily seeking Greater Nagalim, which involves redrawing boundaries to unite all Naga-inhabited areas in the Northeast under one administrative jurisdiction, ultimately aiming for sovereign statehood. It includes various parts of Arunachal Pradesh, Manipur, Assam and Myanmar as well. The demand also includes the separate Naga Yezabo (Constitution) and Naga national flag. It is widely believed that they are Indo-Mongoloids who migrated to India around the 10th century BC.

Naga's Issue: Naga groups are primarily seeking Greater Nagalim, which involves redrawing boundaries to unite all Naga-inhabited areas in the Northeast under one administrative jurisdiction, ultimately aiming for sovereign statehood. It includes various parts of Arunachal Pradesh, Manipur, Assam and Myanmar as well. The demand also includes the separate Naga Yezabo (Constitution) and Naga national flag.

Among all the ethnic groups and tribes living in the Northeast, the Nagas were the first to raise the banner of revolt against the Indian government, on August 14, 1947, under the aegis of the Naga National Council (NNC) led by Angami Zapu Phizo. In July 1948, Phizo was arrested along with some of his associates. They were released in 1949 and Phizo became the President of NNC in 1950. The NNC publicly resolved to establish a sovereign Naga state. In May 1951, the Council held a 'referendum' in which it claimed that 99% of the Naga people supported independence for Nagaland, though this has never been accepted by the government. The NNC boycotted the general elections in 1952 and launched a violent secessionist movement, with Naga insurgents raiding several villages and police outposts. On March 22, 1956, Phizo created an underground government called the Naga Federal Government (NFG) and a Naga Federal Army (NFA). In April that year, the Central

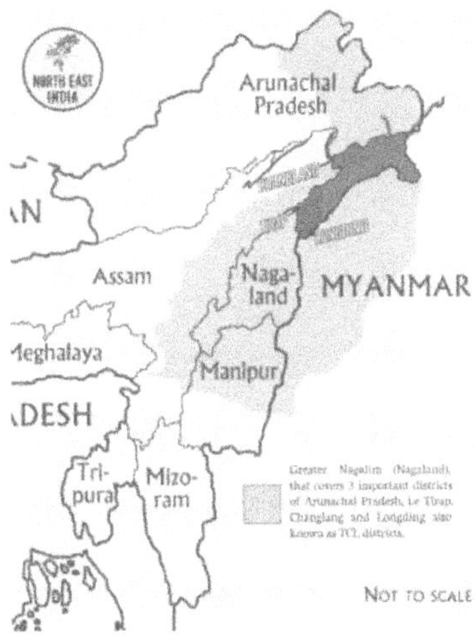

government inducted the army to crush the insurgency in what was, till then, the Naga Hills District of the State of Assam. To deal with the situation, the Armed Forces (Special Powers) Act, 1958, was subsequently enacted. Phizo, however, escaped to the then East Pakistan in December 1956 and, subsequently, to London in June 1960.

After Nagaland attained Statehood on December 1, 1963, a serious attempt was made to bring about a political settlement. In April 1964, a Peace Mission was formed with Jai Prakash Narayan, B.P. Chaliha and Rev. Michael Scott as its members and an Agreement for Suspension of Operation (AGSOP) was signed with the insurgents on September 6. However, the insurgents continued to violate the agreement by indulging in various acts of violence. Six rounds of talks between the insurgents and the Centre resulted in a deadlock and the Peace Mission was dissolved in 1967. In 1972, the Centre banned the NNC, the NFG and the NFA as "unlawful associations" under the Unlawful Activities (Prevention) Act of 1967. The security forces launched a massive counter-insurgency operation and once again brought the situation under control forcing the insurgents to the negotiating table. An agreement known as the Shillong Accord was signed between the Centre and a section of the NNC and the NFG on November 11, 1975. According to the terms of the Accord, the NNC-NFG accepted the Indian Constitution and agreed to come overground and surrender their weapons.

However, a group of about 140 activists of the NNC, who had gone to China for training, repudiated the Shillong Accord and refused to surrender. They formed a new underground organisation called the National Socialist Council of Nagaland (NSCN) under the leadership of Thuengaling Muivah, Isak Chisi Swu and S.S. Khaplang on Myanmarese (Burmese) soil in 1980. With the passage of time, the NSCN emerged as the most radical and powerful insurgent group fighting for the Naga cause, as the NNC-NFG became less active.

The Nagas had always been divided along clan and tribal lines. The majority of the rank and file of the NSCN was from the Konyak tribe, while the command structure was dominated by the Tangkhuls. This created discontent among the Konyaks. There were also apprehensions among the Konyaks and the Myanmerese Nagas that the Tangkhuls were about to strike a deal with the Central government. These factors resulted in a vertical split in the NSCN in 1988. The Konyaks formed a breakaway faction under the leadership of Khole Konyak and S.S. Khaplang, a Hemie Naga from Myanmar. The Tangkhul faction was led by Isak Swu, a Sema from Nagaland, and Muivah, a Tangkhul from Manipur's Ukhrul district. This was followed by severe inter-factional clashes in which hundreds of activists of the rival groups had been killed.

After the death of Phizo in 1990, there was another split in the NNC. Phizo's daughter Adino, an Angami, and Khudhao Nanthan, a Sema and a close associate of Phizo, constituted separate groups on rival lines. In the winter of 1996-97, Khudhao joined NSCN (lM) and is currently the Vice Chairman of the organization. With this move NSCN (IM) was also able to get the support of the Lothas to which Kudao belongs .All factions of the NSCN and NNC (Adino) have been banned since 1991 under the Unlawful Activities (Prevention) Act, 1967.

The NSCN-IM lays primary emphasis on the point that the Naga region was never a part of India and that Nehru's argument was fallacious when he said that India had "inherited" the Naga area from the British. Both Swu and Muivah argue that "the fate of a people cannot be passed on like an inheritance from one party to another". The NSCN-IM has taken an inflexible stand on this point and insists that their demand is not for 'secession' because they have never been a part of the Indian Union.

The Eastern Nagaland Peoples' Organisation (ENPO) conducts public rallies every now and then in six districts to demand the creation of a separate state of 'Frontier Nagaland'. ENPO is the apex body of seven tribal organizations in Mon, Tuensang, Kiphire, Longleng, Noklak and Shamator districts and Extra Assistant Commissioner (EAC) Headquarter, Kiusam in Shamator district. The ENPO started demanding 'Frontier Nagaland' in 2010 lamenting that their area has been left behind in all aspects of development, including education and infrastructure. The six districts under ENPO have 20 legislators.

Peace Initiatives: Shillong Accord (1975): A peace accord signed in Shillong saw the NNC leadership agree to disarm, but dissent among leaders led to a split in the organisation.

Ceasefire Agreement (1997): The NSCN-IM signed a ceasefire agreement with the government to stop attacks on Indian armed forces. In return, the government would stop all counter-insurgency offensive operations.

Framework Agreement with NSCN-IM (2015): In this agreement, the Government of India recognised the unique history, culture and position of the Nagas and their sentiments and aspirations.

D. Tripura:

Tripura- India's 3rd smallest state spanning an area over 10,491 sq km, which is as large as Northern ireland is a natural wonder of the seven sisters with its smooth landscape and laid back atmosphere, and due to its weird border, which was curved out during the partition, 75% of the state is pasted inside the neighbouring country Bangladesh thus making it landlocked. Tripura, with a relaxed land and beautiful people, doesn't feel like any conflict area but like other northeastern states, it too has separatist groups and tribal insurgencies. Over the last 5-6 decades, humanity had to perish many times. With bloodshed between the inhabitants and refugees, refugees and militants, militant and inhabitants tripura had enough of it. One of the ferocious bloodshed in the entire region of North-East, " Mandai massacre" took place in Tripura and the key contributors who took advantage of its regionalism and demographic problems were the Religious leader, religion, neighborhood country's Militancy and various arms consignors.

Before going deeper, let me present the demographic graph of the state which clearly tells us that, 2/3rd of the population are Bengali Hindus and the rest are 19 official indigenous hill tribes and this demographic ratio is considered as the sole cause of 'disturbed tripura'.

Now let's move back to the ancient times when the present region of Tripura and its whereabouts are known as kirat desh (kirata kingdom or kiratas). Kiratas are hindu dwellers of eastern himalayas as per the Mahabharata mythology. As per Rajmala chronicle, a 15th century chronicle written in Bengali verse by the court pandits of Dharna Manikya 1 { ruler of the Manikya Dynasty(1431)} tells us that the ancestors of kings are from the mythological lunar dynasty (chandravansha of Mahabharata). And it was during the 8th century the kingdom's capital had been shifted eastwards along surma rivers in sylhet near present kailashahar town of North Tripura.

The region of Tripura remained under the rule of tripura kings for centuries and the tripura kings belonged to the twipra kingdom (historical kingdom of twipra people in North-East India) of hindu Manikya dynasty with 186 kings. The Monarchy had their capitals in Udaipur, Agartala. The Monarchy was established around the confluence of Brahmaputra, Meghna and Surma rivers by Maha Manikya in 1400 followed by joining the Union of India in 1949. The ancient capital was in Khorongma (present day Bangladesh). In the present day the kingdom is spreaded over India's barak valley, Mizoram, Tripura and Bangladesh.

Tripura people:
Now let's talk about the indigenous people of Tripura, where they are called Tripuri people or Twipra or Tipra or tiprasa. They are basically the ethnic group originated in tripura. They are original inhabitants of the Tripura kingdom (Manikya dynasty) spreaded over India and Bangladesh. The native language of the indigenous tripuri people are kokborok or tripuri or tiprakok that is the reason tripura is also called as Borok nation.

British rule till independence:
Tripura under the British rule of India was called Hill tippera as it was a Monarch with a history of over 2500 years old. The kings retained an estate in british India known as Tippera district, which was a then princely state covering the greater comilla region of Bangladesh and present day Tripura. The capitals of the princely state kept on shifting from udaipur to old agartala during the 18th century and then to new agartala during the 19th century. Bir Chandra was the first king who ascended the throne during the reign of the British period in 1870 and made various Political reforms according to the British system. The next king then Birendra Kishore Manikya (1909-1923) was the ruler when Tripura was incorporated into the province of East Bengal and Assam at the beginning of 20th century. Last Monarch Bir Bikram Kishore Debbarma Manikya (1923-1947) chose to come under the jurisdiction of dominion of India in 1947. But King Bikram Kishore Debbarma died on May 1947 shortly before independence thereafter his son, Kirit Bikram Kishore Debbarma Manikya {(1947-1949) (1949-1978)} titular, who was a minor at that time became a titular king. After that his wife Maharani kanchan Devi (widow) presided over the council of regency that was formed to govern the state. On 13 August 1947, Maharaja signed the Instrument of Accession to join the Union of India. On 9th September 1949, Maharani signed the Merger Agreement which was effective from 15th October, thus making Tripura a centrally administered part C state of India. The last king at present is Kirit Pradyot Manikya, the son of Kirit Bikram Kishore Debbarma Manikya.

After Independence: On 9th sept 1949, tripura became a centrally administered part C state of India. Further in November 1956, Tripura became a Union Territory without legislature. Finally on 21st Jan 1972 tripura gained a full statehood as per the North eastern area (reorganisation) act of 1971.

Change in Demography and threat to ethnicity:
Historically, three phases of Bengali immigration into Tripura can be identified: the immigration occurring in the pre-colonial and colonial era; immigration caused by the partition upon independence in 1947; and immigration during and following the 1971 secession war in East Pakistan/Bangladesh. There is still an on-going low-intensity immigration from Bangladesh due to economic factors and occasional Muslim-Hindu tensions in that country.

From the late middle ages, Bengali cultivators were encouraged by Tripura's tribal dynasties to cultivate rice in the plains in order to collect greater revenue through wet-rice cultivation. Later, towards the mid-nineteenth century, Bengali took up administrative posts in Tripura to manage the land revenue system and the Bengali language became a medium in culture and administration and a lingua franca between the different tribes. Thus, for the tribal rulers, Bengali immigration was a means of economic and administrative consolidation. As long as the tribals had enough land, land alienation did not emerge as a major problem. That changed when Bengali Hindus, fleeing the violence of the partition of India in 1947 and the secession of East Pakistan—now Bangladesh—in 1971 migrated to Tripura, causing a radical demographic change in the state. Between 1947 and 1971, 609,998 Bengali displaced in East Pakistan came to Tripura for resettlement. The impact of the said migration waves on the demographic map of Tripura is shown by the following figures: if according to colonial census data, tribals formed 52 percent of Tripura's population in 1901, the figure was 36.85 in 1951 and 28.95 in 1971, to stabilize at 30.95 in 1991.

Before 1947 (India-Pakistan partition) and prior to the Tripura merger with India Union on 15th October 1949. Tripura then Twipra was a princely independent state, a peaceful self sufficient one with all resources and revenues. After partition, war broke between India and Pakistan (East Pakistan) in the eastern side of India. And on 1949, after the partition and formation of East Pakistan, 6,10,000 Bengali hindus migrated to Tripura as refugees due to religious persecution (which was the state population in 1951). Further adding more 13 lakh Bengali

Hindu refugees during the Bangladesh Liberation War of 1971. Mass genocide of Bengali Hindus by the Pakistani army led to influx of refugees to North-east states also Tripura. Many Hindus were killed, persecuted by the Pakistan military which later took to India Pakistan war of 1971 and Bangladesh was formed. After the war- India government reorganized North-east states which gave a new existence of 3 new states on 21st Jan 1972,- Meghalaya, Manipur and Tripura. Before the partition, merger of Tripura into Union of India and several genocide in Bangladesh, 99% of people in Tripura were borok people which had now reduced to 31% as per 2001 census. This is considered as a massive demographic change till now and as per speculation the borok people will be wiped out within the next 50 years government fails to adapt any concrete measures.

Reason of the beginning of rebellion and insurgency:
Started at the end of 1970, due to the massive change in demography because of the illegal migration of Bengali people who were persecuted in Bangladesh then East Pakistan. The migrants outnumbered the tribals, thus threatening the local economy, culture and social values. Bengali speaking people started to dominate the politics and administration of the tribals were forced to move into the Hilly region. Since the Government has failed to stop the illegal immigration issue therefore it led to a confrontation between Indian nationalism and newly created tripura nationalism thus creating an armed clash between the tribal rebel groups and the forces of India. Further the rise of fanatic Tripura nationalism has resulted in more clashes between the tribal forces and Bengali forces. Countries, organizations and powers who wanted India's North-east to be unstable had heavily invested their stakes through sheltering the militants by providing them arms and proper brainwashing.

The tribal insurgency in Tripura is rooted in the effects of migration from Bangladesh, land-related issues and social marginalization of the indigenous population. Although tribal resistance movements in Tripura existed as far back as 1965, the insurgency's present phase started in 1989 with the emergence of armed groups of which the separatist National Liberation Front of Tripura (NLFT) is the largest and most controversial because of its alleged militant Christian agenda. The NLFT was founded in early 1989 and outlawed inm1997. About 800 fighters strong at its zenith, it is now believed to have some 450 to 500 fighters and 20 to 40 cadres. The NLFT controls some of the more isolated tribal areas along the border with the state of Mizoram and Bangladesh where it is believed to have some 25 safe havens.i

Chronologically rising of the rebel groups:

Senkrak: During the mid 1960's, a first of its kind organised armed tribal movement was started as a reaction or counter to the government's decision of settling down non-tribals refugees in the areas of tribals, which later resulted in various attacks on the government. However it was controlled in the year 1968.

Tripura National Volunteers (TNV) & All Tripura People's Liberation Organisation (ATPLO): Also called Tribal National Volunteers or Tripura National Volunteers force is ·a national militant group of Tripura, formed on 10th Nov 1978 by Bijoy Kumar Hrangkhawl (Leader of Tripura Upajati Juba Samiti) on the ideology of Tripura Nationalism with the objective to separate Tripura from India through arm struggle. The leader was a devout Christian. During the initial days of TNV's establishment, the group managed to gather support from Mizo National Front (MNF). (MNF was formed by the people of Mizoram region of Assam against the central government due to the inaction taken by the latter towards the pathetic famine situation called "mautam" in the year 1959). TNV encouraged its militants to join Christianity as the majority of its members follow it. Binanda Jamatia (member of TNV) backstabbed Bijoy Kumar Hrangkhawl and broke away to start ATPLO on Dec 12, 1980 at Thangnan, Mayami reserve forest in Bangladesh. In 1981, Chunni Kaloi, a member of ATPLO left the organization. In 13th Aug 1982, Binanda Jamatia had a suspect on Chunni Kaloi, that he was supporting Bijoy Kumar Hrangkhawl, which made Binanda Jamatia kidnap Bijoy Kumar Hrangkhawl and his wife. In 3rd Sept 1982, Chunni Kaloi looted arms and ammunition from Manu police station, thereafter attacked the ATPLO camp and rescued Bijoy Kumar Hrangkhawl. In 10th Nov 1982, TNV was revived by Bijoy Kumar Hrangkhawl as president. In 23rd July 1983, Binanda Jamatia surrendered to local police thus making the ATPLO defunct. On the other hand TNV became more powerful, and continued to attack non-tribal and security personnel till 1988. In 12th Aug 1988, TNV surrendered and a tripartite accord was signed by the Government of India, Government of Tripura and TNV. In 2000, TNV merged into a political party called Indegeneous People's Front of Tripura (IPFT).Binanda Jamatia (member of TNV) backstabbed Bijoy Kumar Hrangkhawl and broke away to start ATPLO on Dec 12, 1980 at Thangnan, Mayami reserve forest in Bangladesh. In 1981, Chunni Kaloi, a member of ATPLO left the organization. In 13th Aug 1982, Binanda Jamatia had a suspect on Chunni Kaloi, that he was supporting Bijoy Kumar Hrangkhawl, which made Binanda Jamatia kidnap Bijoy Kumar Hrangkhawl and his wife. In 3rd Sept 1982, Chunni Kaloi looted arms and ammunition from Manu police station, thereafter attacked the ATPLO camp and rescued Bijoy Kumar Hrangkhawl. On 10th Nov 1982, TNV was revived by Bijoy Kumar Hrangkhawl as president. On 23rd July 1983, Binanda Jamatia surrendered to local police thus making the ATPLO defunct. On the other hand TNV became more powerful, and continued to attack non-tribal and security personnel till 1988. On 12th Aug 1988, TNV surrendered and a tripartite accord was signed by the Government of India, Government of Tripura and TNV. In 2000, TNV merged into a political party called Indigenous People's Front of Tripura (IPFT).

Mandai massacre: On June 8, 1980 the largest community violence between the tribals and non-tribals spreaded across the state, more specifically between the ethnic tribe of Tripura and Bengali community at a village called Mandai, which is located at a distance of 30 kms from the state of Agartala. This violence was known for its horribly gruesome killings where 255 Bengalis were killed including children's, pregnant women. As per the data of Indian Army, it was more than the double horrific of My Lai massacre (US Army torture to the Vietnamese people during the US-Vietnam war). As per unidentified sources, more than 1300 people were killed causing massive damage to land and property. This kind of incident became very less after the formation of Tribals Autonomous District Council and counter insurgency operations by the Indian defense forces.

A key event in Tripura were the anti-Bengali riots of May 1979 and June 1980. The riots—which remain a quasi-taboo subject in the streets, markets, and villages up to this day—are believed to have been engineered by TNV members. They resulted in an estimated state-wide death toll of 2,000, with some 20,000 dwellings burned down. They did not only consolidate the TNV as the main tribal militant group but also led to a communitarian polarisation that enhanced the rapid christianization of the tribal population of Tripura. The riots, of course, entrenched animosity and distrust between the tribal and Bengali communities. At the same time, they created a more pertinent need to affirm separate tribal identity vis-a-vis the Bengali Hindu majority in the state. In turn, that led to a larger openness towards Christianity and to Baptism—already present on the grounds—in particular. The rapid growth of tribal Baptism was especially visible in areas where the state and federal government are almost absent, especially with social services. The Baptist Herald, the main organ of the Tripura Baptist Christian Union, describes plenty mass conversions during that period, sometimes involving up to 800 people or entire villages in one day. The Baptist missionaries would often use inducement and superstition to stimulate people to convert, for instance spreading rumors that Christian tribals become more prosperous and would never be affected by disease any longer. Later, a number of young tribal Christians obtained church stipends to study at Christian schools, learn English and advance in life. People started to associate Christianity with access to a better life and modernity." In Tripura also, the void caused by the erosion of traditional tribal culture and the loss over traditional livelihoods is easy to fill with organized religion, whereas health and education programs of church charities play a role in the rise of an educated tribal elite.

Tripura Resurrection Army (TRA): Dhananjay Reang, once Vice president of TNV and President of NLFT formed TRA on 11 Feb 1994 after an attack on him by one of the spliter group of NLFT in his hideout on 10th July 1993 as per the directions of Biswamohan Debbarma and Joshua Debbarma. But the militant organization couldn't sustain or fight back and later surrendered to the Government of Tripura on 5th Feb 1997.

National Liberation Front of Twipra (NLFT): One of the largest militant organization in Tripura's insurgency with its headquarters in Bangladesh and Bhutan. It's ideology was separatism through Tripura Nationalism.
In Dec 1988, a conference was held in rangamura under the leadership of bk, dhanjoy reang and other surrendered tnv members- discussion of future plans and tnv accord. Read showed discontent on the conference and not satisfied with the tnv accord.
In 1988, during the Surrender of tnv d reang was the vp of tnv but he didnot take part in the talks with got or new Delhi as he was unhappy with the resolution therefore in the conference d reang was up for keeping up a armed group for the proper implementation of thevtnv accord. But others disagree to the proposal of d reang.

In 12 March 1989, NLFT was born by former TNV leader D Reang. Its armed wing National Holy Army looted arms from various police stations and made its base at Chakeko Bari.

On 12 Mar 1989, D Reang, former vice president of TNV, expelled from NLFT in 1993, formed another outfit Tripura Resurrection Army (TRA) but surrendered in 1997. After D Reang, Nayanbasi Jamatia took over, later by Biswamohan Debbarma.

Another split in the year 2001 between Nayanbasi and Biswamohan Debbarma occured due to religious conditions and personal ambition, and 2 factions of NLFT was formed. Another split in the year 2003, where Biswamohan Debbarma was removed forcefully by the patrons of NLFT in Bangladesh and a month later Kaloi became the leader. Biswamohan Debbarma formed its own camp with his followers in Tripura Bangladesh border. Later on NLFT was outlawed under UAPA 1967 & POTA 2002.

As we know in the year 1993, D Reang was removed by a coup. And Nayanbasi Jamatiya took over and then Biswamohan Debbarma took command. After that in the year 2004, Nayanbasi faction of NLFT surrendered to the Government of India and Government of Tripura under a MOS. In 2017, NLFT Biswamohan faction selected Sudhir Debbarma as their new president. On 10 Aug 2019, NLFT Biswamohan faction settled MOS with the Government of India as Tripura peace accord by sudhir Debbarma.

Other subgroups of NLFT:
TTVF: Tripura Tribal Volunteers Force
ATVF: All Tripura Volunteers Force
TTDF: Tripura Tribal Democratic Force
ATVA: All Tripura Volunteers Organization
ATSAF: All Tripura Security Armed Force
TRF: Tripura Regimental Force
TNSF: Tripura National Senkrak Force
SDFT: Social Democratic Front of Tripura
TTACF: Tripura Tribal Action Committee Force
THS: Tripura Humkurai Sepoy
LTTF: Liberation of Tripura Tribal Force
ATBSF: All Tripura Bharat Suraksha Force

(These groups were either laid down or being merged with other major outfits later gunned down)

If one looks at the composition of the NLFT's leadership, it is apparent that close to 90 percent of the NLFT's cadres are Christian and almost all first-generation Baptist converts through education channels established by early Baptist missionnary groups. Besides that, almost three-quarters come from the Debarma Tripuri and Jamatiya tribes with 57 percent of Tripura's tribal population, the Tripuri (who gave the state its name) from the main tribal group; the Debarma Tripuri are a clan that comes from the western part of Tripura. The first organized tribal resistance against land encroachment and social marginalization came in mid-1967 with the emergence of the Tripura Upajati Juba Samity (TUJS, Tripura tribal youth association). At that time, only a few thousand tribals in Tripura were Christian, largely Baptist as a result of the missionary efforts by the New Zealand Baptist Missionary Society that opened its Tripura mission in 1938. Although the TUJS had no overt religious agenda, it was backed from the very beginning by the Baptist Church of Tripura which hoped to push back Communist influence among tribals by promoting and expand its role in tribal identity and emancipation. Feeling that its demands went unfulfilled and that Bengali immigration and land encroachment continued, the TUJS formed an armed wing, of which some cadres established contacts with Christian tribal rebel groups in the neighboring state of Mizoram and in Bangladesh. In 1978, the initially 400 strong Tripura National Volunteers (TNV) emerged as a more radical cell within the TUJS. Although the TNV handed no Christian agenda or symbols, the bulk of its leadership consisted of radical TUJS elements who were first-generation Christian converts. Later, in 1988, a peace and power-sharing accord between the rebels and the state government in 1988 led to a complicated factionalist process within the TNV and TUJS that would eventually result in the formation of today's main insurgent group: the National Liberation Front of Tripura.

Traditionally, the NLFT targets Bengali Hindu and fights some 9,000 paramilitary troops bought to quell the insurgency. It also engaged in inter-factional fighting with rival rebel outfits. In addition to the more than 2,000 killed during ethnic riots between tribals and non-tribals near the state capital Agartala in 1979 and 1980, the present insurgency in Tripura claimed over 3,000 lives, 78 percent of whom are civilian casualties. The number of internally displaced is estimated at some

100,000 for the period between 1980 and 2004. Although it is hard to say how much support the NLFT actually has among the tribal population, some estimates put up that about half of the tribal community of Tripura either supports the NLFT or other separatist groups.

Officially, the NLFT's goals are the establishment of an independent Tripura (the "United State of Twipra") through armed struggle; liberation from "Indian neo-colonialism"; instilling consciousness against exploitation; and the promotion of the indigenous languages and culture. To what extent its ideology and agenda are influenced by militant Christianity—and Baptism in particular—is a question that gained prominence since 1998. That year saw a series of raids where NLFT fighters specifically targeted Hindu temples and families of Hindu priests to intimidate local tribals into conversion to Christianity. Later, in early 2001, nearly 125 NLFT fighters and cadres left the group because of what they claimed to be pervasive corruption among the senior NLFT-leadership and the latter's forcible conversion of NLFT cadres and tribal civilians to Christianity.

Yet, contrary to the Christian militias in Ambon, for example, neither the NLFT's name, flag and emblem contain any Christian symbols. The group's 1991 constitution, for its part, also has few references to Christianity or the establishment of any form of religious rule. Article 4, section a. of the NLFT's constitution even states that membership is open to "... any person irrespective of caste, sex or creed who is dedicated (...) and subscribing to the aims and objectives of the movement." The only elements that do have a religious connotation are the NLFT's armed wing's name—the National Holy Army, seldom used in the literature about Tripura—and the obligation for cadres and fighters to make an oath of allegiance "in the name of God" (art. 34).

The reason why the NLFT is included as a case for this article is, that in spite of the absence of Christian references in both its symbols and its consitution, a militant form of Chritianity nonetheless came to play an increasingly large role. One of the main areas where the NLFT's religious turn became visible over the last few years, was its Christian Militantism in Tripura. According to Subir Bhaumik, one of the few scholars who closely monitors the situation in his home state Tripura since the beginning of the insurgency, "contrary to older tribal opposition groups the NLFT increasingly has a more overt evangelical-

Christian angle in its discourse. NLFT leaders repeatedly stated that village leaders should convert. Forced conversion of non-Christian tribals by NLFT fighters using rape as a means of intimidation, was a concern and reality"

Borok National Council of Tripura:
Formed in the year 2000 by Joshua Debbarma through a split between the former and NLFT. Later it went to become one of its arms and carried activities such as abduction and extortion.

IPFT: Indegeneous People's Front of Tripura is a political party existed between 1997 to 2001, later got merged into INPT, further reformed in 2009.
In 2000, IPFT won TTAADC elections where TNV supported and NLFT didn't.
In 2001, TNV merged with IPFT.
In 2002, INPT formed by the merger of IPFT and TUJS.
In 2009, IPFT was revived under the leadership of N.C.Debbarma.
Demand for Tipraland is being put forward by the leadership, a state within TTAADC under article 2 & 3 of the Indian Constitution. Since 2018, the party is under an alliance with Bharatiya Janata Party (BJP) under North East Democratic Alliance (NEDA).

INPT: Indegeneous National Party of Twipra is a political party, formed as a merger between IPFT and Tripura Upajati Juba Samiti in 2002 because of the pressure of NLFT (Political wing). Then Chief of TNV Bijoy Kumar Hrangkhawl was the founder of INPT.

ATTF: The All Tripura Tiger Force (ATTF) was originally founded as All Tripura Tribal Force on July 11, 1990, by a group of former Tripura National Volunteers (TNV) terrorists, who under the leadership of Ranjit Debbarma dissociated themselves from a faction of the TNV led by Lalit Debbarma which surrendered arms in accordance with the August 1988 Accord concluded between the TNV and the Union government.

According to the ATTF, the outfit rechristened itself as All Tripura Tiger Force by substituting the word 'Tribal' with 'Tiger' sometime in 1992.

It was initially a small group of tribal extremists who operated in pockets of North and South Tripura districts. Gradually, it began mobilising manpower by recruiting tribal youth and enhancing the firepower of its cadres. And by year 1991, it emerged as a formidable terrorist group in Tripura.

However, more than 1,600 cadres surrendered by March 1994, under an amnesty scheme offered by the State Government. A group of ATTF cadres which did not surrender revived the ATTF. It was subsequently banned in April 1997 under the Unlawful Activities (Prevention) Act, 1967.

Over the years, the ATTF either formed or was associated with fringe terrorist/criminal groupings such as the Tripura Tribal Youth Force (TTYF), the Tripura Liberation Organization (TLO), the Tripura Young Rifle (TYR), the Tripura Lion Force (TLF) and the Tripura National Army (TNA). Most of these groups, however, have ceased to exist.

Objective: According to the available literature, the outfit's objectives are:
Expulsion of all Bengali-speaking immigrant settlers who entered Tripura after 1956.
Restoration of land to tribals under 'Tripura Land Revenue and Land Reforms Act', 1960.
Removal of names of migrants who entered Tripura after 1956 from the electoral roll.

Leadership and Structure: The outfit is headed by its President, Ranjit Debbarma. Chitta Debbarma alias Bikash Koloi is the Vice-President and Upendra Debbarma is its Organisation Secretary. Malinjoy Reang functions as the outfit's Publicity Secretary, while Subodh Debbarma is its Communication Secretary. Asit Debbarma is the outfit's Finance Secretary.
According to State police sources, the community-wise break-up in the ATTF is as follows. Debbarma- 70 percent, Jamatia- 10 percent, Reang- 10 percent, Tripuri – 5 per cent and others- 5 percent. About 90 per cent of the top ranking ATTF cadres are Hindus and the rest are Christians.
The political wing of the ATTF – Tripura Peoples' Democratic Front (TPDF) – has reportedly set up a parallel government in the remote

areas of the State. The outfit's cadre strength is reported to be about 600. The ATTF headquarters is located at Tarabon in Bangladesh. It also serves as the makeshift headquarters of Arabinda Rajkhowa, chairman of the United Liberation Front of Asom (ULFA).

Other subgroups of ATTF:
TTYF: Tripura Tribal Youth Force
TLO: Tripura Liberation Organisation
TLF: Tripura Lion Force
TNA: Tripura National Army
(These groups were either laid down or being merged with other major outfits later gunned down)

United Bengali Liberation Front (UBLF): The United Bengali Liberation Front (UBLF) came into existence October 1999. The proclaimed objective of the outfit is protection of the Bengali population in the State from attacks by other terrorist outfits such as the National Liberation Front of Tripura (NLFT). Thus, its formation, in a way, demonstrated the clash of interests between the dominant Tribal population and the non-Tribes. The NLFT has, reportedly, carried out targeted attacks against the latter. One such instance cited is the May 20, 2000-massacre in which 15 non-Tribes were killed and approximately 13 injured in the West Tripura district.

At present important leaders of the group include Biplab Das and Bijon Basu among others. The UBLF militants have a modus operandi under which, an attack is always carried out against the Tribes in the State generally, by throwing bombs from a distance. This operation strategy is different from that of the NLFT or the All Tripura Tiger Force (ATTF) in the sense that UBLF terrorists move about in small groups and single out their victims at isolated spots. Their target could be a moving vehicle or a small conglomeration of tribes away from the settlement.

The group, reportedly has been making efforts to establish linkages with the United Liberation Front of Asom (ULFA) and National Democratic Front of Bodoland (NDFB). It is through such organisations that it allegedly tries to reach out sympathisers in the neighbouring countries like Bangladesh. However, official sources have not indicated any clear evidences as regards the same, thus far.

The UBLF is not a proscribed outfit under the Prevention of Terrorism Act, 2002, but has been banned by the State government for its involvement in the activities of selective killings. The UBLF terrorists are also alleged to be involved in activities such as kidnappings, extortion, arson besides the killing of Tribes. Media reports quoting intelligence sources also suggest that the group raises funds from the Kolkata-based business groups, sympathetic to it, who deal in tea, rubber, timber and construction work in Tripura. Moreover, UBLF militants are also reported to be extorting money from State government employees. UBLF has also reportedly secured a large amount of arms and ammunition, which include AK-47 and AK-56 assault rifles from other terrorist groups operating in the Northeast and tried to procure more weapons and high power explosives from Bangladesh in the past. Media reports have also indicated UBLF has been trying to follow the example of terrorist outfits like ULFA in imparting training to its cadres in camps on the international border along with Bangladesh. In this regard it has also been reported to have urged even the Bangladeshi government for help, primarily appealing to the common ethnic link.

Major Incidents in 2001: September 28: Suspected UBLF terrorists kill two and injure two others at Maharanipur in West Tripura. April 26: 8 UBLF terrorists arrested in Tripura

Major Incidents in 2000: October 18: UBLF terrorists kill three, including a woman in South Tripura. September 29: UBLF terrorists kill two tribals in a bomb attack at Teliamura in West Tripura. June 18: UBLF terrorists kill 3 and injure three others in a bomb attack in North Tripura district. May 19: UBLF terrorists kill 8 tribals including two women and a child and injure 11 others in West Tripura district. April, 19: UBLF local action group commander, Biplab Das arrested by the Security Forces (SFs) in Hawaibari West Tripura. A tribal youth killed in North Tripura district by the suspected UBLF terrorists. SFs arrest 19 UBLF supporters in this connection. March 1: Two tribals killed at Kathalcherra, North Tripura by suspected UBLF terrorists. Four others injured in a separate attack. February 6: Suspected UBLF kill Sub-Divisional Officer's (SDO) personal bodyguard and injure the driver.

Christian militancy of Tribals and Political Mobilization
It would be unfair to point the Tripura Baptist Christian Union, or Christianity conversion on the whole, as the main culprit for the

excesses of the NLFT. Although churches supported tribal protests and emancipation movements as a way to expand their social base and counter anti-Christian movements (Communist in the first place), but also tribal Baptist churches also played a mediating role in the peace processes in other strife-torn states like Nagaland and Mizoram. The Tripura Baptist Christian Union also officially distances itself from the NLFT and its actions. On the other hand, it cannot prevent that part of the NLFT leadership highjacked Baptism and uses it as an ideological framework for a separatist agenda and ethnic cleansing. It could also not prevent that a number of individual members and preachers have sympathies for the group and even participate in forced conversions, or that NLFT fighters escorted Baptist preachers to villagers on proselitizing stints.

In his research on Baptism and insurgents in Nagaland, Samir Kumar Das states: "Religious radicalism is a relatively new political currency in the Northeast of India. It first of all underlines the importance of religion in clustering a body of adherents around it and making them chart out a separatist path. Religious radicalism serves as the principle of community formation, to set aside internal differences."

As anthropologist R. K. Ranjit Singh observes: "There is a close interconnectness between the spread of Christianity and modern forms of education among the tribals in Northeast India. That way, the new religion creates ground for regular contacts with different groups of people and establish ties between them and laid the foundation for a bond between the different tribal groups."

Although not necessarily in the form of religious radicalism and not necessarily linear, Baptist Christianity serves the twin purpose of political mobilization and nation-building among hill tribes and their sub-clans that share a common predicament: the gradual loss of traditional livelihoods and control over land and other natural resources by the hand of groups perceived invaders, and by rural–urban migration.

At the same time, there is a need to differentiate from the dominant culture and this is quite obvious in areas that are situated on the "frontline." In 2004, for example, the authors visited a tribal village near the market town of Udaipur in western Tripura that converted to Christianity in 2001 and had two churches for a village of about 30 families or 170 to 200 inhabitants. The village was situated in an area where the river valley had only been affected by Bengali Hindu settlement in the mid-nineties. The authors asked a local doctors, himself of tribal origin, why hill tribes in Northeast India, and Bangladesh too, seem much more prone to convert to Christianity than people from the plains: "Because of migration, land seizure and the roads we are increasingly confronted with the massive cultures from the plains. Our identity and survival are threatened. So our people want to resist assimilation into the Hindu culture. The church is helping us to do that."

All of the aforementioned factors—migration, land alienation, social marginalization, identity crisis—created a social vacuum that is being filled by religion, in this case Baptism although not necessarily in its militant–fundamentalist form.

End of Insurgency
High voltage insurgency and an orgy of violence disrupted civic life and communications, and led to the closure of many educational and financial institutions, threatening the authority of the State. The State took on the problems in a strategic and resolute manner under the sagacious and visionary leadership of Chief Minister Manik Sarkar. It formulated a multi-dimensional and fine-tuned construct to respond creatively to the situation. The control mechanism was subsumed in counter-insurgency operations intent on swift area-domination and ascendancy, as well as psychological operations and confidence-building measures. An accelerated development thrust, management of the media, civic action programmes of the security forces, and the political process were additional factors.

Counter insurgency operations (C.I.Ops), a potent instrument in any fight against insurgency, formed the core of the interventions. These were not set as exclusive, hawkish, one-dimensional combat in the nature of conflict-management. The combat was invested with a broader meaning and constructive contents in the nature of a productive conflict-resolution aimed at defusing insurgency.

Remarkably, the counter-insurgency operations, intensive, extensive and covert as they were, did not take the Army on board — as had happened in other insurgency-bound States. Only the Central paramilitary forces and State police forces were drafted. Special Police

Officers (tribals included) were inducted and channelled into the operations. This proved to be valuable in terms of gathering intelligence and keeping a tab on the activities and movements of the insurgents, collaborators and harbourers. The Central and State security forces were forged into a synergetic, coordinated and cohesive mode to derive optimal gains. Their conduct was under close observation at the highest level (including at the level of the Governor and the Chief Minister), in order to check personnel from going berserk and being ruthless, trigger-happy, oppressive and violative of human rights. This paid off: no complaint of human rights violation, except one or two and that too minor, came up in the course of operations. No antipathy against the security forces or the establishment surrounded the minds of citizens.

Oftentimes, an exclusively combative operation did not result in a sustained and abiding end to conflict. Therefore, here it was discreetly suffused with psychological elements, confidence-building measures and healing touches to achieve a sustained end to the conflict. Psychological interventions were focussed on correcting the tribal person's negative perception about the state and the mainland, and inducing confidence in and credibility about the State's intentions. Psychological operations were forged to work on the minds of the target group — for all conflicts, big or small, begin in the human mind. Brainstorming sessions centred on unwinding the deeds, misdeeds and subversive designs of insurgency and to unmask its hypocritical conduct, promotion of monetary interests, the lavish lifestyle of the leaders in contrast to the abject living conditions of the rank and file, sexual exploitation of women cadre, forced induction of adolescents into the outfits and a game plan to keep the region in perpetual backwardness. This strategy was carried through the media, both print and electronic, art groups, intellectuals, and interactive seminars and discussions. Confidence-building exercises and healing touches encompassed special recruitment to the security forces and other government services, especially in the insurgency-bound pockets. The provision of jobs to tribals in particular, and to the family members of victims, attractive rehabilitation packages comprising monetary benefits, and vocational training to induce insurgents to return to the mainstream and earn a peaceful living and decent livelihood, were other features. The Governor and the Chief Minister, in the course of their public programmes, sought to impress upon those misguided insurgents to see reason, return to the mainstream and be active stakeholders and participants in the well-being and prosperity of the State and the people. There was a good response to this. It brought back a number of them, including an entire group of the NLFT-NB in 2006 along with a cache of arms before the Governor, who was this writer.

Those strategic interventions paved the way for defusing militancy. These helped soothe the ruffled tempers of the tribal people, the pivotal support base of the insurgents. The fire of enmity against the state and the non-tribal population was doused.

As the security forces achieved success in area-domination, no time was lost in implementing governance and developmental interventions swiftly and vigorously. The government reached out to the tribal people with the delivery of basic services such as health care, rural connectivity, drinking water supply, employment generation and income accretion. Socio-economic advancement and a change in the quality of life were ushered in. The impressive gains from development were perceptible to the people in general and the tribal community in particular. They discovered a connect with the mainstream and the state. The outcomes were active community participation in the development process and in the fight against insurgency, the militants' return to the mainstream and consequential retreat from insurgency.

The security forces, both Central and State, spread all over the insurgency-bound pockets as the only visible face of the State, came up with civic action programmes, offered succour and basic services. The work included health care, medical aid and drinking water supply. The provision of study and sports material to students, repair of dilapidated school buildings, construction of community centres, vocational training in computer learning, tailoring, embroidery and so on, and close interaction with the local people, were ensured The security forces thus presented a human face, a pro-citizen, people-friendly, development-oriented face of the State, and earned the trust, admiration and gratitude of the people. Civic action programmes proved to be of tremendous significance in clearing doubts and apprehensions about the intentions of the security forces and the State. This brought forth community participation in the moves against insurgency.

The political process initiated by Chief Minister Sarkar went a long way in dissolving the malaise of insurgency. Peace marches were organised in far-flung insurgency pockets to instil confidence in the people and display the sincerity and commitment of the State towards accelerated development and prosperity for all segments of society. Micro-democratic institutions such as autonomous development councils, gram panchayats and village councils were strengthened, revitalised and legitimised. They turned vibrant and actively functional as local governance modules. This brought all the communities, notably the tribals in particular, into the development stream, bringing about substantial empowerment and a sense of fulfilment.

Tripura scripted a story of triumph over insurgency and conflict-resolution, and demonstrated that insurgency was not an insurmountable phenomenon. What was needed to tackle it was a well-crafted, multi-dimensional strategy, a positive mindset, resolute will, the right vision and direction, sagacious, honest and credible leadership, sincerity of intent, creative responses to the challenge, even socio-economic-infrastructure dispensation to all sections of society, and modulated and humane combat operations intertwined with psychological operations to set a change in the psyche of the turbulent mind.

Tipraland Issue: Tipraland is the name of a proposed state in India for the indigenous Tripuri people in the tribal areas of the Tripura state. They demand the Tripura Tribal Areas Autonomous District Council and some surrounding areas to be made into a Separate State from Tripura. The proposed state covers 68% of the total geographical area of the Tripura and is home to over one-third of the total population of Tripura.

Proposed Tipraland State map: There is also a demand for a Greater Tipraland by adding Tripuris dominant areas outside the Tripura-Mamit district of Mizoram, Kachar and Hailakandi in Assam, and Bandarban, Khagrachari, and Chittagong of Bangladesh.

The formation of "Tipraland", a state within the Tripura Tribal Areas, under articles 2 and 3 of the Indian Constitution is demanded by a political party called the Indigenous People's Front of Tripura (IPFT) as one of their political agenda. Another registered regional political party Tipraland State Party (TSP) also demanding the same demand of Tipraland. The Kingdom of Tripura is a former country which was ruled by 184 Tripuri/Tipra kings. The first king of the Manikya Dynasty of Tripura was Maha Manikya, who ruled the kingdom in the early 15th century. The earlier kings are partly mythological and partly legendary. The second last king was Maharaja Bir Bikram Kishore Debbarman Manikya Bahadur. After his death in 1947, Tipra kingdom joined India as a C-Model State on 15 October 1949 under the name Tripura, and later achieved statehood on 21 January 1972. On January 18, 1982 the Tripura Tribal Areas Autonomous District Council was established.

Tripura Tribal Areas Autonomous District Council: The indigenous Tipra people demanded an autonomous district council, which they finally achieved on 23 March 1979 which is known as Tripura Tribal Areas Autonomous District Council (TTAADC). The politically important TTAADC constitutes two-thirds of Tripura's 10,491 km2 area, which has 12,16,465 (mostly tribals) of the state's 37 lakh population residing in it. The Tribal Welfare Department (Government of Tripura) strictly monitoring the implementation of the Tripura Scheduled Castes and Scheduled Tribes Reservation Act, 1991 (As amended up to February, 2006) for departmental promotion / direct recruitment in all Government Departments / PSUs and local bodies. For admission in schools / colleges, allotment of seats in Medical / Engineering and other Technical and General Courses, 31% reservation for ST is strictly followed. Schedule Tribes in Tripura are exempted from income tax. TTAADC indigenous people language script was Tiprakok script.

E. Meghalaya:

The Insurgency in the state of Meghalaya is part of the wider Insurgency in Northeast India, and was fueled by demands of the Khasi, Synteng and Garo people for a separate state which is basically a frigid armed conflict between India and a number of separatist rebel groups. The state of Meghalaya was separated from the state of Assam in 1971, in order to satisfy the Khasi, Jaintia and Garo for a separate state.

However the creation of a separate state failed to satisfy the tribal groups for various reasons. Such as.
1. It failed to prevent the rise of national consciousness among the local tribal populations which later led to a direct confrontation

between Indian nationalism and the newly created Garo and Khasi nationalisms.
2. A parallel rise of nationalism in the other members of the Seven Sister States further complicated the situation, resulting in occasional clashes between fellow rebel groups.
3. The state wealth distribution system further fueled the rising separatist movements, as funding is practiced through per capita transfers, which largely benefits the leading ethnic group.

Meghalaya shares a border with Bangladesh and has seen decades of migration from the neighbouring country as well as from other parts of India - Bengal, Punjab and Bihar. This has sparked anxieties of indigenous communities who feared becoming a "minority in their own homeland" because of the influx of "outsiders". It was a culmination of these "anti-outsider sentiments" that led to the formation of Meghalaya's first militant group, the Hynniewtrep Achik Liberation Council (HALP), in 1992. Hynniewtrep represented the Khasi and Jaintia communities and Achik represented the Garo community. Hynniewtrep Achik Liberation Council (HALC), formed in 1992, aimed to protect the interests of Meghalaya's indigenous population from the rise of non-tribal ("Dkhar") immigration.
(Note: Dkhar, is a term used by the Khasis to refer to non-Khasi people in Meghalaya. It is non derogatory but some perceived it as derogatory. For Khasis any non-tribal is a dkhar and they address them by that term.)

A conflict of interest soon led to a split of HALC into the Garo dominated Achik Matgrik Liberation Army (AMLA), and the joint Systeng-Khasi alliance of Hynniewtrep National Liberation Council (HNLC). However AMLA passed into obscurity, while Achik National Volunteers Council (ANVC) took its place. The Garo – Khasi drift persisted as HNLC had set up the goal of turning Meghalaya into an exclusively Khasi region, ANVC on the other hand sought out the creation of an independent state in the Garo Hills. A small group of Jaintia region claimed a separate state in the name of the historical kingdom of "Jaintia Rajya".

On 2 April 2014, the UALA, ASAK, LAEF, ANLCA and ANCA militant factions united under the name of A'chik Revolutionary Front, the group aims to create a separate Garoland State in the Garo Hills area.

A number of non Meghalayan separatist groups have also operated in the region, including the United Liberation Front of Assam and the National Democratic Front of Bodoland among others. After Mass surrender and disbandment of ULFA and NDFB, insurgency in Meghalaya has ended for good. Most major Garo militants have also either been killed or have surrendered.

List of Anti Militancy operations: The Meghalaya government had formed a 10 company- strong counter-insurgency force, Special Force (SF) 10, in 2014 to fight the militants. And on 18 March 2015, the government of Meghalaya finally bought the new sanctioned counter insurgency battalion, Special Force 10, the unit that will receive riot management, jungle and urban warfare training. Since then, it has neutralised several top insurgents in the region, including Garo National Liberation Army (GNLA)'s self-proclaimed 'commander-in-chief' Sohan D Shira in February, 2018.

Aravinda Rajkhowa, an ULFA (I) had once narrowly escaped death during an encounter as he had gone to a stream for a bath. As per Meghalaya Police .

On 9 September 2002, ANVC militants killed 6 policemen, after laying an ambush in the vicinity of Chokpot. On 26 September 2003, Indian troops killed 8 ANVC militants in two separate encounters, in the West Garo Hills district.

On 24 July 2007, HNLC chairman Julius Dorphang surrendered to the authorities after abandoning the faction's camp in the Maulvi Bazar district of Bangladesh, four other rebels accompanied Dorphang in his decision. On 12 October 2008, policemen shot and killed top PLF-M commander Pollendro Marak, in the aftermath of an encounter in the area of the Boganol village, East Garo Hills.

On 10 December 2010, four GNLA rebels were killed five were detained in a clash with police officers that took place in the East Garo Hills district. On 5 April 2011, GNLA killed 5 migrant coal miners and injured another in the Goka coal dumping area South Garo Hills district.

On 9 August 2011, 4 GNLA militants were slain, including a senior commander, following a police operation. The events took place in the Bolkengre village, East Khasi Hills district. On 9 August 2012, security forces arrested 5 GNLA separatists in Resubelpara, North Garo Hills district, as the militants were extorting money from a local citizen.

On 20 May 2014, in the aftermath of a police raid 5 UALA militants were killed and one policeman was injured, a weapons cache was also recovered. On 2 March 2015, a bomb blast wounded two petrol pump employees in the West Khasi Hills district, the owner of the pump had previously fallen victim of extortion attempts by GNLA militants. On 5 March 2015, 10 members of the Achik Matgrik Elite Force (AMEF) were nabbed in connection with illegal arms trade operations in the West and North Garo Hills.

Decline in militancy: Over the last several years, militancy in Meghalaya was seen as declining. In 2018, the Centre withdrew the Armed Forces Special Powers Act (AFSPA) from Meghalaya after almost 27 years of witnessing a decline by 80% in insurgency-related incidents.

On 24 September 2014, the heads of the ANVC rebel group and the ANVC Rimpu Marak splinter faction signed a peace accord with the government of Meghalaya. The agreement enhances the autonomy for the Garo Hills Autonomous District and includes financial aid, which will facilitate the socio-economic and educational development of the area. In return the rebels agreed to disband within the period of three months.

Other militant outfits like ANVC, ANVC-B and the UALA have signed a peace agreement with the Meghalaya government, while Khasi Hills-based group HNLC, with a cadre strength of less than 20, is considered largely inactive and has not been involved in subversive activities for many years, sources said.

The ANVC since 2004 has been under an extended ceasefire agreement with the government while the HNLC has been trying to talk peace with the government but on a conditional basis.

Proscribed Terrorist/Extremist Groups

1. Garo National Liberation Army (GNLA)

Active Terrorist / Insurgent Groups
1. Hynniewtrep National Liberation Council (HNLC)
2. Liberation of Achik Elite Force (LAEF)
3. chick Songa An' pachakgipa Kotok (ASAK)
4. United Achik Liberation Army (UALA)
5. Achik National Liberation Army (ANLA)
6. Achik National United Force (ANUF)
7. Achik Tiger Force (ATF)
8. Achik National Liberation Co-operative Army (ANLCA)
9. Achik Matgrik Elite Force (AMEF)
10. United Achik Matgrik Army (UAMA)
11. A'chik National Cooperative Army (ANCA)

Inactive Terrorist / Insurgent Groups
1. Achik National Volunteer Council (ANVC)
2. People's Liberation Front of Meghalaya (PLF-M)
3. Achik Jatna Remikkangipa Kotok (AJRK)
4. Achik National Liberation Central Army (ANLCA)
5. Hynniewtrep People's Liberation Front (HPLF)
6. Achik National Liberation Front Army (ANLFA)
7. United Achik National Front (UANF)
8. Hynniewtrep Tiger National Front (HTNF)
9. Achik National Security Defence (ANSD)

People's Liberation Front of Meghalaya (PLF-M)
Formation: People's Liberation Front of Meghalaya (PLF-M) is a relatively new terrorist group operating in the Garo Hills of Meghalaya. Reports suggest that the outfit has been re-christened as Hynniewtrep Achik National Council (ANC). When the Hynniewtrep Achik Liberation Council (HALC) split in 1992, it resulted in the formation of the Hynniewtrep National Liberation Council (HNLC), which represents the Khasis in Meghalaya, and the Achik Liberation Matgrik Army (ALMA), which wanted a separate Garland State for the Garos. The PLF-M is an offshoot of the Achik Liberation Matgrik Army (ALMA). Most of the ALMA terrorists surrendered in 1994, but a few formed the Achik National Volunteers' Council (ANVC) in 1995. The PLF-M consists of some of these "surrendered rebels" of the erstwhile ALMA who returned underground after their rehabilitation scheme failed. The exact strength of the outfit is not known.

Objectives: The claimed objective of the PLF-M is economic development of the Garo Hills, as well as better educational opportunities for the Garo tribes in Meghalaya. It also demands a separate state for the Garos. In this regard, Chengku Momin, the "minister for information and publicity' of the PLF-M had warned all the non-Garos, in March 2001 not to contest the State Assembly and district council elections slated for 2003.

Leadership: The chairman of the outfit is Vincent Sangma and Nimush Marak is the Commander in Chief. Besides that L K Sangma is one of the 'area commanders.

Area of Operation: The outfit is primarily active in Dainadubi, Williamnagar, in East Garo Hills, and Dalu in West Garo Hills. Among its activities include extortion of money to generate funds for its activities. In July 2000, the PLF-M had slapped extortion notices even on some Member of Legislative Assemblies (MLAs) and including two ministers, from the Garo hills.

Linkages: The PLF-M reportedly maintains close connections with the Achik National Volunteer Council (ANVC).

Garo National Liberation Army (GNLA)
Incidents and Statements involving Garo National Liberation Army: 2017, 2016, 2015, 2014, 2013, 2010, 2012.

Formation: The Garo National Liberation Army (GNLA) was formed in 2009. Since its formation, the GNLA has been involved in killing, abduction, extortion, bomb blasts and attacks on Security Forces (SFs). In the current situation, the State Government is still examining the activities of the outfit before declaring it an outlawed group. The outfit is believed to have around 70 active members, of whom 45 have completed training. The law and order situation in the Garo-dominated areas has deteriorated after the outfit was formed. According to media reports, the Central Government is considering banning the outfit.

Objectives: The GNLA is fighting for a 'sovereign Garland' in the Western areas of Meghalaya.

Leadership: The outfit was formed by a former Deputy Superintendent of Police (SP), Meghalaya, Pakchara R. Sangma alias Champion R. Sangma, after deserting the Police Force. He is the 'chairman' of the outfit and Sohan D. Shira, former Achik
National Volunteers Council (ANVC) 'area commander for the East Garo Hills is the 'Commander-in-Chief' of the outfit. The cadre base of the outfit is mainly formed by deserters from ANVC, Liberation of Achik Elite Force (LAEF) and National Democratic Front of Bodoland (NDFB).

Area of Operation: The outfit operates in the three Districts of Garo Hills in Western part of Meghalaya. Though the main area of operation of the GNLA was in East Garo Hills and South Garo Hills, it has started to expand its network in coal-rich borders of West Khasi Hills bordering South Garo Hills. Dorengchigre village located in East Garo Hills District is the heartland of GNLA. Also, GNLA 'chairman' is reportedly in Bangladesh seeking support and seeing the probability of setting up a base in Dhaka.

Linkages: The GNLA has forged close operational links with other North-East-based militant groups like the United Liberation Front of Asom (ULFA) and the NDFB. It also has links with the National Socialist Council of Nagaland--Isak-Muivah (NSCN-IM). The outfit has also forged an alliance with the Bangladesh-based militant group, A'chik Special Dragon Party, which operates along the India-Bangladesh border in the western part of Meghalaya Peace Process. The Government, which initially dismissed the GNLA as a "bunch of criminals", on December 12, 2010, invited the group for talks to "facilitate their surrender". Reacting to the proposal, the 'chairman' of the outfit, Pakchara R. Sangma, on May 21, 2011, said, "The GNLA will come forward for talks only if the Centre requests it." He, however, refused to surrender.

Meghalaya's Tribes
Khasi Community: Khasi people are an indigenous ethnic group of Meghalaya in north-eastern India. They have a distinctive culture and are the largest tribe of Meghalaya. Both inheritances of property and succession to tribal office run through the female line, passing from the mother to the youngest daughter. The Khasi speak the Mon-Khmer language of the Austroasiatic stock. They are divided into several clans.

Wet rice (paddy) provides the main subsistence; it is cultivated in the valley bottoms and in terrace gardens built on the hillsides.

Garo Community: The Garos, who call themselves Achiks are the second largest tribe in Meghalaya. The Garos have a strong tradition that they have come from Tibet. They have a number of dialects and cultural groups. Each of them originally settled at a particular area of the Garo Hills and outlying plain lands. However, the culture of the modern Garo community has been greatly influenced by Christianity.

Jaintia Community: The Pnar, also known as Jaintia, are a sub-tribal group of the Khasi people in Meghalaya, India. 4) The Pnar people are matrilineal. They speak the Pnar Language, which belongs to the Austro-Asiatic language family and is very similar to the Khasi language. The Pnar people are natives of West Jaintia Hills and East Jaintia Hills District of Meghalaya, India. They call themselves as "Ki Khun Hynñiew Trep" (Children of 7-hut). Their main festivals are Behdeinkhlam, Chad Sukra, Chad Pastieh and Laho Dance.

The name "Pnar" is an endonym, while "Jaiñtia" and "Synteng" are exonyms. The word "Jaiñtia" is derived from the name of a former kingdom, the Jaintia Kingdom, whose rulers were Syntengs. One theory says that the word "Jaiñtia" is ultimately derived from the name of the shrine of Jayanti Devi or Jainteswari, an incarnation of the Hindu goddess Durga. Another theory says that the name is derived via Synteng from Sutong, a former settlement; the myth of Jayanti Devi was probably created after the Hinduisation of the Jaintia kingdom. As with all sub-tribes of the Khasi tribe, the Pnar sub-tribals have no recorded history of their own. However, they are mentioned in the Buranji chronicles of Assam and the British records.

F. Manipur:

Manipur is one of the seven states of North east India, and one of the Seven Sister States. The state is bounded by Nagaland in the north, by Mizoram in the south, by Assam in the west, and by Myanmar in the east as well as in the south. The state capital of Manipur is Imphal. The capital lies in an oval-shaped valley of approximately 700 square miles surrounded by mountains and is at an elevation of 790 metres above the sea level. Physiographically Manipur may be characterised in two distinct physical regions – an outlying area of rugged hills and narrow valleys, and the inner area of flat plain, with all associated land forms. Manipur has a population of 2,388,634. Of this total, 58.9% live in the valley and the remaining 41.1% in the hilly region. The hills are inhabited mainly by the Nagas, Kukis (Chin-Mizos)and smaller tribal communities and the valley mainly by the Meiteis (including Meitei Muslims known as Meitei Pangal or Pangal and "Bhamons" who are literally non-Meiteis). Some Naga and Kuki settlements are also found in the valley region. Racially, Manipuri people are far more similar to South East Asians than to mainland Indians.

Manipur is known for its ethnic and cultural diversity. But the State has been plagued by internecine conflicts among different ethnic groups and tribes. The State is home to the Meiteis -- the major ethnic group in the State -- who embraced Hinduism in the seventeenth century. There are about 30 different tribes inhabiting Manipur. Some of the larger tribes include Nagas, Kukis, Paites, Thadous, Simtes, Vaipheis, Raltes, Gangtes and Hmars. Unlike the Meiteis, who occupy the Imphal Valley, the other tribes inhabit the surrounding hill districts. The Meiteis constitute more than 50 per cent of the population but occupy only one-tenths of the State's area.

The Meiteis do not belong to the Scheduled Tribe (ST)-category while the hill tribes enjoy certain privileges like job reservation, protection of their lands from settlement and ownership by non-STs even if they are Manipuris. This has been strongly resented by the Meiteis who perceive that the hill tribes are garnering benefits disproportionate to their population.

Manipur has been in the cross-currents of India's oldest insurgent movements.
Naga - The Naga movement (1950s) is the country's longest-running insurgency which fights for the Greater Nagaland or Nagalim.
Kuki - Kuki groups also have fought the Indian government for an 'independent Kuki homeland', spread across Manipur. The Kuki insurgency gained momentum after ethnic clashes with the Nagas of Manipur in the early 1990s.
Meitei - The Meiteis in Manipur also opposed the merger agreement between the Manipuri king and the Indian government (1949).
In 1964, the United National Liberation Front (UNLF), a meitei insurgent group, was formed, demanding secession from India.

Subsequently, numerous Meitei insurgent (valley insurgent) groups like the People's Revolutionary Party of Kangleipak (PREPAK) and the People's Liberation Army (PLA) came into being.

History: Royal chronicles, Cheitharol Kumbaba, document the history of Manipuri kings of Ningthouja dynasty to 33 AD, one of the longest-ruling dynasties of India. The kings and people of Manipur followed an indigenous faith known as Sanamahism until the 18th century. At the very beginning of the 18th century, some scholars say in 1704, king Charairongba converted to Hinduism along with his family. Meidingu Pamheiba (named Garib Nawaz by Muslims) was the son of king Charairongba, who is known for his conquest of the Burmese capital. In the year 1891 Manipur became a Princely State under British Rule after the Anglo-Manipur war. In 1947, Maharaja Budhachandra signed a Treaty of Accession merging Manipur into India. Manipur became a Union Territory in 1956 and in the year 1972 it was granted the status of full fledged state.

Manipur was merged fully with the Indian Union on October 15, 1949, but it became a full-fledged State more than two decades later, in 1972. This delay in granting statehood caused discontent among the Meiteis who felt that their identification with 'Hindu India' brought them no political or economic benefits. This gave rise to secessionist tendencies among a section of the Meiteis and a number of separatist groups emerged thereafter. On November 24, 1964, Samarendra Singh founded the United National Liberation Front (UNLF) to achieve independence and establish a socialist society. In December 1968, a breakaway group of the UNLF, led by Oinam Sudhir Kumar, established a government-in-exile called Revolutionary Government of Manipur (RGM) with headquarters in Shylhet, in the then East Pakistan. The RGM was backed by Pakistan. The primary objective of the RGM was to 'liberate' Manipur through an armed struggle. The RGM maintained an elaborate underground organisation. Its administrative and civil set-up included a home minister, a finance minister, a foreign minister and an army chief of staff with Sudhir Kumar as General Secretary.

However, the Meitei secessionist movement received a serious jolt when most of its leaders were arrested during the Bangladesh liberation war in 1971. The movement gradually fizzled out with the rest of the leaders accepting the amnesty offered by the then Chief Minister of the State, R.K. Dorendro Singh.

Some of the Meitei rebels, including N. Bisheswar Singh, were detained in Tripura jails in the company of Naxalites-leftwing extremists. Bisheswar Singh and his associates were indoctrinated there into Maoist- thought. After his release from jail, Bisheswar, along with a team of 16 other Meitei rebels, left for Lhasa in Tibet, on June 14, 1975, to seek Chinese assistance. The team returned to Manipur in 1976 after receiving extensive training in guerrilla warfare . On September 25, 1978, Bisheswar formed the People's Liberation Army (PLA) to achieve independence through armed struggle.

Apart from the formation of the PLA, Manipur witnessed the growth of a number of Meitei underground organisations with similar objectives in the late seventies and early eighties: People's Revolutionary Party of Kangleipak (PREPAK) led by R.K. Tulachandra in 1977 and Kangleipak Communist Party (KCP) in 1980. Some lesser known insurgent groups such as Poirei Liberation Front (1979), Meitei State Committee and United People's Revolutionary Socialist Party also sprang up.

Meitei insurgents stepped up their activities during 1979-81. They unleashed a violent campaign looting banks and treasuries and killing many security force personnel. The number of persons killed in acts of violence went up from two in 1978 to 14 in 1979, 36 in 1980, and 51 in 1981. In order to tackle the situation, the entire Imphal Valley was declared a disturbed area and the Armed Forces (Special Powers) Act, 1958, was imposed on the Valley in September 1980. Subsequently, security forces arrested Tulachandra, the leader of PREPAK, while the leader of the rival PREPAK faction, Maipak Sharma, surrendered in the same year. Security forces also succeeded in destroying several bases of the Meitei insurgent groups. Security forces, while raiding a PLA camp in Tekcham, Thoubal district, killed nearly its entire top-leadership and arrested Bisheswar on July 6, 1981. On October 26, 1981, the PLA, PREPAK and the KCP were notified as unlawful organisations. Counter-insurgency operations continued and on April 13, 1982, the new PLA leader, Thoundam Kunjabehari and eight other activists were killed in an encounter in Kadampokpi, near Imphal.

Following these setbacks, the PLA failed to keep up the momentum, though sporadic low-level terrorist activities continued. But two other Meitei insurgent groups - PREPAK and the KCP found it difficult to recover from the losses suffered during counter-insurgency operations.

By the end of the eighties, Manipur was once again engulfed in insurgency. Meitei extremists groups, particularly the PLA, stepped up their activities. PLA militants killed Vandana Mallick,an Indian Police service (IPS) officer in an ambush near Imphal on April 8, 1989. Importantly, the PLA reorganised itself and formed a political wing called the Revolutionary People's Front (RPF) in the same year. The RPF seeks the secession of Manipur from India. The RPF established a government-in-exile in Bangladesh's Shylhet district, with Irengbam Bhorot Singh as the president. The RPF had a vice-president, a general secretary, secretaries in charge of various departments: home, finance, foreign affairs, publicity and communications, social welfare, health and education. The armed wing of the RPF -- the PLA -- was similarly reorganised on the lines of a disciplined army. The PLA had set up two camps in Myanmar and five in Bangladesh. Reports indicate that about a thousand PLA recruits received arms training in these camps. The PLA also formed a united front of Meitei extremists called the Revolutionary Joint Committee (RJC) along with PREPAK and KCP. In its bid to enlist the support of the people, the PLA launched an armed campaign against social evils. It took to enforcing total prohibition and gunning down rapists, besides launching a vigorous drive against drug peddlers, in the early nineties.

Moreover, Meitei insurgent groups sought to project a pan-Mongoloid identity. They rejected the Bengali script, which they believed suppressed their language and culture. To assert their separate identity, they revived the practices of old the Meitei religion - Senamahi.

The insurgents also began to raise their voice against the Mayangs (outsiders) settled in Manipur. They perceived that domination by outsiders was largely responsible for their economic and social backwardness. The Pangals or Manipuri Muslims who constitute over seven per cent of the population had been considered as Mayangs. In May, 1993, more than 90 people, including women and children, were killed in a series of clashes between the Meiteis and Pangals, in Thoubal and Imphal districts. Reports indicate that the People's Republican Army (PRA) that was set up in the early nineties instigated the communal clashes. Reports also suggest that a section of the Pangals established links in Bangladesh and with Pakistan's Inter Services Intelligence (ISI) for weapons and other assistance. Besides, a number of new outfits such as People's United Liberation Front (PULF), North East Minority Front (NEMF), Islamic National Front, Islamic Revolutionary Front (IRF) and United Islamic Liberation Army (UILA) had been formed in order to protect their community.

While Meitei outfits remained active in the Imphal Valley, the major Naga insurgent goup - National Socialist Council of Nagaland--Isak-Muivah (NSCN-IM), unleashed a reign of terror in the Naga-inhabited areas in four of Manipur's five hill districts, namely, Ukhrul, Senapati, Tamenglong and Chandel. The NSCN-IM used Ukhrul district particularly (where its leader Muivah was born) as a base for collecting funds and recruiting cadres. The NSCN-IM carried out several terrorist acts in Manipur in the nineties. On June 29, 1993, NSCN-IM militants killed 26 security force personnel and eight civilians in an ambush on National Highway No. 39. During May-September 1993, NSCN-IM militants killed as many as 120 security force personnel. On July 31, 1995, they attacked a Manipur Rifles post, in Kangohud, Senapati district, and looted 22 weapons and 3,784 rounds of ammunition. Again in August 1995, NSCN-IM militants made a vain attempt on the life of the Deputy Chief Minister, Chaoba Singh.

The ethnic conflict between the Nagas and the Kukis - a major tribal group in Manipur, constituted another problem of the State. Clashes between the two groups are now not heard of. A number of Kuki outfits like Kuki National Army (KNA), Kuki National Front (KNF) and many others had been struggling for a separate State within the Indian Union since the late eighties. The ethnic conflict had an added dimension as a result of a bitter struggle to control drug trafficking and smuggling of contraband through the border town of Moreh. The NSCN-IM controlled this illegal commerce till Kuki-Naga clashes erupted in 1992. The Kukis captured it from the Nagas, but the NSCN-IM remained determined to drive its rival out of Moreh, as well as out of Kuki settlements in the Naga dominated hill districts. The conflict had resulted in the death of nearly a thousand people and an enormous loss of property. Over 2,000 houses were burnt and hundreds of villages were affected.

The entire State's polity remained polarised along ethnic lines. In addition to Meitei, Kuki and Naga rebel groups, several other tribes, such as the Paite, Vaiphei and Hmars had also launched their own terrorist groups in recent years. There had also been frequent internecine conflicts, particularly between the Kukis and the Paites. Violence between the Kukis and the Paites had peaked in 1997-98, when clashes claimed over 1,000 lives, with 4,600 houses torched and hundreds of thousands of rupees-worth of property destroyed. However, there were no violent incidents between these two tribes since the signing of an agreement between their leaders in October 1998.

What are the major ethnic conflicts in Manipur?
Naga-Kuki clash - Land that the Kukis claim to be their 'homeland' in the Manipur hills overlaps with the Greater Nagaland or Nagalim. The NSCN-IM entered a ceasefire agreement with the Indian government only in 1997.
Kuki-Zomi - In 1993, a massacre of Kukis by the NSCN-IM left thousands of Kukis homeless. The Kuki-Zomi tribes organised various armed groups as a reaction to this aggression of Nagas.
Meiteis and Meitei Pangals (Muslims) - Similar clashes were taking place between them which led to the formation of the Islamist group People's United Liberation Front (no longer active).

What is the Kuki-Zomi movement?
The Kuki-Zomi movement started as a defence against aggression by other groups. It later transformed into a call for Kukiland and later diluted to simply a call for a separate state. Kukiland – an imagined country spreading across the Kuki-Zomi inhabited areas of India, Myanmar and Bangladesh.

What are the dominant valley insurgent groups?
The United National Liberation Front (UNLF) is considered the mother of all Meitei insurgent groups. Out of the valley insurgent groups, the UNLF remained the most powerful till recently. Few other powerful groups are the Kangleipak Communist Party (KCP) and the Kanglei Yawol Kanna Lup (KYKL). These groups emerged over time and now function out of camps set up in Burmese territory. Over the years the power of the valley groups has waned, even UNLF is at its weakest. Amongst the Naga groups, the NSCN-IM remains the most prominent group.

What was the Government's reaction towards these clashes?
The Indian government enacted the Armed Forces Special Powers Act (AFSPA) in 1958 in reaction to the Naga separatist activity in Nagaland and parts of Manipur.
When the valley movement gained momentum, the AFSPA act was extended to the entire state. In the 1980s, Manipur was declared a disturbed area. A tripartite Suspension of Operation (SoO) agreement between the Centre, the state and the Kuki-Zomi groups was signed in 2008 after several peace talks. With the gradual improvement of law and order AFSPA has been repealed in several areas. The Manipur government recently decided to withdraw from the SoO agreement. The Valley Insurgent Groups which remains active never entered an agreement with the Centre or participated in any peace talks.

What is the history of ethnic conflicts in Manipur?
During British era: The Kangleipak kingdom, then a British protectorate, was repeatedly raided by Naga tribes who came down from the northern hills.

The British political agent in Manipur is believed to have brought the Kuki-Zomi from the Kuki-Chin hills of Burma to protect the valley from plunder by acting as a buffer between the Meiteis and the Nagas.

The Kukis, like the Nagas, were fierce headhunting warriors — and the Maharaja gave them land along the ridges, where they could act as a shield for the Imphal valley below.

Kuki-Meitei divide: Ethnic tensions between the hill communities and the Meiteis have existed from the time of the erstwhile kingdom, but the friction started escalating with the advent of the Naga national movement in the 1950s, and the call for an independent Naga nation.

The Naga insurgency was countered by the rise of insurgent groups among the Meiteis and Kuki-Zomi.

Movement for 'Kukiland': In the 1990s, as the NSCN-IM pushed harder for self-determination, the Kuki-Zomi groups began to militarize, and the Kukis launched their own movement for 'Kukiland'.

Even though the Kukis had started out as protectors of the Meitei people, the Kukiland demand created a rift between the communities.

Naga-Kuki clashes of 1993: During the Naga-Kuki clashes of 1993, NSCNIM cadres allegedly went from village to village in areas they claimed as belonging to Nagas, emptying them of Kuki residents.

Many Kukis fled to Churachandpur, a district dominated by the Kuki-Zomi people.

Meitei nationalism: The Naga and Kuki movements fuelled Meitei nationalism, and numerous groups sprung up in the valley. Concerns over demographic change and shrinking of traditional Meitei areas started to surface in the 1970s. The Meitei population feared the possible creation of Greater Nagalim would lead to shrinking of Manipur's geographical area

There were some demands for Scheduled Tribe status for Meiteis. The Meiteis contend that in a state where the government is the largest employer and there are very few other opportunities, reservation for STs in jobs amounts to an unfair advantage.

Extension of Ceasefire: In 2001, the Indian government's decision to extend its ceasefire with the IM to states other than Nagaland led to widespread violence in Manipur.

Demand for an Inner Line Permit (ILP): In 2015, as the Meiteis of the valley protested demanding ILP in Imphal city, equally intense protests were seen in Churachandpur countering the demand, and protesting the introduction of laws by then Chief Minister Okram Ibobi Singh, one of which said the state would determine who was a Manipuri and who was not.

What are some of the historical factors responsible for violence in Manipur in 2023?

Historical conflict: Historical ethnic conflicts and tensions between Kukis (Hill tribe) and Meiteis in Manipur have contributed to the unrest, as both communities compete for political representation, resources, and cultural recognition.

The Ethnic Fault lines: Meiteis comprise a little more than half of the population while the tribals, Kukis and Nagas, are nearly 40% of which 25% are Kukis and 15% are Nagas. Most of the Meiteis live in the Imphal valley while the tribals live in the hill districts. The Meiteis are more educated and also better represented in business and politics of the state than Kukis and Nagas.

Meitei dominance:

Demographic dominance: Meiteis form 52% of the population of Manipur and predominantly reside in valley areas which are 10% of the total land of the state.

Political dominance: Meitei dominate the political establishment in Manipur with 40 out of the 60 Assembly constituencies. People from the hill areas claim that despite hill districts of Manipur comprising 89% of the geographical area, there were only 20 MLAs from these areas in the Manipur Assembly.

Land issues: Meiteis are limited to only around 10% of the land in the state, as the rest of the state is classified as tribal areas. They live in the small patch of plain area in the state, the Imphal Valley, while the Kuki (tribals) reside in the protected Hill Areas, exclusively reserved for them. Being classified as non-tribals, Meitei people can't buy land in over 90% of the state. According to STDCM (Scheduled Tribes Demand Committee of Manipur) Meiteis have been gradually marginalized in their ancestral land as they cannot buy land in tribal /hill areas of Manipur and are confined to 10% of the land. While the tribals can buy land in Imphal Valley, thereby further reducing the land availability. The Hill Areas in Manipur comprising 90% of the total land in Manipur are declared by the government under the provisions of Article 371C of the Constitution.

Issues in Delimitation Process: In 2020, as the Centre began the first delimitation process in the state since 1973, the Meitei community alleged that the Census figures used in the exercise did not accurately reflect the population break-up.

Drug trafficking and cross border crime: The proximity to the Golden Triangle and porous international borders make Manipur vulnerable to drug trafficking and other cross border criminal activities. These illegal activities can fuel violence and social unrest in the region.

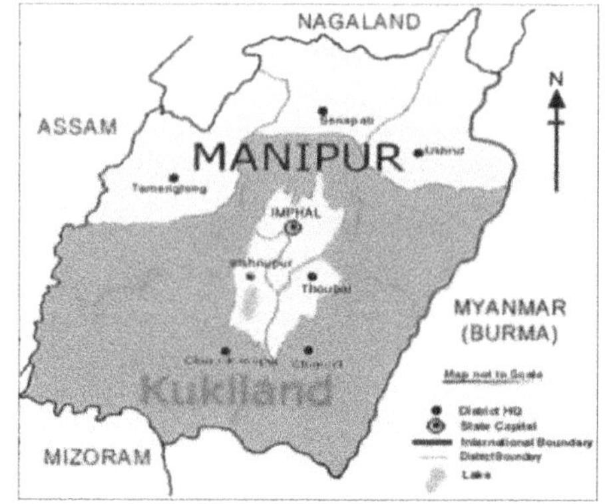

Influx of Migrants: The coup in Myanmar has led to a refugee crisis in India's Northeast. Meitei leaders have alleged that there has been a sudden mushrooming of villages in Churachandpur district.

Chief Minister N Biren Singh has repeatedly echoed and fed these fears — pointing to the presence of Myanmarese in Churachandpur, and linking them to the cultivation of poppy, and repeatedly making references to "foreigners" and "outsiders".

Demand for autonomy: Ethnic groups, particularly the Nagas and Kukis, seek greater political autonomy or the creation of separate administrative units. These demands are often rooted in historical claims and cultural identities.

Presence of Insurgent groups:

Insurgent Organization	Ethnic Group	Primary Location	Demands	Current Status
National Socialist Council of Nagaland-Isaac Muivah (NSCN-IM)	Naga	North of Imphal Valley	Creation of independent Nagalim – Nagaland	Secret Framework agreement signed, temporarily ending hostilities
Kuki National Organisation (KNO)	Kuki/Zomi	South of Imphal Valley and Sadar Hills areas to the north	Creation of new Kuki (Zomi) State – "Zalengam," or Freeland	Signed secession of operations agreement, currently in political negotiations
United People's Front (UPF)	Kuki/Zomi	Same as KNO	Creation of new Zomi (Kuki) State or territorial council within Manipur	Same as KNO
Various "Valley-based" organizations	Meitei	Imphal and on eastern border with Myanmar	Independence or increased autonomy of Manipur	Most refuse to negotiate with India

Application of AFSPA: The implementation of the Armed Forces (Special Powers) Act (AFSPA) grants extensive powers to the military. This has resulted in allegations of human rights abuses. The act's presence is seen as a symbol of oppression and has catalyzed protests and demands for its repeal.

What are some immediate factors which triggered Manipur violence?

Meitei Community's Demands for ST Status: Since 2012, there has been a constant demand led by the Scheduled Tribes Demand Committee of Manipur (STDCM) for granting the Scheduled Tribe (ST) status to the Meitei community.

The Meitei Tribe Union had filed a petition before the Manipur High Court and had argued that the Meitei community was once recognised as a "tribe" before the merger of the princely state of Manipur with the Union of India in 1949 and that it lost its identity as a tribe after the merger.

Manipur High Court direction: On 20 April 2023, a judge of the Manipur High Court directed the state government to "consider the request of the Meitei community to be included in the Scheduled Tribes (ST) list".

The Kukis feared that the ST status would allow the Meiteis purchase land in the prohibited hilly areas. The tribal groups called for a total shutdown on 28 April 2023 in protest of the state government actions.

Government eviction drive: In February 2023, the government of Manipur evicted a small settlement of 16 Kuki tribal households, claiming that they were encroaching on protected forest land.

However, tribal groups protested that the eviction drive was targeting legitimate residents.

Suspension of Operation agreements: The SoO agreement with Kuki was signed in 2008 as a ceasefire agreement between the Indian government and various Kuki militant groups operating in the northeastern states of Manipur and Nagaland.

Under the agreement, the Kuki militant groups agreed to stop carrying out violent activities and come to designated camps to be monitored by security forces.

In return, the Indian government agreed to suspend its operations against the Kuki groups.

On March 10, 2023 the Manipur government decided to withdraw from the Suspension of Operations (SoO) agreement with two militant groups, Kuki National Army (KNA) and Zomi Revolutionary Army (ZRA), alleging their involvement in inciting agitation among forest encroachers.

Why is the administration not able to control Manipur violence?

Position of Hon'ble Chief Minister of Manipur: The Meiteis community wants CM Biren Singh to continue while the Kukis want CM Biren Singh to resign. Thus have created a serious law and order crisis in the state.

Imposition of President's rule (Art 356): In order to restore normalcy there is need to impose President's Rule (Article 356) in the state as the present Manipur government has been able to control violence and does not enjoy the confidence of all Manipuris. Ruling party feels that the resignation of C.M. Biren Singh or imposition of President's Rule would be seen as admission of guilt that its government was not able to handle the situation

Complex ethnic dynamics: Manipur's diverse ethnic landscape, with multiple tribes and communities, makes it difficult to address the grievances of all at one table. The ongoing conflicts between Meiteis, Nagas, Kukis, and other tribes make it challenging to find a solution that satisfies everyone.

Lack of coordination among forces: There are instances of lack of coordination among various forces deployed in Manipur like Assam Rifles, Indian Army, CRPF, State police. This has led to multiple standoffs between Assam Rifles and Manipur police.

Armed men disguise in police uniforms: There have been instances of men in uniform, firing at Central security forces deployed in buffer zones using automatic weapons, preceded by blockade and protest by women-led groups. As per the officials, police uniforms are readily available in the state while weapons looted from police armories are being sold in black market.

Lack of development: Manipur faces significant developmental challenges, including poor infrastructure, limited access to resources, and high unemployment.

These factors exacerbate existing tensions and make it harder to resolve unrest.

Influence of external factors: Military coup in Myanmar and subsequent crackdown has led to an influx of refugees who have further influenced the unrest in Manipur. External factors add another layer of complexity to the situation in Manipur. There is a possibility that the recent coup in Bangladesh may further exacerbate the situation in Manipur.

What is the role of surrounding countries in Manipur unrest?

Myanmar: Many communities in Manipur, such as the Kukis, Nagas, and other tribal groups, share ethnic, cultural, and linguistic ties with similar groups in Myanmar, particularly in the Chin State and Sagaing Region. The Chin and Kuki-Zo people are among the large number of refugees who have arrived, escaping brutality and persecution at the hands of the Myanmar military. The lack of effective control by the Myanmar government and the ongoing conflict in Myanmar provide the insurgent groups with spaces to regroup, train, and launch operations against Indian security forces. The India-Myanmar border is a significant route for drug trafficking, particularly heroin and synthetic drugs like methamphetamine. In August 2023, Home minister of India stated that the situation in Myanmar had added to the ongoing conflict in Manipur and announced that the porous border between Manipur and Myanmar would be fenced and the free movement regime (FMR) would be suspended.

Bangladesh: There are historical and cultural connections between certain Manipur communities and those in Bangladesh, especially those of Bengali descent. In the past, some insurgent groups from Northeast India, including Manipur-based insurgent organizations like the United

National Liberation Front (UNLF) and the People's Liberation Army (PLA), have used Bangladeshi territory as a base for training, regrouping, and launching operations. The presence of Bangladeshi migrants in the Northeast, including Manipur, has been a contentious issue. Local communities sometimes view these migrants as competing for jobs and resources, adding to existing social tensions. Bangladesh Ex Prime Minister Sheikh Hasina recently revealed that several Western nations, including the United States and Britain, are reportedly conspiring to create a Christian state by annexing parts of Bangladesh, Myanmar, and India. This agenda has found secret allies in the Kuki-Chin National Front (KNF) and other regional insurgent groups.

Bangladeshi authorities have noted connections between the KNF and other groups in India and Myanmar, suggesting a coordinated effort to establish a separate eastern state. The KNF's alliance with the Islamist militant group Jamaat Ul Ansar Fil Hind Al Sharqiya (JAFHS) is seen as a strategic move to destabilize the region and further their own agenda under the guise of religious conversion and militancy.

China: There are logical historical reasons to look at the probable Chinese involvement in aggravating the current conflict especially when the region was witnessing a relative peace over the last nine years and was on path of development under Act East policy of the Modi government. China sees the Act east policy as an attempt by India to tilt the balance of power. Various insurgent outfits in the Northeast, including Manipur, continue to have links with armed groups such as Arakan Army and United Wa State Army in Myanmar from where Chinese weapons are finding their way into the Northeast.

What are the implications of the Manipur violence?

Loss of Human life: According to government figures, as of 3 May 2024, 221 people have been killed in the violence and 60,000 people have been displaced.

Other details of the violence include: Over 1,000 injuries, 32 people reported missing, 4,786 houses burned, and 386 religious structures vandalized. Mass burial of 87 tribals in the hill district of Churachandpur, Manipur.

Violence against women: Incidents of sexual violence have garnered both national and international attention, bringing to light the harrowing reality faced by women in Manipur. Meitei mobs have repeatedly targeted women as a means of control of the rival faction, including burning homes and subjecting them to assaults, and even forcing women to strip under threats of violence or shooting them in the face, causing disfigurement. In a shocking charge, the CBI has alleged that personnel from the Manipur Police allegedly drove the two women to a mob of around 1,000 people, which stripped and paraded them before they were gang-raped, in an incident that shook the nation. The 26-second clip showed two Kuki tribal women paraded naked by a mob of men who were groping their genitals and assaulting them.

Economic Development: Violence and instability have markedly impeded infrastructure projects. Exports of handwoven textiles, medicines and food items have fallen by nearly 80 per cent. Economic stagnation fuels a cycle of poverty and further unrest, as disenfranchised youth are often recruited by insurgent groups.

Growth of militancy: Prolonged unrest could provide fertile ground for militant groups to expand their influence and recruit more people, leading to a rise in extremist activities and further destabilizing the region. Tension with neighboring countries: The unrest in Manipur could have implications on India's relations with neighboring countries like Myanmar, Bangladesh, and China.

Challenges to India's Act East Policy: The unrest in Manipur could impact India's Act East Policy, which aims to boost economic and strategic ties with Southeast Asia.

Internal displacement: As per the report published by the Genevabased Internal Displacement Monitoring Centre (IDMC) Manipur violence accounted for 97% of displacements in South Asia in 2023.

It is the highest number of displacements triggered by conflict and violence in India since 2018.

What steps should be taken to normalize the situation in Manipur?

Rehabilitation of victim: It is important to identify the victims and rehabilitate them and those in rehabilitation camps, with the help of the

Govt and the civil society. The government should foster the participation of the civil society of the region in the decisionmaking process to instill a sense of ownership and belonging.

Disarming of the Civil Society: A huge quantity of weapons and ammunition are still being held by the warring communities in the conflict-driven state of Manipur. The entire civil society needs to be disarmed on priority.

Prevent Fake News: Discourage International/national media from bias reporting by exposing fake news being pedaled.

Inclusive dialogue: Engage all stakeholders, including various ethnic groups, in a dialogue to understand their grievances and find common ground. The Mizoram Accord of 1986 between the Government of India and the Mizo National Front (MNF) serves as an example of successful engagement with all stakeholders.

Transparency and Fairness: In order to remove the trust deficit, the government should ensure that the legal system is fair and transparent to prevent the misuse of power by security forces.

Evaluation of Criteria for declaring a community as SC/ST: There is need to evaluate the criteria for ST status for all, as per present status, in line with recommendations given by Committees like:- The Lokur Committee (1965) which recommended 5 criteria for identification, namely, primitive traits, distinct culture, geographical isolation, shyness of contact with the community at large, and backwardness.

Surveillance of the International Border: The Government should increase surveillance along the Myanmar Border to keep check on infiltration.

One District One Force (ODOF): ODOF will result in better coordination and operations to restore normalcy. Under ODOF arrangement, personnel of one security force will be responsible to maintain law and order in one district. This will increase accountability and reduce the possibility of conflict amongst the security forces.

Repeal of AFSPA: The repeal of AFSPA, Armed Forces Special Powers Act 1958, is necessary to improve the human rights situation in the region. The government should ensure that the legal system is fair and transparent to prevent the misuse of power by security forces.

G. Mizoram

Origin: The origin of the Mizos, like those of many other tribes in North Eastern India is shrouded in mystery. They were generally accepted as part of a great Mongoloid wave of migration from China and later moved out to India to their present habitat. It is possible that the Mizos came from Shinlung or Chhinlungsan located on the banks of the river Yalung in China. They first settled in the Shan State and moved on to Kabaw Valley to Khampat and then to the Chin Hills in the middle of the 16th century. The earliest Mizos who migrated to India were known as Kukis, the second batch of immigrants were called New Kukis. The Lushais were the last of the Mizo tribes to migrate to India. The Mizo history in the 18th and 19th Centuries is marked by many instances of tribal raids and retaliatory expeditions of security. Mizo Hills were formally declared as part of the British-India by a proclamation in 1895. North and South Hills were united into the Lushai Hills district in 1898 with Aizawl as its headquarters.

According to K.S.Latourette, there were political upheavals in China in 210 B.C. when the dynastic rule was abolished and the whole empire was brought under one administrative system. Rebellions broke out and chaos reigned throughout the Chinese State. The Mizos left China as part of one of those waves of migration. Whatever the case may have been, it seems probable that the Mizos moved from China to Burma and then to India under forces of circumstances. They first settled in the Shan State after having overcome the resistance put up by the indigenous people. Then they changed settlements several times, moving from the Shan State to Kabaw Valley to Khampat to Chin Hills in Burma. They finally began to move across the river Tiau to India in the Middle of the 16th Century.

The Shans had already been firmly settled in their State when Mizos came there from Chhinlung around 5th Century. The Shans did not welcome the new arrivals, but failed to throw the Mizos out. The Mizos had lived happily in the Shan state for about 300 years before they moved on the Kabaw Valley around the 8th Century.

It was in the Kabaw Valley that Mizos got the opportunity to have an unhindered interaction with the local Burmese. The two cultures met and the two tribes influenced each other in the spheres of clothing, customs, music and sports. According to some, the Mizos learnt the art of cultivation from the Burmese at Kabaw. Many of their agricultural implements bore the prefix Kawl which was the name given by the Mizos to the Burmese.

Khampat (now in Myanmar) is known to have been the next Mizo settlement. The area claimed by the Mizos as their earliest town, was encircled by an earthen rampart and divided into several parts. The residence of the ruler stood at the central block call Nan Yar (Palace Site). The construction of the town indicates the Mizos had already acquired considerable architecture skills. They are said to have planted a banyan tree at Nan Yar before they left Khampat as a sign that town was made by them.

The Mizos, in the early 14th century, came to settle at Chin Hills on the Indo-Burmese border. They built villages and called them by their clan names such as Seipui, Saihmun and Bochung. The hill and difficult terrain of Chin Hills stood in the way of the building of another central township like Khampat. The villages were scattered so unsystematically that it was not always possible for the various Mizo clans to keep in touch with one another.

Before the British moved into the hills, for all practical purposes the village and the clan formed units of Mizo society. The Mizo code of ethics or Dharma moved around 'Tlawmngaihna", an untranslatable term meaning on the part of everyone to be hospitable, kind, unselfish, and helpful to others. Tlawmngaihna to Mizo stands for the compelling moral force that finds expression in self-sacrifice for the service of others. The old belief, Pathian, is still used in the term God today. The Mizos have been enchanted by their new-found faith in Christianity with so much dedication and submission that their entire social life and thought process have been transformed and guided by the Christian Church Organisation and their sense of values has also undergone drastic change.

Their sojourn in Western Burma, into which they eventually around the seventh century, is estimated to last about two centuries. They came under the influence of the British Missionaries in the 9th century, and now most of the Mizos are Christians. One of the beneficial results of Missionary activities was the spread of education. The Missionaries introduced the Roman script for the Mizo language and formal education. The cumulative result is a high education percentage of 95 % (as per the National Sample Survey 1997-98) which is considered to be the highest in India. The Mizos area distinct community and the social unit was the village. Around it revolved the life of a Mizo. Mizo Village is usually set on the top of a hill with the chief's house at the center and the bachelor's dormitory called Zawlbuk, prominently. In a way, the focal point in the village was the Zawlbuk where all the young bachelors of the village slept. Zawlbuk was the training ground, and indeed, the cradle wherein the Mizo youth was shaped into a responsible adult member of the society.

About: Mizoram is a mountainous region which became the 23rd State of the Union in February 1987. It was one of the districts of Assam till 1972 when it became Union Territory. Sandwiched between Myanmar in the east and south and Bangladesh in the west, Mizoram occupies an area of great strategic importance in the north-eastern corner of India. It has a total of 630 miles of boundary with Myanmar and Bangladesh. Mizoram has the most variegated hilly terrain in the eastern part of India. The hills are steep and are separated by rivers which flow either to the north or the south creating deep gorges between the hill ranges. The average height of the hills is about 900 metres. The highest peak in Mizoram is the Phawngpui (Blue Mountain) with a height of 2210 metres. Mizoram has a pleasant climate. The state of Mizoram was carved out of Assam and attained statehood in 1987. Mizoram is the second least populated state of India. Over 91 percent of the geographical area of the state is covered by forests. Since a significant portion of the state's boundaries are shared with Myanmar and Bangladesh, the state has gradually become a transit point for trade and commerce between these two countries. A major chunk of the population still practices the traditional agriculture method of 'jhum' cultivation or shifting agriculture. Various ethnic groups inhabit the state of Mizoram and the topography is mainly hills, rivers and lakes. Mizoram has recently quashed insurgency in its state that lasted for decades, even before it was carved out of Assam. The Indian government had made several efforts ever since 1966 to quash insurgency including air strikes in the capital of Mizoram, Aizawl. Tribal Group Distribution: Mara, Paite, Lai, Hmar, Bnei Menashe, Tanchangya, Chin, Chakma, Faihriem

History of Mizoram's formation: The process of the consolidation of the British administration in tribal dominated areas in Assam started in 1919 when Lushai Hills along with some other hill districts was declared a Backward Tract under government of India Act. The tribal districts of Assam including Lushai Hills were declared an Excluded Area in 1935.

It was during the British regime that a political awakening among the Mizos in Lushai Hills started taking shape the first political party, the Mizo Common People's Union was formed on 9th April 1946. The Party was later renamed as Mizo Union. As the day of Independence drew nearer, the Constituent Assembly of India set up and Advisory Committee to deal with matters relating to the minorities and the tribals. A sub-Committee, under the chairmanship of Gopinath Bordoloi was formed to advise the Constituent Assembly on the tribal affairs in the North East. The Mizo Union submitted a resolution of this Sub-committee demanding inclusion of all Mizo inhabited areas adjacent to Lushai Hills. However, a new party called the United Mizo Freedom (UMFO) came up to demand that Lushai Hills join Burma after Independence.

Following the Bordoloi Sub-Committee's suggestion, a certain amount of autonomy was accepted by the Government and enshrined in the Six Schedule of the constitution. The Lushai Hills Autonomous District Council came into being in 1952 followed by the formation of these bodies led to the abolition of chieftanship in the Mizo society.

The autonomy however met the aspirations of the Mizos only partially. Representatives of the District Council and the Mizo Union pleaded with the States Reorganization Commission (SRC) in 1954 for integrated the Mizo-dominated areas of Tripura and Manipur with their District Council in Assam.

The tribal leaders in the North East were laboriously unhappy with the SRC Recommendations: They met in Aizawl in 1955 and formed a new political party, Eastern India Union (EITU) and raised demand for a separate state comprising of all the hill districts of Assam. The Mizo Union split and the breakaway faction joined the EITU. By this time, the UMFO also joined the EITU and then understanding of the Hill problems by the Chuliha Ministry, the demand for a separate Hill state by EITU was kept in abeyance.

MAUTAM FAMINE:
In 1959, Mizo Hills was devastated by a great famine known in Mizo history as 'Mautam Famine'. The cause of the famine was attributed to flowering of bamboos which consequent resulted in rat population boom in large numbers. After eating up bamboos seeds, the rats turned towards crops and infested the huts and houses and became a plaque to the Villages.

The havoc created by the rats was terrible and very little of the grain was harvested. For sustenance, many Mizos had to collect roots and leaves from the jungles. Others moved out to faraway places with edible roots and leaves from the jungles. Others moved out to faraway places while a considerable number died of starvation.

In his hour of darkness, many welfare organizations tried their best to help starving villagers to facilitate supplies to the remote villages, with no organised porters, animal transport to carry the air-drop food supplies. This event in Mizoram shows the failure of the Indian government to provide adequate relief to the native people of the state.

Earlier in 1955, Mizo Cultural Society was formed in 1955 and Laldenga was its Secretary. In March 1960, the name of the Mizo Cultural Society was changed to 'Mautam front' During the famine of 1959-1960, this society took lead in demanding relief and managed to attract the attention of all sections of the people. In September 1960, the Society adopted the name of Mizo National Famine Front (MNFF). The MNFF gained considerable popularity as a large number of Mizo Youth assisted in transporting rice and other essential commodities to interior villages.

Beginning of Insurgency: The Mizo National Famine Front dropped the word 'Famine' and a new political organization; the Mizo National Front (MNF) was born on 22nd October 1961 under the leadership of Laldenga with the specified goal of achieving sovereign independence of Greater Mizoram.

Seen retrospectively, a perceived sense of loss of identity to Assamese domination was one of the basic factors that worked continuously to the dissatisfaction of a section of the Mizos. Mizoram was previously the Hill District Council of Assam State. Alleged discrimination against the Mizo people in various fields, including incommensurate representation at various levels of governance was another contributing factor. Finally, the alleged neglect of the sufferings of the Mizos during the 1959-famine by the Assam and Union governments, among others, worked as the immediate cause that led to the launching of the insurgency in Mizoram.

The insurgency in Mizoram started as early as 1966 when the Mizo National Front (MNF) launched Operation Jericho under which they attacked the Indian defence forces stationed in and around Mizoram. Large scale disturbances broke out on 28th February 1966 government installations at Aizawl, Lunglei, Chawngte, Chhimluang and other places simultaneously.

Operation Jericho was created to systematically capture the power in the Mizo district. The MNF aimed at taking over the treasuries and the petrol pumps, neutralizing the police force, and capturing all the important non-Mizo ("Vai") officials. The MNF flag was to be hoisted at Aizawl on 1 March 1966, followed by a victory parade on 2 March 1966. The MNF arsenal would be supplemented by capturing the armories of 1 AR, the Border Security Force (BSF), and the local police. The MNF leaders had hoped that they would have a large number of sympathizers among the local police, the government officials, and the AR, which would make the takeover peaceful. They also hoped that if they could keep their flag flying in Aizawl for 48 hours, other countries such as Pakistan would recognize the Mizo territory as a sovereign nation and take up their case in the United Nations. The volunteers and the sympathizers of MNF were promised a prosperous future in the proposed sovereign state.

Mizoram was a part of the Assam state in the 1950s. The security forces stationed in the Mizo Hills district included the 1st Battalion, Assam Rifles (1 AR) headquartered at Aizawl, the 5th Battalion, Border Security Force (5 BSF) and the local police. On the night of 28 February/1 March 1966, the MNF launched a series of simultaneous attacks on the 1 AR garrisons at Aizawl, Lunglei and Champhai and the 5 BSF posts at Chawngte, Demagiri, Hnahlan, Marpara, Tipaimukh, Tuipang, Tuipuibari, Vaphai and Vaseitlang.

The first attack by MNF began at about 10:30 pm IST on 28 February 1966, at the sub-treasury at Lunglei. A group 500–1000 strong attacked the camp of the security forces and the AR post. The attack was repulsed, leaving two AR personnel and a few MNF militants dead, and three more AR personnel wounded. The AR camp was surrounded and starved by the MNF militants for three days. The IAF Helicopter at last flew over the camp to supply the prior needs of Assam Rifles. On 5 March, the insurgents kidnapped R.V. Pillai, the Sub-divisional Officer. By 7 March, they had captured the AR post as well as the Border Roads Task Force camp at Lunglei.

On the night of 28 February 1966, the MNF insurgents entered Aizawl after cutting all the telephone lines, so that the local authorities could not seek immediate help from Shillong or Silchar while on the same day, the MNF distributed copies of the two-page declaration of independence.

At 02:00 IST, on 1 March 1966, the insurgents attacked the telephone exchange, Aizawl District Treasury and looted money, arms and .303 ammunition at Aizawl further paralysing the civil administration.

Around this time, several MNF leaders had gathered in Aizawl on the pretext of a General Assembly. A few of the MNF leaders strongly opposed the violence, and asked Laldenga to withdraw his orders for an armed action. However, it was too late to discontinue the operation, as the rebels had already attacked multiple places including Lunglei, Champhai and Demagiri.

On 1 March, Laldenga made a declaration of independence, and exhorted all the Mizos to join the revolt against the "illegal Indian occupation" of the Mizo territory.

The same day, the insurgents released all the prisoners from the Aizawl jail, who looted the shops of the non-Mizos ("Vai"s), and also burned several huts in the Aizawl bazaar.[6] Due to the AR's refusal to surrender, the victory parade proposed to be held on 2 March was postponed to 10 March.

On 5 March, the insurgents led by Pu Hruaia plundered the Public Works Department office in Aizawl, looting items for the "Mizoram

Sawrkar" ("Mizoram Government") Office. On 11 March, the insurgents burned the houses of the senior officials of the Mizo Union.

Government response: During that time the Chief Minister of Assam was Bimala Prasad Chaliha, and the Indian Home Minister was Gulzari Lal Nanda. And tge later showed up in the Indian parliament on 3 March, stating the total number of rebels in Aizawl, Lunglei, Vairengte, Chawngte and Chhimluang as 800–1300.

On 2 March 1966, the Government of Assam invoked the Assam Disturbed Areas Act, 1955 and the Armed Forces (Special Powers) Act, 1958, proclaiming the entire Mizo district as "disturbed". Bimala Prasad Chaliha condemned Laldenga for his "betrayal", while Gulzari Lal Nanda promised "stern action" with "all the force" at the Government's command. A 24-hour curfew was imposed in Aizawl on 3 March, and reinforcements were sent for 1 AR by helicopters.

Airstrikes: On the afternoon of 4 March 1966, the IAF jet fighters strafed the MNF targets in Aizawl using machine guns, allegedly causing few civilian casualties. The IAF was asked to carry the troops in Mi-4 helicopters into the besieged AR camp, accompanied with fighter escorts, but failed due to heavy and accurate fire by the insurgents. The Toofani fighters of 29 Squadron operating from Kumbhirgram and Hunter fighters of 17 Squadron operating from Jorhat undertook independent missions to escort the troop reinforcements and to suppress the insurgents. In the history of independent India, this remains the only instance of the Government of India resorting to air strikes in its own territory. Locals claim that Rajesh Pilot and Suresh Kalmadi were among the IAF pilots who dropped the bombs. Pu Zoramthanga, who went on to become the Chief Minister of Mizoram in 1998, once said that the main reason he joined the MNF and became a rebel was the "relentless bombing of Aizawl in 1966". The people of Mizoram now observe Zoram Ni ("Zoram Day") to commemorate the air raids.

Ground operations: The operations were overseen by HQ Eastern Command under Lt. Gen. Sam Manekshaw. The local responsibility for the army operations was given to 101 Communication Zone under Maj. Gen. Sagat Singh. And by the end of the march had regained control of Mizoram. Later, when the GOC Eastern Command, Lt. Gen. Sam

Manekshaw, flew over parts of Mizoram in 1968, his helicopter was fired at by the insurgents.

Withdrawal of MNF forces: The insurgents had managed to capture all the posts of 1 AR except their headquarters at Aizawl. Their chances of capturing the AR headquarters were low after the IAF airstrikes. When the MNF leaders heard about the likely arrival of the Indian Army in Aizawl on 7 March, they decided to retreat to Lunglei, which was under the MNF control. After some resistance, the MNF rebels withdrew from Lunglei on 13 March, taking away some arms, ammunition and vehicles with them. The security forces secured Lunglei on 14 March, and Champhai on 15 March. The 5th battalion, Parachute Regiment (5 Para), was flown in by helicopters to Lunglei on 14–15 March, set out for Demagiri and secured it on 17 March. By the 25th, all the important towns and the posts had been freed from MNF control.

By the end of March 1966, the Indian security forces had captured 467 muzzle loading guns, 332 shotguns, 175 rifles, 57 pistols/revolvers and about 70,000 rounds of ammunition from MNF. However, MNF had also managed to obtain a large amount of ammunition from the captured security forces posts. Its weapon cache consisted of: around 1500 shotguns, 600 rifles (mostly .303 bore), 75 sten-guns, 30 revolvers/pistols, 25 carbines and 20 light machine guns.

The MNA headquarters, originally located in Aizawl was moved multiple times during the conflict: first to South Hlimen (on 3 March), then to Reiek (on 18 March) and finally to the Chittagong Hill Tracts in East Pakistan.

New phase: The Mizo insurgency entered a new phase of intensity with the MNF adopting guerilla tactics. Counter-insurgency operations, therefore, became more difficult as MNF cadres mixed themselves up with the local civilian population. The SFs suggested resettlement of villages as a counter-strategy. Named 'Operation Accomplishment', it was launched in January 1967, after the Union Home Ministry gave its consent. Accordingly, 109 villages were relocated into 18 group centres of what was called Protected and Progressive Villages (PPVs), closer to either side the of Vairengte -Aizwal-Lunglei main road. In the ensuing counter-terrorism operations, 36 MNF cadres were killed. 75 security force personnel also lost their lives between January 4 and February 15,

1967. The SFs also arrested 100 MNF cadres. Phase II of Operation Accomplishment was launched in 1968-69. During the operation, approximately 240,000 persons constituting some 80 per cent of the total population in the Mizo Hills were organised into 102 groups by the year 1972. The idea was to isolate the terrorists from the civilian population. The terrorists, this way, would head to the nearby jungles. Security operations would be, consequently, directed against the insurgents and civilian deaths could be minimised.

Operation Accomplishment was supplemented by Operation Blanket during the later half of 1960s. Self-contained groups of 10 to 15 SF personnel would station in a particular location for a prolonged period of 15 to 20 days under this strategy. This was to give a feeling that their presence was not for a short duration and they were there to stay for the safety of the local population. The villagers would thus feel secured in the presence of the SFs. This was also done to encourage the local population to associate themselves with counter-insurgency operations, and to win their confidence. Also, information about the MNF would come through; it was felt, in the wake of diminishing fear of reprisal by the latter.

The following period saw intensified military action against the MNF. The Bangladesh War and its subsequent liberation from Pakistan in 1971 also led to erosion in the MNF's support and strength. The Union government, after securing a military advantage over the insurgents, offered a surrender package to the MNF. In August 1968, the Union government offered the first amnesty package to the Mizo insurgents. This included pardon to surrendered terrorists for waging war against India, and compensatory money for depositing the arms they possessed. 1,464 unarmed and 64-armed terrorists surrendered under the scheme.

The Mizo National Front was outlawed in 1967. The demand for statehood was gained fresh momentum. A Mizo District Council delegation, which met prime Minister Mrs Indira Gandhi in May 1971 demanded a full fledge state for the Mizos. The union government in its own offered the proposal of turning Mizo Hills into a Union Territory in July 1971. The Mizo leaders were ready to accept the offer on condition into a Union Territory in July 1971. The Mizo leaders were ready to accept the offer on condition that the status of U.T would be upgraded to statehood sooner rather than later. The Union Territory of

Mizoram came into being on 21st January, 1972. Mizoram get two seats in Parliament, one each in the Lok Sabha and in the Rajya Sabha

Way of formation: Rajiv Gandhi's assumption of power following his mother's death signaled the beginning of a new era in Indian politics. Laldenga met the Prime Minister on 15th February 1985. Some contentious issues, which could not be resolved, during previous talks referred to him for his advice.

All trends indicated that neither the Centre nor the MNF would pass up the opportunity that has now presented itself to have a full lenient and flexible. New Delhi felt that Mizo problem had been dragging on for a long time, while the MNF was convinced that bidding farewell to arms to live as respectable Indian Citizens was the only ways of achieving peace and development.

Statehood was a prerequisite to the implementing of the accord signed between the MNF and the Union Government on 30 June 1986. The document was signed by Laldenga, on the behalf of MNF, and the Union Home Secretary RD Pradhan on behalf of the Government, Lalkhama Chief Secretary of Mizoram, too signed the agreement.

Mizoram Accord - 30.6.1986 and Statehood -20.2.1987: The MNF volunteers came out of their hiding and surrendered arms to makeshift bamboo huts up for the purpose at Parva and Marpara. A total of 614 activists gave themselves up in less than two weeks in July. Large quantities of small and big firearms including LMGs and rifles were received from them.

While the MNF kept its part of the bargain, the Centre initiated efforts to raise the status of Mizoram to a full fledged State. A constitution Amendment Bill and another to confer statehood on Mizoram was passed in the Lok Sabha on 5 August 1986.

The formalization of Mizoram State took place on 20th February, 1987. Chief Secretary Lalkhama read out the proclamation of statehood at a public meeting organised at Aizawl's Parade Ground. Prime Minister Rajiv Gandhi flew in to Aizawl to inaugurate the new state. Hiteshwar Saikia was appointed as Governor of Mizoram.

Insurgency after statehood: The year 2000, however, was not so peaceful. On June 30, 2000 suspected BNLF terrorists killed seven members of the anti-terrorist Hunter Force of Mizoram police and injured four others in an ambush laid along the India-Bangladesh border in the Mamit district. Barring this lone incident, no major terrorist activity was reported in Mizoram. 13 terrorism-related incidents occurred in the State between December 1998 and March 2000. These included the killing of five police personnel by suspected Manipur-based People's Liberation Army (PLA) cadres, at the Vaitin foothills, near Sakerdawi in Aizawl district, on March 24, 1999. This incident again occurred in the border areas of Mizoram.

After the Mizo Peace Accord was signed, the Hmars, another tribe inhabiting Mizoram began an armed struggle with secessionist agendas. This tribe demands the formation of a separate tribal autonomous district called Hmar Ram. Their organisation, the Hmar Peoples Convention Democrats (HPCD), claimed responsibility for explosions in Aizawl city in 2014. (Halliday, 2015)

China and Pak supported Mizo insurgency, reveals Mizo National Front leader in a new book. Zoramthanga talks about his meeting with Mao Zedong and Zhou Enlai in his autobiography. The two-volume book, to be called 'MILARI' in Mizo language, is currently being translated into English and the Mizo National Front President Zoramthanga plans to make it into a Hollywood movie in future with the potential of being at par with the flicks on the life of legendary revolutionary Che Guevara. Once a dreaded militant and now a leading politician in North East, Zoramthanga has completed writing his autobiography, which, he terms, will be a very controversial book and is likely to be objected by both Pakistan and Chinese governments because of detail accounts of their "support" to the insurgency in Mizoram. The book will have detailed descriptions of his 20 years of underground days, which will include how Dhaka had failed with the capture of Lieutenant General AAK Niazi's one lakh troops by Indian forces, he added. Zoramthanga informed that MNF cadres were mixed with commandos of East Pakistan and were captured by Lieutenant General JS Arora, but later all escaped and went into the jungle again.

The Mizo Model? Counter-insurgency operations: In February,1966, an ethnic separatist organisation called the Mizo National Front (MNF) overran the entire State in a series of simultaneous and surprise attacks and captured even Aizawl, its capital. The Indian government and its security forces lost control of Mizoram almost as completely as the Pakistani security forces have now lost control of Swat, which has an area of only 1772 Sq Kms with a population estimated at 1.5 million in 1998.

It took the government of India and its security forces 20 years to re-establish the government's writ over the state by making it clear to the MNF that violence would not pay and by reaching a political solution on the future of the Mizo people, which would enable them to remain a part of India with considerable political and economic rights.

The counter-insurgency operations carried out by the Indian security forces in Mizoram are considered a model for others to learn from and emulate. It has today India's leading counter-insurgency school and even the US sends its military officers to the school to learn from India's success in dealing with the insurgency.

The Swat District of the North-West Frontier Province of Pakistan came under the virtual total control of the Tehrik-e-Nifaz-e-Shariat-e-Mohammadi (TNSM) in 2007. The hilly terrain in Swat is somewhat similar to that in Mizoram The area affected by the TNSM insurgency is much smaller than the affected area in Mizoram.

The MNF movement was an ethnic separatist movement. The TNSM movement is a religious fundamentalist movement. Apart from this, there was another major difference between Mizoram and Swat. The Mizos constituted a small number of people confined to Mizoram. They had to fight against the Indian security forces unaided by other non-Mizo tribal groups in the region. The tribals of Swat are part of the Pashtun tribe, which is spread over a vast area in the Pashtun belt across the Pakistan-Afghanistan border. They are not fighting alone against the Pakistani security forces. They are supported by the Pashtuns in the surrounding areas.

An Interesting story about MNF and Zoramthanga during the insurgency days: Words after Zoramthanga took oath as the chief minister of Mizoram for the third time.

Zoramthanga went underground for 20 years (1966-1986), living in hideouts in Chittagong (now in Bangladesh), Arakan (Myanmar) and

Islamabad before the Mizo Accord was signed in 1986, paving the way for his mentor, Laldenga, to become the chief minister of Mizoram. MNF received funding and training from Pakistan's Inter-Services Intelligence (ISI).

In 1971, when the Bangladesh war was yet to begin, I was first sent by my underground government in Dhaka (then in East Pakistan) to hold discussions with an officer from R&AW. He was Mr Subramaniam. But till date, I have no idea whether Subramaniam is his real name or not. We met in Shillong (the then capital of Assam). But soon, the war started, and further talks were halted.

During the war, we all fled from Dhaka and started living in Chittagong. In Chittagong, all Pakistani army commandos were captured, but we (MNF guerrillas) managed to escape. I became a party member in 1965. I was then a student of DM College, Imphal. The next year, I went underground and remained so for 20 years. Initially, I was handling the affairs of the northern part of Mizoram. Till the beginning of 1969, I was roaming around in the forests of Mizoram. Then we shifted our base to East Pakistan.

In 1969, I became secretary to MNF president Laldenga. I was then 25 years old. We were all in Chittagong. During the war, we escaped to Arakan hills (in Myanmar) before reaching West Pakistan. It was a James Bond-type escape. The director general of the ISI later told us in Islamabad that they couldn't imagine how we had managed to escape. Many Pakistani army personnel were killed, caught and imprisoned. We joined a group of refugees and somehow reached the Akyab (now called Sittwe, a famous port in Myanmar). We were there for a month or so. Finally, we took a Pakistani flight from Rangoon to Karachi. Between 1972 and 1975, we were based out of Islamabad. Earlier in 1970, I accompanied party president Laldenga to China. It was a secret mission from Dhaka to Beijing. We first reached Canton (Guangzhou) before landing in Beijing. We then visited Shanghai before returning to Dhaka. During our stay in China, we had a talk with the then Chinese premier Zhou Enlai and other important functionaries. Mr Zhou Enlai asked me: You look very young, how old are you?' I said I was 26 sir. He laughed and said, You are younger to me by almost 50 years. Going to China and getting arms training turned out to be difficult. We sent two batches of MNF boys - about 150 boys in total - to China through

Kachin (Myanmar) for training. But the journey itself, from Chittagong to China, was strenuous. It took about three months, one way.

While in Pakistan, between 1972 and 1975, we held a number of secret talks with R&AW officials. We came back to Delhi in 1976. Then the formal peace talks began, which concluded in 1986 when the Mizo Accord was signed. We all came overground when Laldenga became the chief minister of Mizoram. He died in 1990. I then became the MNF president and have remained in the post for the last 28 years.

MNF's secessionist movement started in 1966 and came to an end in 1986, when it signed the Mizo Peace Accord with the Government of India and created a separate state of Mizoram.

When the Mizo National Front (MNF) formed the government in 1987 under the leadership of Laldenga, Zoramthanga looked after Finance and Education departments. In 1990, when Laldenga died, he became the president of the MNF.

Conclusion: In 1986, the Mizoram Peace Accord was signed between the MNF and the government of India. Since then, Mizoram has been at the forefront of electoral democracy with high voter turnouts at every local, state and national election. (Sirnate and Verma, 2013) But the transition from insurgency to democracy hasn't been a smooth one. Though only 13 civilians were reported to have been killed, this attack left a deep scar in the heart of the Mizos and gave rise to an insurgency that would grow for the next two decades. (Buhril, 2016)

3. Border Disputes among Northeastern States

1. Assam and Arunachal Pradesh

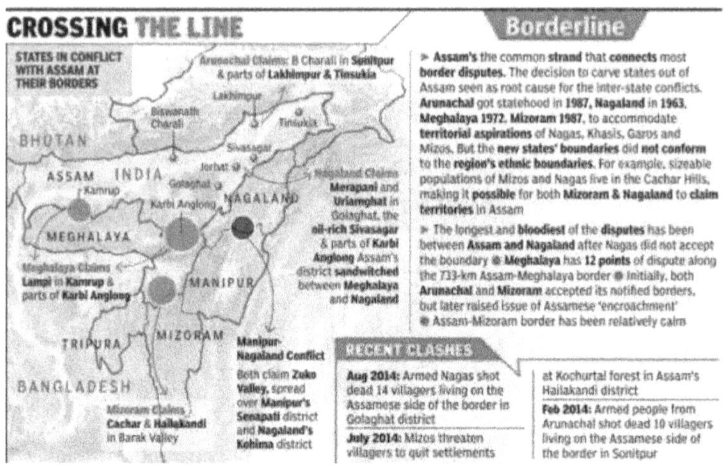

Assam shares an 804 km-long boundary with Arunachal Pradesh. This area 'separated' from Assam was initially called North East Frontier Tracts and during British rule, there was a law which involved setting boundaries between plains and hills which was later known as North East Frontier Tracts (NEFT). However, after independence, the Assam government was in control of the NEFT. This, in 1954, became the North East Frontier Agency (NEFA). It was under the administrative jurisdiction of Assam post- Independence. In 1972, NEFA was renamed as Arunachal Pradesh and granted status of union territory and it became a full-fledged state in 1987. But before it got its present boundaries, a tripartite committee headed by former Assam chief minister Gopinath Bordoloi transferred around 3650 sq km of territory, which was earlier with NEFA, to Assam. This transfer done without consultations with the people or administration of NEFA is the prime bone of contention between both states as Arunachal Pradesh doesn't recognise it. Arunachal Pradesh, which was made a union territory in 1972, has been maintaining that several forested tracts in the plains traditionally belonging to hill tribal chiefs and communities and these were "unilaterally" transferred to Assam earlier.

Also the border dispute between the two states has its genesis in 1873 when the British started the inner-line regulation creating an imaginary boundary between the plains and hills areas north of Assam. The inner-line regulation, which still exists, requires people from outside Arunachal Pradesh to take permits before entering the state.

However, that 1951 report which claimed over 3,000 sq km of the Arunachal Pradesh area had been transferred to Assam led to frequent issues eventually, While there were no tensions reported earlier. Arunachal Pradesh has constantly held that this area was transferred without the consent of its people, while Assam has maintained that the transfer was legally carried out. People have alleged that residents of one state go to the other side and encroach on the land. This did not just lead to disputes but also violence. A lawsuit on the issue has been pending in the Supreme Court since 1989. Eventually, in 1989, Assam filed a case in the Supreme Court stating "encroachment" by Arunachal Pradesh.

Assam and Arunachal Pradesh share 804.1 K.M of inter-state boundary having 8 districts of Assam and 12 districts of Arunachal Pradesh. The State of Arunachal Pradesh claimed 123 villages on historical and other grounds before the Local Commission in 2007. As per the decision taken in the meetings held in Guwahati in the month of January and April, 2022 between the Chief Ministers of Assam and Arunachal Pradesh, 12 Regional Committees were constituted for joint verification of these 123 villages. On July 15, 2022 the Historic Namsai Declaration was signed between the states of Assam and Arunachal Pradesh at Namsai, Arunachal Pradesh wherein the 123 claimed by Arunachal Pradesh were minimized to 86 villages.

Based on the recommendations of the 12 Regional Committees, an MOU has been signed by the two Hon'ble Chief Ministers at New Delhi in the presence of Hon'ble Union Home Minister, Govt. of India on 20th of April 2023. 71 of the 123 villages have been amicably resolved by the MoU and timelines have been fixed for finalization of the boundaries of the remaining villages.

As of July 2024, The Arunachal Pradesh government has re-constituted six regional committees to examine and exercise the present status of border dispute with Assam.
A notification issued by the Home and inter-state border affairs department on Thursday said that the Terms of Reference (ToR) for the regional committees, as established, will continue to be governed by

the provisions set forth in the original notification issued on June 1, 2022.

The remaining six districts of the state where border dispute with Assam still persists as people from both states have not agreed to demarcation of villages along the inter-state border includes, Pakke Kessang, Papum Pare, Kamle, Lower Siang, Lower Dibang Valley and Longding district respectively.

2. Assam and Nagaland

If we go back to the history, the Assam-Nagaland relationship is marked by cooperation and Competition. The Nagas belong to the Mongolian racial group and lived in the hills area of undivided Assam from Doiyang to Burhidihing region. The Nagas first came in contact with the plains during the Ahom period, The Ahom administration came in contact with the people living in the Hills area such as Lotha, koinak, Aao and Nokte tribe and also maintained a good relation with the "Wangso" Naga living in the Tirap district of Arunachal Pradesh. It has been proved in historical record that the names of Naga tribe such as Khamjongia, Namsongia, Bannferia, Bannsungia were given by the people living in the plains. During the reign of the Ahom king Pratap Singha the "POSA" system was introduced for the purpose to allow the Hill tribes to earn some taxes or foods from the particular areas of Ahom kingdom. Pratap Singha also allotted some "KHAT" to the Nagas and it was also found that Nagas in return of that also used to pay Certain tributes to Ahom king. But this situation was totally changed after the outbreak of Moamoria Rebellion in the last part of 18th Century and till the beginning of 19th Century. After the Rebellion, Because of loss of pride and prestige the Nagas stopped to pay tribute to Ahom kings. Therefore, the relation between Ahom rulers and Nagas changed dramatically and the Nagas attacked the Ahom kingdom during the reign of Kamaleswar Singha in the years 1807 and 1809 respectively.

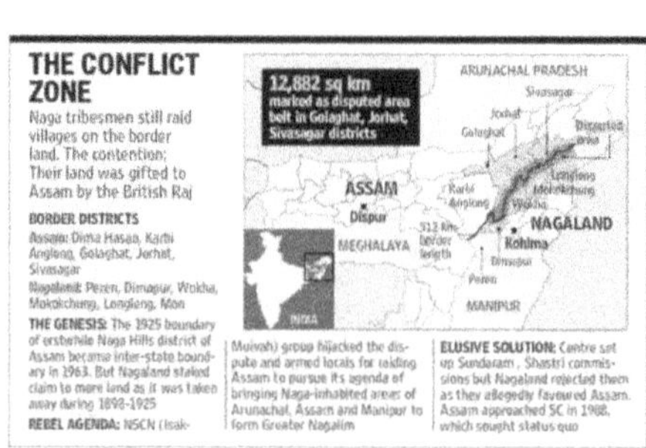

Assam and Nagaland share a total of 512.1 kms including the jorhat, Sivasagar, Golaghat, Karbi Angling and Dima Hasao districts of Assam. The Naga Hill district was created by British ruler in 1866 as a part of the Assam province after they took charge from the Yandaboo Treaty in 1826 and Naga hill district remain as part of Assam till 1957. Since 1979, for administrative purposed the entire border areas between Assam and Nagaland was divided into Six Sectors vis A,B, C, D, E and F.

As a separate state Nagaland was created in 1 December 1963 cutting down from the earlier Naga Hill District of Assam. Nagaland state Act defined its borders as per the demarcation of the British on 25" November 1925, which was unacceptable to the Nagas. Nagaland basically comprised the earlier Naga Hill District and the Naga tribal areas (later known as Tuensang Areas).

It has been observed that the dispute always came from the Naga people with the claim of restoration. For which an agreement as 16-point was submitted by "Naga Congress" in 1960 to the then Prime Minister of India. They included the "Restoration" of all Naga Territories that had been transferred out of Naga Hill District after 1826. But the Government of Assam strictly denied this claim and stand with the demarcation created on 1st December 1963. This started the border clashes in the border areas in 1965, 1968, 1969, 1979 and 1985 and again in 2014, 2015. There is a blame game also started over the clashes in which Assam Government argued that the Nagaland encroached 80% of the reserved forest of Assam in Sivasagar, Jorhat, Golaghat and Karbi Anglong Districts which include approximately 59,159.77 hectres. On the other hand NSCN (IM) (National Socialist Council of Nagaland) wants the entire Assam tract South of the Guwahati - Dibrugarh Railway track in Sivasagar, Jorhat, Golaghat and Karbi Anglong to be included in the projected "Greater Nagalim".

Causes of the dispute:
There are some root causes of the border dispute between Assam - Nagaland. These are -
1. Insurgency
2. Failure of the Government
3. Encroachment of Reserved Forest Land
4. Role of Neutral Forces
S. Break of Interim Agreement

1. Insurgency: To some extent successful solution of the Assam-Nagaland border dispute depends on the successful resolving of the

Naga Insurgency problem. The National Socialist Council of Nagaland (NSCN) wants to establish a "Greater Nagalim" including the Naga inhabited areas of Assam, Manipur and Arunachal Pradesh and in addition some portions of Myanmar. The proposed "Greater Nagalim" will cover approximately 1,20,000 sq. km. in contrast to the present state of Nagaland that has an area of total 16,527 sq. km. .

2. Failure of the Government: There is a blame game going on between the Government of Nagaland and Government of Assam. It has been noticed that whenever the Government of Assam starts the eviction operation in its Reserved Forest Areas, the Nagaland Government criticizes the Assam Government for letting loose a reign of terror among Naga Villagers.

3. Encroachment of Reserved Forest Land: Dispute over encroachment of Reserved Forest Land is one of the major cause of Assam-Nagaland border crisis. A vast area of Geleki bordering Nagaland in Sivasagar District is encroached upon by Villagers from the state and also more than 80% of the land in Desoi Valley, Desoi and Tiru Hills reserve forest under the Mariani forest Range in Jorhat District is also under the occupation. The encroached areas are mainly in Mariani Revenue Circle areas, Teok Revenue Circle areas, Sonari, and Nazira Revenue Circle in Sivasagar and also in Golaghat and Sarupathar Revenue Cicle in Golaghat District.

4. Role of Neutral Forces: A Neutral Force was deployed in Assam-Nagaland border areas since 1971, Especially in Golaghat District areas. The Neutral Forces were deployed in the B sector under Golaghat District which has always remained the key point of disputes. But sometimes, the role of Neutral Forces cannot easily be acceptable for the inhabitants in the deployed areas.

5. Break of Interim Agreement: Break of the Interim Agreement between Assam and Nagaland by both side is a major factor in border dispute. The Interim Agreement was signed in 1972 to maintain a good relation between the two parties and to sort out the problem. The Interim Agreement was signed after the recommendation of the K.V.K. Sundaram committee report.

Continuity of the dispute till Present time: Since the creation of Nagaland the dispute over their territorial demarcation has developed and Nagaland regularly involved in some cross border activities with Neighboring states particularly with Assam in Golaghat and Jorhat District bordering areas. The dispute had grabbed world attention with the infamous Merapani incident in 1985. And in 2007 the all Assam Student union (AASU) threatened the rebel side that they would march into Nagaland.

The 'AASU' called economic Blockade against Nagaland in July, 2017, when Geleki region of Sivasagar district incidented an aggressive behavior by Naga People and kill two residents and torched several houses. The Assam government has already filed original suit No. 02/1988 before the honorable Supreme Court for identification of boundary and resolving the boundary dispute. In 2014 Under Dhansiri Subdivision of Golaghat district an incident happened again. The root of the couflict and politics on it still prevalent since the first Naga assailment came in on 29 December 1959 and government property at Uriamghat. There is always a tension on Ronkham areas of border in Jorhat district.

As on Aug 2021, The Nagaland Assembly adopted a three-point resolution to resolve border tensions with Assam, PTI reported. The development came nearly a week after the two states agreed to withdraw their armed police forces from disputed areas in the Dessoi Valley reserve forest. Members of the Assembly agreed to form a 10-member committee led by Nagaland Chief Minister Neiphiu Rio to study all aspects of the matter. The committee will prepare a report and submit it to the House within three months.

Steps Taken so far: The Government of India formed a commission under the leadership of K.V.K. Sundaram in 1971 to observed the border dispute between Assam and Nagaland and give some recommendation on it. On the basis of the Sundaram report, four Interim Agreement were signed between Assam and Nagaland. First and second agreement were signed in March 1972 . It demarcated the border of Geleki reserve forest, Roads of Amguri - Tuli, Tiru Hill, Desoi Reserve Forest and from Teok river to Dikhow river. Again in May 1972, the third agreement was signed. It demarcated the border of Desoi Valley and Doiyang Reserve Forest with the consent from both sides. The border area covered from Desoi river to Kakodonga river crossing the Goroijan Lake. The fourth agreement was signed in May 1972 again. This would demarcated the border of Goroijan Lake under

Kakodonga Forest and the border of Kakodonga river's bordering areas. The Prime Minister and Home Minister of India jointly wrote a letter on the border issue between Assam and Nagaland to the Chief Minister of Nagaland on 25' January 1979 to resolve the problem and after that in 1985 and enquiry committee was formed under B.C. Mathur (later under S.K. Shastri) to examine the clash between two sides and committee submitted its full report in 1987.

3. Assam and Meghalaya

History: Assam, the elder sister of all the states in the North Eastern Region, has experienced border disputes with practically all of its neighbors. Northeast India now has four interstate border disputes: Assam-Arunachal Pradesh, Assam-Nagaland, Assam-Meghalaya, and Assam-Mizoram. Before 1972, Meghalaya was a constituent state of Assam, with Shillong serving as the state capital. Everything was fine between the Khasi, Jaintias, Garos, and Assamese before 1972. However, as Assam grew and developed, it can be seen on many levels, whether in health care or education and more advanced when it comes to public administration, many policies that the Assam government tries to implement are now considered anti-people or against those who do not speak Assamese. An independent state from Assam is one of the key reasons that the people of the United Khasi, Jaintia Hills, and Garo Hills seek. Language assimilation and making it essential to speak Assamese, particularly for official purposes, presented a threat to other minor languages. Following the passing of the Assam Language Act of 1960, many non-Assamese-speaking communities felt inferior or marginalized by the Assam government.

Assam and Meghalaya share a border of roughly 723.2 kilometers. Before 1971-72, the Assam Reorganisation (Meghalaya) Act, of 1969 was approved, and the people of Meghalaya were granted autonomy. The leaders of the Hills State Movement, on the other hand, are unwilling to recognize the 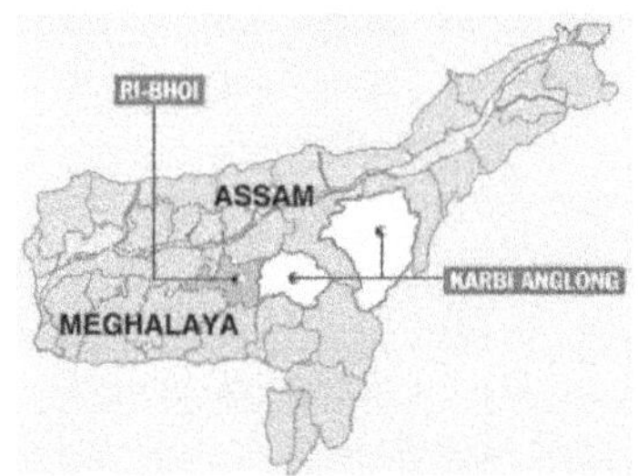

Autonomous state. Many politicians believed that having an autonomous state would imply partial independence, but the Assam government still controls the lock and key. As a result, Hill leaders lobbied for a distinct state, and then-Indian Prime Minister Indira Gandhi responded to their demands and awarded Meghalaya a separate state under the North Eastern Areas (Reorganisation) Act of 1971. The bill was introduced and passed in the Indian Parliament, and it went into force on January 21, 1972, the day the state of Meghalaya was founded.

The geographical boundaries of Meghalaya shall be determined by Section 3 of the Assam Reorganisation (Meghalaya) Act, 1969. According to the aforementioned constitutional provisions, the following regions will be incorporated into the state of Meghalaya: 1. The United Khasi and Jaintia Hill District 2. The Garo Hill Region. The United Khasi and Jaintia Hills District shall be construed to include the regions formerly known as the Khasi states and the Khasi and Jaintia Hills District under subparagraph (2) of paragraph 20 of the Sixth Schedule of the Constitution of India, as amended by paragraph 14 of the Eight Schedule to the North-Eastern Areas (Re-organisation) Act, 1971. To understand and grasp the border between Assam and Meghalaya, read paragraph 20 sub-paragraph 2 of the Sixth Schedule to the Indian Constitution. However, the regions indicated in the Sixth Schedule are neither demarcated delineated. The creation of the new State was based on the Assam Reorganisation (Meghalaya) Act of 1969, which the Meghalaya government refused to accept. But Why Meghalaya government refused to accept the state reorganisation act?

The 1969 Act had followed the recommendations of a 1951 committee to define the boundary of Meghalaya. On that panel's recommendations, areas of the present-day East Jaintia Hills, Ri-Bhoi and West Khasi Hills districts of Meghalaya were transferred to the Karbi Anglong, Kamrup (metro) and Kamrup districts of Assam. Meghalaya contested these transfers after statehood, claiming that they belonged to its tribal chieftains.

Position of Assam on the dispute: Assam said the Meghalaya government could neither provide documents nor archival materials to prove its claim over these areas.

Dispute narrowed down to 12 sectors: After claims and counter-claims, the dispute was narrowed down to 12 sectors on the basis of an official claim by Meghalaya in 2011.

Efforts to resolve the Assam-Meghalaya border dispute.

A. Joint official committee formed in 1983: In 1983, a joint official committee was formed to address the border issues. The panel recommended that the Survey of India should re-delineate the border, teaming up with both the states.

B. Independent panel of 1985: An independent panel, spearheaded by Justice YV Chandrachud, was set up in 1985. Meghalaya rubbished the report.

C. Border demarcation with the help of Survey of India. In 1991, about 100 km of the border was demarcated with the help of the Survey of India. However, Meghalaya did not accept it.

D. In 2011, Centre comes into picture: In 2011, the Meghalaya Assembly passed a resolution for intervention of the Centre and the establishment of a boundary commission. The Centre asked the two governments to appoint nodal officers to discuss the dispute.

E. Three regional committees constituted in 2021: The two States had in June 2021 adopted a give-and-take policy to start the process of resolving the boundary dispute. For this, they constituted three regional committees each. The draft resolution, released in January 2022, was prepared on the basis of the recommendations of these regional panels. In March 2022, a historic MoU was signed between the two states resolving the dispute in 6 of 12 sectors.

Assam - Meghalaya Border Pact: In March 2022, Assam and Meghalaya partially resolved a 50-year-old border dispute in six of the 12 sectors along their 884-km boundary. The six sectors where disputes remain are Langpih, Borduar, Nongwah-Mawtamur, Desh Doomreah, Block 1 & Block II, and Psiar-Khanduli.

The Agreement: As per the agreement, out of the disputed 36.79 sq. km land, Assam will get 18.51 sq. km of the disputed areas and Meghalaya will get the remaining 18.28 sq.km. About 70% of the inter-State boundary has now become dispute-free with the signing of the agreement. The problem in the six other areas will be resolved in the near future.

What lies ahead? The freshly demarcated border will have to be passed by Parliament by amending the North Eastern Region (reorganisation) Act, 1971. This will then have to be ratified by the legislative assemblies of both the states.

Firing incident at the border village of Mukroh and suspension of talks: Three months later, in November 2022, 6 persons, including an Assam Forest Guard, were killed in a clash between Assam Police and a mob. This incident took place in a clash between a mob and a contingent of police and forest guards from Assam in pursuit of a truck allegedly smuggling timber across the inter-state border. This firing incident was a setback before phase 2 began. It led to the suspension of talks. Assam chief minister Himanta Biswa Sarma and his Meghalaya counterpart Conrad K Sangma resumed talks to resolve remaining border disputes in six boundary areas between both the states.

4. Assam and Mizoram

Assam and Mizoram share a 165 km-long border. The length of Assam Mizoram Inter-state Boundary is 164.6 Km (Source Survey of India) and it touches the districts of Cachar, Hailakandi and Karimganj of Assam with Mizoram's Aizawl, Mamit, and Kolasib districts.

History of Assam and Mizoram Border Dispute: The border dispute between Assam and Mizoram is a legacy of two British-era notifications of 1875 and 1933, when Mizoram was called Lushai Hills, a district in Assam.

The 1875 notification differentiated Lushai Hills from the plains of Cachar and the other demarcated boundary between Lushai Hills and Manipur. While Mizoram became a state only in 1987 following years of

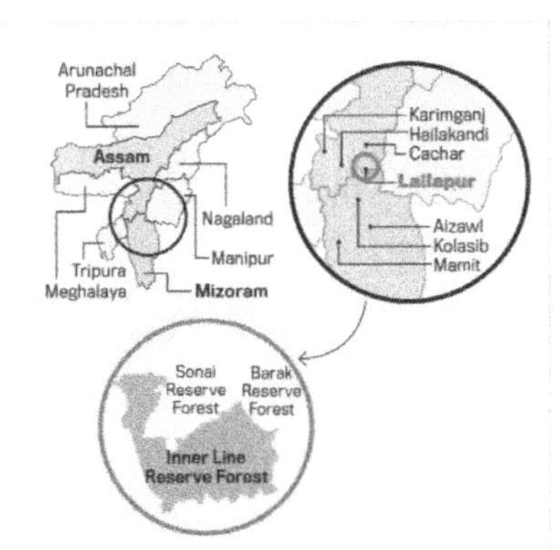

insurgency, it still insists on the boundary decided in 1875. Assam, on the other hand, wants the boundary demarcated in 1986 (based on the 1933 notification).

Lets look into broader concept: The **Assam-Mizoram border dispute** is rooted a century and a half back. The dispute stems from two notifications passed under British era. First, **notification of 1875,** that differentiated Lushai Hills from the plains of Cachar. Second, **notification of 1933,** that demarcates a boundary between Lushai Hills and Manipur.

The British drew a boundary between the Lushai Hills (presently in Mizoram) and the Cachar plains (presently in Assam) in August 1875. People of Mizoram accepted this boundary as it was drawn with the consultation of their state chiefs. Further Mizoram believes the **boundary should be demarcated on the basis of the 1875 notification,** which is derived from the **Bengal Eastern Frontier Regulation (BEFR) Act, 1873.**

Later, in 1933, a notification demarcated the princely state of Manipur and defined all the boundaries of northeast India. Conflicts arose when Mizoram officials denied acknowledging the notification of 1933. According to them, this division did not include any consultation of Mizoram officials. Mizo leaders are against the demarcation notified in 1933, according to them, the **Mizo society was not consulted.**

On the other hand, the **Assam government follows the 1933 demarcation.** As a result both states continue to have a **differing perception of the border** and that is the point of conflict.

The Indian Government carved out Mizoram from Assam as a Union territory in 1972 and made it a state in 1987. Assam's districts, Cachar, Hailakandi, and Karimganj, share a boundary of 164 km with Mizoram's Aizawl, Mamit, and Kolasib districts. Both the states kept accusing each other of usurping land, from 1987 onwards.

The first skirmish took place after 7 years of Mizoram's formation in 1994. Regardless of countless discussions organised by the Central Government between these 2 states over their dispute, the hostility continued.

Violent clash between the two states on Aug 2021: Violent border clashes between India's north-eastern states of Assam and Mizoram last week left several dead and many more injured. Tensions with Assam escalated on 26 July after clashes erupted between police on either side of a contentious border point. The two sides fired at each other, leaving seven dead and 60 people injured. Six of those killed were policemen from Assam. Mizoram officials alleged that 200 policemen from Assam, led by a senior officer, overran one of their police outposts at the border town of Vairengte. The evicted policemen, barely 20 of them, were joined by reinforcements, according to locals - and they retaliated after taking position in the hills overlooking the camp. Local Mizos also burnt down buses that had carried the Assam policemen to the border and clashed with villagers from Assam backing up their force. "For a while, it was like a war between two countries," said Pu Gilbert, a villager in Vairengte. The two states have filed murder cases against senior officials on the other side. Assam even advised locals against travelling to Mizoram. Mizoram said it is now facing an "economic blockade" with Assam preventing vehicles to travel to Mizoram. Mizoram depends on supplies from Assam, a much bigger state that is home to some 30 million people. Under colonial rule, Lushai Hills, as Mizoram was then known, was part of Assam. It was carved out as a centrally administered territory in 1972 and later upgraded to a full-fledged state following an agreement between Delhi and the separatist MNF, which waged a 20-year-long guerrilla campaign against India.

Reasons that Ignited Mizoram and Assam Border Dispute

Although the **Assam-Mizoram border dispute** commenced a century ago, several incidents stirred up bitterness along the way. It started from a disagreement over an imaginary line between these states, but continued through several skirmishes and casualties.

The primary reasons that have been sparking this dispute are as follows:

Assam claims that Mizoram has trespassed their claimed boundary. On the other hand, Mizoram lay charges on the unilateral movement of Assam inside their territory.

Governments of both states have appointed officials under numerous sections of the Indian Penal Code to resolve this tension. This includes Assam's Chief Minister as well.

On top of everything, the Assam Government advised their citizens not to travel to Mizoram. Furthermore, it asked its citizens residing in Mizoram to maintain utmost vigilance.

Besides, Mizoram accuses Assam as being culprits for obstructing NH-306 and removing railway tracks. These, especially NH-306, are considered a lifeline of Mizoram and jamming it results in an economic blockade.

Current Situation of Mizoram and Assam Border Dispute: The Union Government constantly kept trying to settle this disagreement by organising discussions between these 2 states. While Mizoram depends on Assam for supplies and accuses them of creating an economic blockade, Assam denies all accusations.

Therefore, India's Home Ministry deployed CRPF as a neutral force to maintain the state of affairs and avoid further clashes. Far delayed, both states expressed a willingness to alleviate the disagreement through a peaceful resolution. The joint statement ensures that none of these states will send any forces to specific areas that have already faced disturbances. Assam, Mizoram to hold ministerial-level talks to resolve border disputes. As per ANI news on Aug 9, 2024.

Possible Solutions for Assam-Mizoram Border Dispute: Deploying the Central force and maintaining the state quo will not bring peace back. For a peaceful resolution of such inter-state border disputes, both Central and State governments should consider the following aspects:

Both these states must come forward proactively to settle the dispute cordially by forming a committee. It must include civil societies and other contributors for an extensive understanding of the issue.

The committee also must consider both the states' local leaders and chiefs. Every recommendation made by this committee must be obligatory to both states. In addition, civilians must not interpret any mandatory decisions as a drawback. The Local Government must propagate the bright side of this resolution. Lastly, the Supreme Court must implement a strict deadline to resolve all the existing conflicts.

Why do inter-state border disputes remain unresolved?

Ans: Linguistic Idea of Reorganization: Although the States Reorganization Commission, 1956 was based on administrative convenience, states reorganized largely resembled the idea of one language one state.

Geographical Complexity: The other complexity has been terrain — rivers, hills and forests straddle two states in many places and borders cannot be physically marked. Colonial maps had left out large tracts of the northeast outside Assam as "thick forests" or marked them "unexplored".

Indigenous Communities: Indigenous communities were, for the most part, left alone. Boundaries would be drawn for administrative convenience when the "need" arose.

The 1956 demarcation did not resolve the discrepancies. When new states were carved out of Assam (Nagaland in 1963, Mizoram, Meghalaya, Tripura and Manipur in 1972, and Arunachal Pradesh in 1987), it was still not addressed.

What are the Other Methods of Resolution of Border Disputes in India?

Ans: **Through Exclusive Original Jurisdiction of SC:** The Supreme Court has exclusive original jurisdiction as per Article 131 of the Constitution of India, which means no other court can hear these cases:

It can hear disputes between the Government of India and one or more States.

It can hear disputes between the Government of India and any State(s) on one side, and one or more other State(s) on the other.

It can hear disputes between two or more States if the dispute involves a question of law or fact on which the existence or extent of a legal right depends.

Limitations on Jurisdiction: The Supreme Court's jurisdiction does not extend to disputes arising out of treaties, agreements, covenants, engagements, or similar instruments entered into before the commencement of the Constitution and continuing in operation, or if the instrument provides that the jurisdiction shall not extend to such disputes.

Through Inter-State Council: Article 263 of the Constitution empowers the President to establish an Inter-state Council if it appears that the public interests would be served by such a Council.

It serves as a forum for discussion and resolution of disputes between states, as well as for investigating and discussing subjects of common interest among states or between the Union and one or more states. In 1990, the Inter-state Council was established through a Presidential Order. In 2021, the Council was reconstituted.

4. Northeast security forces (State Police and commando)

A. Nagaland Police: Nagaland police is the ultimate law enforcement agency of the state with its headquarter located in Police Reserve Hill (PR Hill), Kohima, Nagaland. Controlled by the Department of Home Affairs, Government of Nagaland the Police force is headed by the Director General of Police.

About the state: The State of Nagaland was formed on December 1st, 1963, as the 16th State of the Indian Union. It is bounded by Assam in the west and north west, Myanmar (Burma) on the east, Arunachal Pradesh and part of Assam on the North and Manipur in the South.

Departments:
Nagaland Police SMS Based Vehicle Monitoring System (NPSVMS): In order to address the issue of thefts and losses of vehicles, an IT system is being developed by the Nagaland Police.

Forensic Science Lab (FSL): The FSL of Nagaland Police is located at Dimapur.

Intelligence (INT) unit: The intelligence unit is headed by a Inspector General of Police (INT)

Nagaland Police Telecommunication Organization (NPTO): Also known as the Police wireless wing helps in better communication and is headed by a DIG.

Training:

Nagaland Armed Police Training Centre (NAPTC): Formed on 1st Oct' 1969 with its base at the Police Complex, Chumukedima, Dimapur on the National Highway 39.

Duties and Responsibilities: Basic training to new recruits, In-service training, other courses by the government.

Nagaland Police Training School (NPTS):

Established on 1st November 1966 wit its base at the Police Complex, Chumukedima, Dimapur on the side of National Highway 39.

Duties and responsibilities: Basic training to new recruit constable/havildar/ASI (both men/women), In-service training, other courses by the government.

Nagaland Armed Police Battalions of Nagaland Police:

1st NAP Chumukedima, Dimapur.

2nd NAP Alichen, Mokokchung.

3rd NAP Tuensang

4th NAP Thizama, Kohima

5th NAP Phek

6th NAP Tizit, Mon.

7th NAP Bhandari, Wokha.

8th NAP Naltoqa, Zunheboto,

9th NAP (IR) Saijang, Peren.

10th NAP (IR) Zhadima, Kohima.

11th NAP (IR) Riizhaphema

12th NAP (IR) Tuli, Mokokchung (Paper Nagar).

13th NAP (IR) Yajang°C'

14th NAP (IR) Kiphire

15th NAP (IR) Chumukedima, Dimapur.

Current Update: In 2018, Nagaland became the second state in North East India to establish a Tourism Police or Tourist Police in order to facilitate tourism in the state.

According to the report of 'Data on Police Organizations' 2021, released by the Bureau of Police Research & Development (BPR&D),

Nagaland is the only State in India with more police force than sanctioned.

B. Mizoram Police: Mizoram police is the ultimate law enforcement agency of the state with its headquarter located at Khatla, Aizawl, Mizoram. Controlled by the Department of Home Affairs, Government of Mizoram, the Police force is headed by the Director General of Police.

About the state: Mizoram was an administrative unit under the state of Assam known as Mizo District Council. The administrative unit council was headed by the police force of the then Superintendent of Lushai Hills. The first SP was posted in 1960. It became a UT on 21st January, 1972. Shri I.J Verma (IPS) was the first I.G.P of Mizoram UT. Shri L. B Sewa (IPS) was the first DIG of Mizoram.

Training Branch, PHQ: The first Training Branch was established in the year 1984 and the first i/c of the Training Branch was 'Pu Vanlalzuata' Inspector of Police. In the year 1988, the 'Training of Police Officers' was brought under "DIG (Training)" and to supervise training, "Pu C. Dothanga, IPS" was posted as the first DIG (Training) in the year 1988.

Police Training School: The Police Training School at Thenzawl is the premiere and the only Training Centre/School in Mizoram which was established in 1973 under the aegis of 1st Battalion Mizoram Armed Police at Lungverh, Sakawrtuichhun and continued as such till 31st March 1986. The Training Centre was officially recognized and established w.e.f. 1st April 1986. The Training Institution has since been under the charge and supervision of an officer of the rank of Superintendent of Police, designated as Principal. On May 2011, Police Training Centre Lungverh was shifted to Thenzawl, Serchhip District, since then, it was declared as a full fledged Police Training Centre (instead of temporary headquarters of 4th India Reserve Battalion)

CID Crime: Set up in 1975 along with the Anti-Corruption Branch the CID (Crime) is a part of the State Police Organization, where the primary function is covering all the aspects of prevention, investigation and detection of crime.

CID Special Branch (SB): Created and started functioning in the year 1973. Presently the Headquarters office is set up at CID Complex, Bungkawn, Aizawl and it is headed by Sr. Superintendent of Police under the supervision and guidance of DIG (CID). A.K. Roy, APS was the first Superintendent of Police of CID(SB). At present, CID (SB) is having 16 (sixteen) Sector Offices in various strategic locations within the state.

Subsidiary Multi Agency Centre (SMAC) under CID (SB): This centre helps in sharing intelligence report between the state Agencies and directly follows the instructions of Ministry of Home Affairs.

Battalions:
1st Battalion MAP - 1973
2nd Battalion MAP - 1987
3rd Battalion MAP - 1992
1st Indian Reserve Battalion - 1993
2nd Indian Reserve Battalion - 2001
3rd Indian Reserve Battalion - 2007
4th Indian Reserve Battalion - 2007
5th Indian Reserve Battalion - 2008
SP Security - 1994
S.P, Traffic - 2008

Mizoram Police Radio Organisation (MPRO) - 1972
CID Crime - 1975
Central Police Workshop - 1983

Mizoram Tourist Police comprises police personnel trained in soft skills, communication skills and equipped with knowledge of tourist places. The Tourist Police will initially be deployed in five (5) major tourist attractions:
1). Entry and Exit Point at Lengpui Airport,
2). Solomon's Temple, Aizawl,
3). Millennium Centre, Aizawl,
4). Thenzawl, Serchhip District,
5). Zokhawthar, Champhai District.

After Arunachal & Nagaland, Mizoram gets its tourist police unit. These specially-trained police personnel are equipped with thorough knowledge about tourist destinations, language skills and other amicable soft skills.

The Union Territory of Mizoram attained Statehood on 20.02.1987 with three districts viz. Aizawl, Lunglei and Chhimtuipui district. The Police Sub- Division, Police Station and Outpost in 1987 are as follows:-

Name of District - Sub-Division - P.S - O.P
Aizawl - 5 - 18 - 6
Lunglei - 2 - 6 - 2
Chhimtuipui - 2 - 6 - 3

Mizoram Tourist Police: Hon'ble Home Minister Pu Lalchamliana launched on 18th October 2019, Mizoram Tourist Police which will be responsible for safety and security of the tourists during their travel, stay and visit to various Tourist Destinations in the state. As per the Data on Police Organisations (DoPO) 2021 report which is published periodically by the Bureau of Police Research and Development under the Union home ministry. The percentage share of women at officer level is highest in Mizoram and Tamil Nadu with 20.2.
The DoPO report is published periodically by the Bureau of Police Research and Development under the Union home ministry. Nationally, the share of "women officers" stands at 8.2 per cent. In 11 states and Union territories, the share of women at officer level is five per cent or less.

Kerala police has three per cent women officers, and West Bengal has 4.2 per cent. The best performing states on this count are Tamil Nadu and Mizoram, which have the highest share of women officers at 20.2 per cent.

The worst are Bihar and Himachal Pradesh which have recorded a sharp decline in the share of women police officers. In 2019, Bihar reported 25.3 per cent officers, which dropped to 17.4 per cent, and in Himachal Pradesh, it dropped to 13.5 per cent in 2020 from 19.2 per cent in 2019, according to the report.

C. Manipur Police: Manipur Police comes under direct control of the Department of Home Affairs, Government of Manipur. The Manipur Police is headed by Director General of Police (DGP)

Pre-British Period: There was no formal policing in Manipur, as such, before the arrival of the British on the scene. There was a system known as the Lallup System, which meant free labour of the people to the King. The people were allotted a plot of land for which they were not required to pay revenue, instead had to serve the state 3 months in a year, or 10 days in every 40 days, to be precise. This service of the people was used by the King in various parts of the administration such as guards, construction work and in providing some sort of informal policing. Since the same person was not continually employed for the purpose nor paid any salary, it would be easy to appreciate that in tracking down of criminals and keeping a watch on their activities, the system was most inadequate and could hardly be called policing.

British Period: On 27th April 1891, during the reign of Maharaja Shri Kulachandra Singh, the British Government took over the administration of Manipur after a decisive battle with the ruling Prince at Khongjom. It was then that the British organized properly for the first time the State Military Police of Manipur, the forerunner of Manipur Rifles, under Political Agent, Mr. Crawford, who was appointed the first Commandant of the force.

The Civil Police was also organized properly when Imphal Police Station was established in January 1893 having jurisdiction over the entire State of Manipur except hills. This Police Station is still functioning under the same name and is the oldest Police Station. The first Officer in-Charge of this Police Station was Sub-Inspector, Shri A. Ramlal Singh alias Meino Singh of Sagolband. In 1911 Jiribam Police Station was opened on the Cachar border to prevent export of cattle and smuggling.

As stated earlier, the Imphal Police Station did not have jurisdiction over the hills nor over the Chowkidars posted there. But considering the need for the maintenance of law & order in hill areas, a special Police force known as Hill Lambus was then organized under the Sub-divisional Officers of Ukhrul, Tamenglong and Churachandpur.

In 1953 Civil Police and Manipur Rifles were reorganized. The armed branch of the Civil Police was merged with Manipur Rifles, which was declared as the armed wing of Manipur Police.

In 1959 a Tear Gas Squad was raised in Manipur Rifles. It had a total strength of 2 JCOs and 22 other ranks.

The most important event during 1962-63 was the increase of the strength of Manipur Rifles by another battalion (2nd Bn.MR), which was raised on 1st November 1962.

The Manipur Rifles Battalions, 3rd and 4th Battalions, are missing. The land earmarked at Pallel and Churachandpur for these Battalions continues to be with BSF even today.

The 5th Bn. Manipur Rifles was raised on 19/12/72 and trained at Pangei.

During 1976-77, following the signing of the Shillong Peace Accord in November 1975 by the Underground Nagas, there was comparative peace. Sporadic incidence of violence, however, continued to take place as there were still some elements that were opposed to the accord.

To augment the strength of the Police,

The 6th Bn. MR was raised on 16/3/78 with its HQs at Imphal.

The 7th Bn. MR was raised on 11/8/80 with its Hq. at Khabeisoi at Imphal.

A City Police Control Room was established on 14th July 1981 at Imphal.

In January 1982, Crime Branch was established as an independent unit under the overall charge of DIGP (CID) at Imphal. This was a significant addition to the police set-up.

During 1982-83, the security forces and the police achieved considerable success in their operations against the Meitei extremist groups. The activities of Meitei extremist groups were reduced to a very low profile. PREPAK and KCP became almost defunct, and PLA suffered a severe blow after several casualties and arrests of some of its top leaders in Tekcham and Kodompokpi areas.

In 1986 two important additions were made to the functioning of the Police Department. In April 1986, Manipur Police Housing Corporation was established as a separate body to look after construction of police buildings. Soon after in September 1986, a Central Motor Transport Workshop was also established for repairing vehicles of the Police Department under one roof and command in Imphal itself.

Manipur Rifles
Battalion with Location and Commandants
1st MR - Imphal West - S. Ibomcha Singh, MPS
2nd MR - Imphal West - Victoria Yengkhom, MPS
5th MR - Khongjarol - Ningshem Vashum, IPS
6th MR - Ukhrul - G. Jenkhansuan, MPS
7th MR - Khabeisoi
8th MR - Leikun - T. Thongzapao, MPS

India Reserve Battalion
Battalion with Location and Commandants
1st IRB - Churachandpur - Lunkhomang Khongsai, MPS
2nd IRB - Naranseina(Bishnupur) - T. Lalboi Haokip, MPS
3rd IRB - Khangabok(Thoubal) - S. Somorjit Singh, MPS
4th IRB - Thengu Chingjin(Imphal East) - K. C. Lokho Mao, MPS
5th IRB - Thengu Chingjin (Imphal East) - Amang Haokip, MPS
6th IRB - Pangei - Thangboi Kuki, MPS
7th IRB - Jiribam(Uchathol) - Mangkhojang Kipgen, MPS
8th IR(CDO)Bn. - Khabeisoi (Imphal East) - N. Madhunimai Singh, MPS
9th IR(Mahila)Bn. - Khuman Lampak (Imphal East) - Khoisnam Sarma Devi, MPS
10th IRB - Imphal - Sh. Jugeshwar Sharma, MPS
11th IRB - Imphal - Th Vikramjit SIngh, MPS

Manipur Police Training College: The Manipur Police Training College, Pangei was established on 2nd January, 1967 as a Police Training Centre with Shri W.Damudor Singh, IPS (Retd. Inspector General of Police) as its first Officer In-Charge. The Training Centre was upgraded to the status of a training School on 22/10/1972 and the officer In-Charge designated as Principal, MPTC which was again re-designated as Director, MPTS on 05/01/2005. The Manipur Police Training School has subsequently been upgraded to the status of a College on 23/09/2009.

D. Meghalaya Police: The Meghalaya Police is the ultimate agency for law & order in the state and until 1972 was a part of Assam police when Meghalaya was created. The Meghalaya Police is headed by a Director General of Police (DGP) with the headquarters at the Secretariat Hill, Shillong. The Total Sanctioned Strength of Meghalaya Police is 12,911 personnel, with an actual strength of 10,956. All serve in various positions. (2022 sources)

Organisations under Meghalaya Police:
Infiltration Branch: Meghalaya shares long International border (423 kms) with Bangladesh on the South and West and another long inter-state boundary with Assam (566 kms) on the North and East. The main objective of the State Infiltration Branch is to prevent and check the influx and illegal entry of foreign nationals detecting, prosecuting and deporting them after concrete evidence is established against them.

Criminal Investigation Department (CID): CID administrated by the Addl. Director General of Police, CID further assisted by Inspector General of Police, CID, Dy. Inspector General of Police, CID/ACB/Vig, Spl. Superintendent of Police, (CID), Superintendent of Police, SCRB, Dy. Superintendent of Police, CID & ACB including other non-gazetted staff.

CID performs the following functions :- Investigation of complicated cases, confidential enquiries, organized crime, Publication of the Criminal Intelligence Gazette every month, Maintaining Narcotic Cell, Maintaining a Photographic Cell, Maintaining, Law and Research Cell, Maintaining Dog Squad, Maintaining Juvenile Guidance Bureau, Keeping Liaison with the Forensic Science.

The State CID comprises the following Units.
Cell-I - Record Cell.
Cell-II - Specialized Cell
Cell-III - Investigation Cell
Cell-IV - Manpower Management / Reserve Branch.
Cell-V - Human Rights Cell.
Cell-VI - Overall Coordination both intra and Inter office.
Cell-VII - Anti Corruption Branch.
Cell-VIII - S.R. Cell.

State Crime Records Bureau (SCRB): SCRB was created in the year 1988 by the Meghalaya Police on the recommendation of the NCRB (National Crime Records Bureau). SCRB, Meghalaya is headed by the Superintendent of Police (SCRB), Shillong, Meghalaya.

Meghalaya Fire & Emergency Service: The overall command and control of Meghalaya Fire & Emergency Service Organization is vested upon the Addl. Director General of Police (F&ES) Meghalaya, Shillong. The prime duty of Fire & Emergency Services Organization is to combat fire and to render effective fire fighting operations, fire prevention, Search & Rescue operations etc.

Meghalaya Police Training School: The Meghalaya Police Training School near Golf Links, Shillong was established on April 18, 1977. It was established with an aim of imparting basic Training to Unarmed Branch Constables, Assistant Sub Inspector and Sub-inspector of Police. However the Basic Training for Sub Inspectors was discontinued from the year 1988 with the establishment of the North Eastern Police Academy (N.E.P.A.), Umsaw.

Meghalaya Police Radio Organisation (MPRO): Headed by the Director, MPRO has message control offices in the seven districts with its headquarter at Golf Links, Shillong. At the head of the hierarchy is the Director, MPRO, assisted by one Addl. Superintendent of Police, three Dy. Superintendents of Police and other subordinate officers and staff to run the message control offices, both at the Shillong headquarters and in the seven districts. They play a vital role in the transmission of important messages for the Meghalaya Police. The organization also maintains a central MPRO Training Centre at Golf Links, Shillong.

Forensic Science Laboratory Meghalaya: State Forensic Science Laboratory Meghalaya, had been established with effect from January 1987.

Meghalaya Police Battalion:

1st Meghalaya Police Battalion (MLP): The 1st MLP Battalion at Mawiong, Shillong was originally the 7th Assam Police Bn. of the erstwhile composite State of Assam which was converted into the 1st MLP Bn. on 01.5.72 after the creation of the State of Meghalaya.

2nd Meghalaya Police Battalion: The 2nd Meghalaya Police Battalion is situated at Goeragre, about 13 Kms from Tura on the Tura Guwahati road. It was started in 1982 on a land measuring 30.83 hectares, overlooking the Ganol river which flows from east to west.

3rd Meghalaya Police Battalion / 1st IndianReserve Battalion(IRBn) is located at Khliehtyrshi, Jowai

4th Meghalaya Police Battalion/2nd India Reserve Battalion(IRBn) is located at Siejlieh, Nongstoin.

5th Meghalaya Police Battalion/3rd India Reserve Battalion(IRBn) is located at Samanda, Williamnagar.

6th Meghalaya Police Battalion/4th India Reserve Battalion(IRBn) is located at Camp Shillong.

Meghalaya Special Force 10: Also known as 'Meghalaya Multipurpose Special task force', or 'SF 10' is a 'special force' which was created and specially trained to deal with internal security challenges such as counter insurgency as well as riot control and disaster management. Since its inception in 2015, the first batch of SF 10 Commandos and Rangers, have been deployed into the sensitive and tactical areas of Garo Hills in Meghalaya.

The Tactical Unit of SF 10 in Western Range has been focusing on counter insurgency ops to fight against militancy for the most part while the rangers on Law and Order. The (SF-10) second batch of this elite forces has received specialized commando training from the Assam Rifles Commando Training School in Dimapur, Nagaland and a few from them acquired specialized commando training with the Grey Hounds in Telangana. This elite commando has been extremely reliable with their results and brought a lot of peace by bringing down one of the most dreadful militant outfit GNLA in their initial days.

E. Tripura Police: The state which shares 80% (Approx) of its area with the International border, covered by Bangladesh from three sides, sees a lot of Insurgency, drug trafficking, human and animal trafficking problems. And therefore the Tripura Police works with zeal to maintain the law and order in the state, protecting the rights of the people and ensuring a congenial and secure society for them to live in.

The Tripura Police headquarters is located at Agartala, the capital of Tripura state. Entire Tripura Police is divided into two ranges, The Southern Range consisting of West, Sepahijala, South, Khowai, Gomati districts and the Northern range consisting of North, Dhalai. Unakoti districts. It had in all 77 police stations across the state.

The state approximately has a 28,031 strong police force in the Republic of India including Women Police, supported by a sanctioned strength of 3,036 Home Guards Volunteers, 4,011 Special Police Officers (SPO) and 989 Ministerial Staffs. We serve a population of over 31 Lakhs residing in this state spread over an area of 10,491 square kilometers.

History: The history of policing in Tripura is as old as the history of this state.

Policing under Manikya Dynasty: Raja Ratna Manikya (1325 - 1350) was considered to be the first king of Tripura who brought a considerable reform in the administration as well as in the indigenous police system in the line of Muslim administrative system of Bengal during his regime. The Nawab of Bengal said to have conferred the title of 'Manikya' on him. He brought three experienced Bengalis with him to Tripura who helped in establishing administrative system on Muslim pattern. The plain Tripura, then known as Tipperah, and its adjacent areas were under direct administration of the King. There were 'Binidias', special type of Police, under direct control of king, who acted as conduits to inform tribal chiefs about the orders/formans of the King and also were empowered to arrest any person for defiance of king's order etc. The distant regions were ruled through regional administrators known as 'Laskars' who exerted their authority as Police officers in collection of taxes from tribal chiefs.

Raja Amar Manikya introduced the title of 'Thanadars' during last part of 16th century and exercised authority as provincial ruler. There was no written code, no court of law and no jail before 1870.

When the British domination and supremacy started on the erstwhile kings in 1761, the kings had to take permission from the British ruler to purchase or to collect even a rifle.

However, modernization of administrative system in 'Independent Hill Tipperah' began following several administrative reforms introduced by Raja Birchandra Manikya in the line of British administration during his regime from 1862 to 1896. The courts of Tripura dispensed justice according to primitive system of equity and good conscience till 1873-74, since there was no judicial procedure. Afterwards, Tripura King adopted Acts of Government of Bengal and Acts of British India. Nine enactments were passed in 1873-74 including Criminal Procedure Code, Police Code, Cattle Trespass Act and Civil Procedure Code etc.

In addition to the main duties of maintenance of peace and law & order, the police officers/men were Collectors of Forest revenue, Cotton revenue, Chowkidari tax and in some places of Land revenue also. There was also a contingent of 'Binindias' or 'Tipperah Burkandazes' whose main duty was to serve processes on the hill people. No regular system of village police was in existence in the kingdom. Chowkidars as a rule were employed only in the headquarter stations. Crime and other occurrences of interior areas were reported by the village head men.

In 1886-87, 4 new posts of Head Police officers with the designation of 'Superintendent' were created to control and supervise Police and cotton departments and also for revenue work of 4 divisions who were subordinate to the Sub-Divisional officers.

Maharaja Radha Kishore Manikya (1896-1909) brought separation of Police and Revenue Department. Mr. Ananda Mohan Guha was the first Superintendent of Police appointed by the Raja after such separation. Kumar Brajendra Kishore was made the head of police administration.

During the regime of Maharaja Birendra Kishore Manikya Bahadur (1909-1923) the State Civil Service was reconstituted on 31/03/1916 for recruitment of high officials of the state including the post of Superintendent of Police and Deputy Superintendent of Police. The new Arms Act and the Penal Code Amendment Act were passed in 1911. Mr. Kamini Kumar Sinha was the Superintendent of Police then.

The Superintendent of Police had to go for extensive tour and inspect Thanas.

Maharaja Bir Bikram Kishore Manikya Bahadur was the last King who reigned from 1923 to 1947. This period was most turbulent period in the history of Tripura and India also. Political activities got new momentum. During communal riots in Bengal, large number of refugees entered the state causing demographic change and ethnic tension in some places. The Reang-revolt led by Ratan Moni Reang was suppressed by taking stern Police action. During his governance, the police and military force turned into an organised force. The Indian Criminal Law Amendment Act, 1908 (Act XIV of 1908) as amended up-to-date was adopted in 1942.

Policing after merger with India: At the end of several hundred years of rule by 184 Kings, the erstwhile princely state came under the control of the government of India on Oct 15, 1949 according to a merger agreement signed between Kanchan Prabha Devi, the regent maharani, and C. Rajagopalachari, the Governor General of India. After merger, the State of Tripura became a centrally administered part C State under a Chief Commissioner. The Tripura Administration Order 1949 kept in force all earlier laws prevailing in Tripura. Tripura was one District Territory with one District Magistrate & Collector and one Superintendent of Police up to 31/08/1970.

Afterwards, 3 Districts were created with appointment of 3 DM & Collectors and 3 Superintendents of Polices as heads of Civil and Police Departments of the District. A separate post of Superintendent of Police, CID was created with Headquarters at Agartala. Tripura Armed Police was reorganized under a Commandant.

On attaining Statehood on 21st January 1972, the status of Chief Secretary of Tripura was upgraded to the status of Joint Secretary of Govt. of India. A common cadre of IAS, IPS & IFS cadres was created under the title Manipur-Tripura Cadre. The strength of IAS officer was increased to 21, IPS to 8 and IFS to 4.

In January 2012, Vice President of India conferred the President's Colour on Tripura Police, the fourth Police force in India to receive this honour, for its success in combating the three decade old insurgency in the State and ensuring that there was no human rights abuse. In 2012, on Statehood Day, the number of Districts has been increased to 8 from 4 to reach out to people for better service delivery. Subsequently Tripura got full-fledged separate cadre of IPS officers in 2015.

Central Training Institute (HG&CD) commonly known as CTI was set up in Tripura in 23rd August, 1980.

Functions and Charter of Duties: CTI was mainly created as a Combined Training Institute for both Home Guards & Civil Defense Volunteers . It conducts various types of training viz. Basic training, Refresher training, Special Arms training for Home Guards and Rescue Operation training, Fire fighting and First aid training for CD (civil defense) Volunteers. The Central Training Institute has been declared as 'State Nodal Institution for imparting Practical Training on Disaster Management for both the official and non official in the State.

Border Wing Battalion Home guards: The Border Wing Home Guards Battalion was raised in Tripura in 1977 following an order issued by the Ministry of Home Affairs, Govt. of India along with 3(three) other Eastern States namely Assam, Meghalaya and West Bengal.

KTDS Police Training Academy: The state of Tripura has got only one training academy for the police personnel. It was set up on 01.05.67 at A.D. Nagar in the barracks of Tripura Armed Police Battalions as a training school for the police personnel. With the passage of time it was elevated to the status of Police Training College and was shifted to Narsingarh, Tripura (West) under Airport PS about 14 km away from Agartala Headquarters on 23.9.85. As per order of Home Department, Govt. of Tripura on 12.06.2009, it was officially renamed as KTDS Police Training Academy 24.06.2009

Tripura State Rifles: In view of growing insurgency in Tripura during 1980s, Tripura State Rifles was raised on the pattern of Central Para Military Force (CPMF). Subsequently, Tripura Legislative Assembly passed Tripura State Rifles Act. 1983. Based on that Act, the 1st Bn TSR came into existence on 12th March, 1984. This was followed by raising of other TSR Battalions. Presently, there are 12(twelve) Battalions of TSR in the State, out of which 9 Battalions are India Reserve (IR) Battalions.

Key Functions of TSR:
Counter insurgency operations in the State.
Assisting the civil Police in maintaining Law & Order.
Assisting the civil administration in relief and rescue work especially during natural calamities.
Providing security in trouble prone areas by establishing protective Camps.
Security of VIPs/ vital installations etc.
Performance of escort duties etc.
Protection of life and property in the event of any disturbances.
Security duties to ONGC & OTPC.
Railway protection duty in the interior locations.

Establishment of TSR Training Centres:- To maintain the high professional standards of the force, there are two dedicated training centres for the Tripura State Rifles:

A.Ch. Rama Rao, TSR Training Centre, R.K. Nagar, West Tripura:- The Centre was set up in the year 2007 to impart progressive professional in-service training to the TSR personnel. The Centre imparts training in Basic Courses, Cadre Courses, Driving & Maintenance Courses, field craft and tactics etc.

Counter Insurgency & Anti Terrorist (CIAT) School, Kachucherra, Ambassa, Dhalai Tripura: The School came in existence in the year 2012 with the assistance from the BPR&D, MHA, Govt. of India. The School imparts training in CI Ops and jungle warfare tactics not only to TSR personnel but also to CPMFs like CRPF, RPF and RPSF etc.

Special Armed Force: The Special Armed Force was established in the year 1993 with a view to accommodate the retrenched Border Wing Home guards' personnel. The Border Wing Home Guards Battalion was raised in the year 1977 to help the B.S.F. in the deployment along the International Border of Tripura with Bangladesh. The 1st Commandant of SAF was Shri G. S. Khan, EEx- BSF officer.

Mobile Task Force: The Mobile Task Force in Tripura has been functioning since 1970. Initially it was a small unit under the Supervision and control of the District Superintendents of Police. Subsequently, on 20/11/1975 a separate unit was set up independently to tackle the problem of illegal immigration. Besides, MHA (Border

Management Division) had sanctioned 144 temporary posts under the MTF/PIF scheme in 1974. The important function of Mobile Task Force is primarily detection, prosecution and deportation of illegal Bangladeshi immigrants from this country. Apart from the above, MTF carries out the tasks of conducting inquiry in respect of suspected Nationality, fake/doubtful nationality certificate, involvement of Bangladeshi nationals in fundamentalist and anti Indian activities and also collection of intelligence involving trans-border crimes/issues etc.

Office of the SP (SCRB): Tripura has been established as an independent Unit with the posting of SP, SCRB. The idea behind this is that SP SCRB would keeper by building a strong digital database to aid the investigating agency in their endeavour to prevent and detect crime. Following sections are functioning under the guidance and supervision of SP (SCRB), Tripura.

Photography Cell:- The Photography Cell renders assistance to the investigation team by taking photographs of SOCs (scene of Crimes) and other related things.

Fingerprint Cell : Experts and Officers of Finger Print Cell play an important role in recording and searching ginger impression slips of arrestee and retrieval of chance prints found at scenes of crime. Finger Print is going to acquire

AFIS (Automated Finger Print Identification System) which will have palm print capabilities and scalability and extensibility to include Iris and facial image recognition applications.

CCTNS Cell: Crime and Criminal Tracking Network and System is a Mission Mode Computerization Project under Nation Level E-Governance Plan (NeGP).
Objectives:
Sharing Crime and Criminal information across States & Country.
Sharing intelligence.
Enhancing tools for Investigation, Crime Prevention, Law & Order Maintenance, Traffic Management, Traffic Management etc.
Improving service delivery to Public/Citizen/Stakeholders.
Enabling easier and faster analysis of data.
Increasing Operational efficiency.

Dog Squad : Tripura Police Dog Squad started functioning in 1967 in Special Branch Organization with one Tracker dog namely, 'Mili'.

Police dog squad in functioning in 03(Three) separate category i.e. Sniffer, Track were and Narcotics, Sniffer Dogs are mainly functioning to detect the explosive items and Anti Sabotage checking in VVIP/VIP programme venue Hon'ble Governor TPA and Hon'ble C.M. TPA programmes, all minister's residence, shopping malls, bus satads, markets, fairs Exhibitions, Mela groud and on religious occasions. Tracker dogs are used in detection murder, theft, robbery and burglary cases. Narcotics dogs are specially trained to find out 'Ganja' from hidden places,

AQ & PQ Cell :- The AQ & PQ Cell is a very important segment of SCRB and replies to all crime related Assembly Questions and Parliament Questions after collecting crime data from the Districts.

Statistics Cell: Statistics Cell maintains all crime related data of the State. A total of 49 periodical returns including fortnightly, monthly , quarterly, half yearly & yearly returns are being sent from this section, Besides, different statements are being furnished of demand to the higher authority as well as to the Government. SCEB has been earmarked as the Nodal Unit for sending all returns/statements to the Government and also to NCRB etc.

Anti – Human Trafficking Unit: Preparation of monthly and yearly Statement of Anti-Human Trafficking cases and sending the same to the Director, NCRB, New Delhi.

Preparation of monthly and yearly Statement of missing/kidnapped persons and sending the same to the Director, NCRB through AIGP (Crime), Tripura.

Preparation of Yearly Statement of missing/Kidnapped Children. Keeping records in respect of Special Juvenile Police Units of the State. Quarterly updating of the records of Juvenile Units and dealing with all matters related to Juveniles.

F. Arunachal Pradesh Police: Arunachal Pradesh Police is the ultimate law enforcement agency of the state with its headquarter located in Itanagar. Controlled by the Department of Home Affairs, Government of Arunachal Pradesh the Police force is headed by the Director General of Police.

Special agencies or departments:
Intelligence Unit
Security Battalion
Commando Force
Civil police
Tourist police force.

History: Under the British regime, the subcontinent was governed under the Assam Frontier (Administration of Justice) Regulation, 1945 for resolving any disputes and cases, both civil and criminal. The britishers formed the North-East Frontier Tract (NEFT) by dividing the tribal areas from some districts under the Assam Province. After independence in 1947 the NEFT became a part of the Assam state. In 1951, it was renamed as the North-East Frontier Agency (NEFA). The district headquarters of the erstwhile NEFA were established between 1953 and 1955. The North-East Frontier Agency was renamed Arunachal Pradesh and it became a union territory in January 1972. The security and policing of the area before it became a UT was entrusted to the Assam Rifles. The security and control was at standstill till 1959 but it grew hot and tempted after repeated Chinese intrusions and sizing up the scenario the Indian counterpart placed the Assam Rifles under the operational control of the Army. Assam Rifles continued as Civil Police in certain forward areas even after the Chinese invasion in 1962 whereas CRPF was inducted policing much later. After facing unprecedented security, law and order issues the Govt. of India sanctioned a small crew in order to set up a Civil Police in October 1967. Gradually with time small police stations and headquarters are being developed. The force functioned under one AIG with its headquarter at Shillong.

In 1969 Shri G.C. Singhvi (IPS), joined as the first DIG of Arunachal Pradesh Police at the headquarter in Shillong. He tried his best in setting up a full fledged Arunachal Pradesh Police. Later in 1971, Shri L.B. Sewa (IPS) was handed over the charge and responsibility of setting up the Arunachal Pradesh Police. His efforts created wonders in establishing the force. He is and will be known as the Architect of Arunachal Police.

In 1971, the first batch of 30 SIs and 18 ASIs were recruited followed by their training at the Assam Police Training College, Deregaon. In 1973 the first Police Training Centre of Arunachal Pradesh was set up at Banderdewa. In 1974 the Indian Police Act 1861 was enacted in the UT of Arunachal Pradesh followed by creation of the post of Inspector General of Police in March 1976. And in March 1977, Shri K.P. Srivastava assumed office as the first IGP of Arunachal Pradesh. Since then several categories of police stations were established such as A Class Police Stations for DC, B Class PSs for ADC and C Class PSs for other Administrative Centres.

On 20th February, 1987, Arunachal Pradesh became a full fledged State and Government of India directed the state police to be headed by Director General of Police on Feb 13, 2002. And the first Director General of Police of Arunachal Pradesh Police was Sh. Suresh Roy (IPS)

Present Status:
There are 3 Ranges, 26 Police districts, 132 notified Police Stations (out of which presently, 93 Police Stations are functioning), 21 Out Posts and 38 Check Gates, CI Post 3, 2 AAP Bns and 5 India Reserve (IR) Bns in Arunachal Pradesh Police force.

Arunachal Pradesh Police Battalions:
1st A. A. P. BN. HQ. ITANAGAR
2nd A. A. P. BN. HQ. AALO

India Reserve (IR) Battalions:
1st I. R. BN. HQ. Namsangmukh
2nd I. R. BN. HQ. Diyun
3rd I. R. BN. HQ. Seijosa
4th I. R. BN. HQ.Jully
5th I. R. BN. HQ. Pasighat

Current Update:
In 2018, Arunachal Pradesh became the first ever state in North East India to establish a Tourism Police or Tourist Police in order to facilitate tourism in the state. Arunachal Pradesh launches "tourism police" to facilitate tourism in the state. The Arunachal Pradesh state police documented 2021-2026 themed 'SMART police for safe Arunachal'.

G. Assam Police

History: Policing in Assam during Ahom Rule: Before the advent of the British, there did not seem to be any organised police force in Assam, either under the Ahom Kings or earlier.The army as well as the various officers of the kingdom were responsible for the maintenance of peace and safeguarding the lives and properties of the people. Towards the end of the Ahom rule, during the reign of Kamaleswar Singha (1795-1811), an armed force on the British model was raised to serve the dual functions of maintenance of law and order and border defence. It was, however, not a regular and fully organised police force.

Assam Police during British Rule: On taking over the administration of Assam, after the Yandaboo treaty of 1826, the British also did not immediately introduce any revolutionary changes and the army was employed in the task of maintaining law and order. Army outposts were also set up at different places for this purpose. However, the high expenditure in maintaining a large body of troops reduced the number of troops to just four regiments by 1839-40. Steps were taken to increase the armed component of the Civil Police in the province. The necessity of raising a separate force under the civil government apart from the armed civil Police was also felt and the first unit of this new organisation was formed. This was the 'Cachar Levy', formed in 1835 by the Civil Service Officer, in-charge of Nowgong district, Mr. Grange, to guard new settlements and tea estates. It consisted of 750 officers and men of different ranks, viz., Inspectors, Head Constables and Constables. Three years later, a similar body, called 'Jorhat Militia', was formed to protect the border areas against frequent border transgressions. It was also known as the 'Shan militia', as the recruits were mostly from the Shan community. Eventually it was merged with the 'Cachar Levy', which was subsequently renamed as 'Frontier Police' in 1883 and then as 'Assam Military Police' in 1891 and then again as 'Assam Rifles' in 1920. After 1862, the British deployed regular troops in several parts of Assam to consolidate its occupation and a police establishment consisting of one Darogah, one Jamadhar and a number of constables was maintained at each district headquarters. The duties included guarding the Eastern Frontier of Assam from the Brahmaputra River to Cachar. The Levy was a force of a semi-military nature. This development saw the gradual induction of Assamese youth into the police force. The Police Act of 1861 was introduced in Assam in 1862 and the Criminal Procedure Code was also brought into operation in the same year. Till 1874, Assam was administratively a part of the British-ruled province of Bengal and was administered through an agent of the Governor-General. The Police officers were home in the Bengal Cadre and the control and supervision of the Police Department were under the central administration. Following this, there were new administrative developments, and one such was in respect of law and order and prevention of crime. Under the Police Act of 1861, eleven Police Districts were created in Assam. These were : (1) Goalpara, (2) Kamrup, (3) Darrang, (4) Nagaon, (5) Sibsagar, (6) Lakhimpur, (7) Garo Hills, (8) Khasi and Jaintia Hills, (9) Naga Hills, (10) Cachar and (11) Sylhet. The police administration was run from Shillong, the provincial capital. The first Inspector General of Police was Chichele Plowden, who was a civil servant. The police was divided into four branches:

(i) Civil Police, employed in the districts for maintenance of law and order and prevention of crimes and other miscellaneous duties generally entrusted upon the police.

(ii) Frontier Police, a quasi-military force entrusted with the responsibility of protection of the border.

(iii) Municipal Police, created to look after the law and order in the towns, and was subsequently amalgamated with the Civil Police in 1882, and

(iv) Rural Police, a security force to handle the law and order in the villages.

While the Rural and the Municipal police occupied an insignificant position, the mainstay of the police force in Assam was the Civil and the Frontier Police. Civil Police was the principal Police force in the Province and its total strength in 1874, at the time of constituting Assam as a Chief Commissioner's province was 3,352. This was done in accordance with the decision of the Government of India on March 5, 1878 as a part of its reorganisation of the police force. The force was classified into two categories viz. (i) Civil Police for the discharge of ordinary Civil functions and (ii) The Frontier or armed Police for quasi-military work.

Although the Frontier Police (which was, as stated earlier, renamed as Armed Police in 1891) was created to defend the frontiers, it was also used very often to assist the civil police. At the beginning of 1881, there were Municipal Police at Goalpara, Guwahati, Dibrugarh, Sylhet, Sibsagar, Silchar and Shillong but from the 1st April of the year, the

Municipal Police excepting those at Sylhet and Shillong, were amalgamated with the ordinary Civil Police. In addition to these two broad categories, a new police force called "Punitive Police" was formed in 1880 under the Police Act of 1861 and was deployed in Sylhet and Goalpara to handle the recurrence of disturbances there. Later on it was deployed in the Khasi Hills. It was known as "Punitive" because it realised the cost of its maintenance from the erring inhabitants. Five years later, the Railway Police Force was created in April 1885 with one Head Constable and 4 Constables to assist the Railway Survey Party.

The Assam Police Frontier regulation of 1882 provided for the maintenance of proper discipline in the force and fixed the terms and conditions of service in the Assam Frontier Police. Further changes were witnessed in 1883 when the Frontier Police was re-organized to give it a distinct military role and the defence of the entire Frontier line was placed in its hands. The Frontier Police was organized into four corps which was stationed in Cachar, Lakhimpur, Garo Hills and Naga Hills. With the exception of these four districts the duties of guarding the Jails and Treasuries were taken over by the Civil Police.

The New Province of Assam came into existence in 1912. During that year, the formation of a new battalion for the North-East Frontier was sanctioned and a scheme for the re-organisation of the whole Military Police Force into four uniformed Battalions of equal strength was drawn up and submitted to the Government. A Finger Print Bureau was set up at Shillong. The Criminal Investigation Department(CID) was established in 1913 under the special Superintendent of Police and A.E.H. Shettleworth was the first to occupy this position with three branches under his jurisdiction-the Special Branch, concerned with Intelligence and extremist activities, the Investigation Branch, the Finger Print Bureau as already mentioned. Considering the importance and volume of work, the post of Deputy Inspector General of Police(CID) was created in 1935 and R.R.Cuming became its first DIG.

The Assam Civil Police Committee constituted in 1929 under the chairmanship of Sir Syed Mohammad Saadullah, after making a detailed study and seeking the opinion of various sections of the public.

World War II and the Japanese Invasion: Additional duties thrust upon the Police increased enormously with the progress of the war. The

Assam Police faced an entirely novel set of circumstances during 1942. It became clear in the early part of the year that the triumphal march of the Japanese armed forces could not be stopped and the fate of Burma was hanging in the balance.

The preparation for the invasion of India by the Japanese forces created new problems of internal security which the Assam Police was called upon to tackle. The Naga Hills and Manipur became the main targets of attack by the Japanese forces and the Assam Police supplied officers and men to augment the local Police forces and helped in establishing intelligence screens in these areas. When the threat of the Japanese to the railway and other vital communications was at its height, the Police, stationed in the airfields bombed by the enemy, in the isolated pockets and in the threatened areas, remained firm.

Assam Police in Independent India: The year 1947 saw the transfer of power from British to Indian hands. The preliminaries to Constitutional changes as well as the aftermath threw an unprecedented strain on the Police Force. Two important changes affected the Assam Police. The first was the transfer of the Sylhet district to Pakistan and second was the complete separation of the administration of the Assam Rifles from the Police. The retirement of a large number of service officers mainly British, the release of personnel opting for Pakistan and the absorption of those serving in Sylhet who opted for India were some other major factors which caused a temporary setback in the strength and resilience of the Police force immediately after Independence. The disturbed conditions in the Naga Hills arising out of the activities of the followers of A. Z. Phizo claiming independence for the Nagas posed a new problem to the Assam Police in 1956 and in the following years. The Police force in the Naga Hills had to be reinforced and a large number of platoons of the A. P. Battalions were drafted to cope with the situation. It is a matter of pride that the Assam Police gave a good account of themselves and proved equal to the task and as good as any armed force deployed in the area. When the Naga Hills district was separated from Assam in 1958, the Assam Police was withdrawn in stages but they continued to man the outposts on the Naga Hills border.

Training Institutes: There are four training institutions in Assam, all located at Dergaon, in the district of Golaghat to train the Assam Police personnel. These are :

1. Police Training College
2. Armed Police Training Centre
3. Battalion Training Centre and
4. Recruit Training School.

These training institutions provide: Basic in-service training, Basic training to new recruits, training to police personnel of various ranks belonging to the different branches of Assam Police and guided under supervision of the DIG (TAP/EB) located at Dergaon.

Police Training College: Established: 1948 at Salonibari, a place about 12 km north of Tezpur town. Mr. D. C. Dutt, IP, was the first Principal of the Police Training College. The College was shifted from Salonibari to Dergaon on April 1, 1949.

Roles:

1. Before the establishment of the North East Police Academy (NEPA) at Barapani, near Shillong and the police training institutions for all other units of the North East, the police officers upto the rank of Deputy Superintendent of Police from Arunachal Pradesh, Manipur, Maghalaya, Mizoram, Nagaland and Tripura were imparted training at the Police Training College, Dergaon.

2. The College imparts training for a few weeks to the IPS Probationers allotted to the Joint Cadre of Assam and Meghalaya after they pass out of the Sardar Vallabhbhai Patel National Police Academy at Hyderabad.

3. It also provides basic training to the newly recruited Assam Police (APS) officers, Sub Inspectors of the Unarmed Branch, Assistant Sub Inspectors of the Unarmed Branch and Women Constables.

4. It also runs in-service training courses as well as pre-promotion cadre courses for Unarmed Branch officers and the Women Police.

5. It has a Horse Riding School and a Motor Driving and Maintenance Training School.

6. Recently, the college has undertaken a training course for the Enforcement Inspectors of the Transport Department of the Government of Assam.

Recruit Training School:
Established: 1973
Roles: It imparts training to the constables belonging to the Unarmed Branch of the Assam Police.

Armed Police Training Centre: Established: April 1, 1974 at the headquarters of the 5th Assam Police Battalion, Kahilipara, Guwahati under Shri B. Barthakur, IPS. The training center was eventually shifted to Dergaon in 1977.

Roles: The center has the responsibility for giving basic training to the armed wing of the police force of Assam. The Central Arms Repair School (CARS) of the Assam Police functions under the aegis of the APTC.

Battalion Training Centre: Established: March 1980 at Dergaon.

Reason and Role: A comprehensive in-service training courses for the police personnel to sharpen and refresh their professional skills and consequently.

Also runs some specialized courses like map reading, capsule courses for non-commissioned officers as well as Instructors' courses.

All pre-course training for the police personnel selected to undergo any specialized course in central police organizations such as NSG, CRPF, BSF, ITBP and other training institutions is conducted at the BTC Dergaon.

Mounted Police: Police personnel patrolling on the horse back. Established in the year 1964 at 5th A.P. Bn, Kahilipara, Guwahati. Horses & Manpower were also sanctioned for training of cadets at the Riding School of the Police Training College, Dergaon.

Purpose: Crowd control, Traffic control & management, mobs during processions, Area patrolling like river banks, ghats, parks.

River Police: Established: 1979

Purpose: To maintain law & order on the Brahmaputra river districts (districts surrounding the Brahmaputra river). Such as Goalpara, Kamrup and Darrang district comprising 4 (four) River Police Stations and 6 (Six) River Police Out Posts during that time.

Functions: a) Prevent crime and maintenance of law and order in the char areas of the river Brahmaputra. b) prevent and detect illegal infiltration through the riverine routes of the river Brahmaputra from Bangladesh.

Some River Police Stations (RPS): Goalpara River Police Station (Pancharatna) located in Goalpara district, Sualkuchi River Police

Station, Tezpur River Police Station located in Sonitpur district, Biswanath Ghat River Police Station located in Biswanath district.

Some River Police Out Post (RPOP):
1. Buraburi (Mahamaya) River Police Out Post, Dhubri district.
2. Nagarbera River Police Out Post, Kamrup district.
3. Beki River Police Out Post, Barpeta district.
4. Aye River Police Out Post, Bongaigaon district.

CM's Special Vigilance Cell: Chief Minister's Special Vigilance Cell (CM's SVC) was created in the year 1984 with its Headquarters at Guwahati.

The main objective of the creation of this Cell was to enquire and investigate into the special & sensitive offenses committed by the State Government officials under the Prevention of Corruption Act, 1947 (Amended in 1988), offenses U/S 406 to 409 IPC, 417 to 420 IPC, 417 to 477(A) IPC and also under Official Secrets Act, 1923, only when referred to by the Chief Minister of Assam.

Special Branch: The Special Branch came into existence in 1965.

The branch deals with the collection, collation and dissemination of intelligence having security and law and order implications. It usually deals with sensitive matters like public agitation, subversive activities which carry potential and real danger to the security of the state and the nation. Security matters of the vulnerable persons, vital installations and key industries also fall within its purview.

The work of the Special Branch is carried out through two different setups:
1. Headquarters set-up
2. District Special Branch (DSB) setup in the districts.

There is a Special Operations Unit (SOU) to deal with activities of militant organizations and important cadres which has been notified as a Police Station. The S.P. of Special Operations Unit exercises the power of an Officer in Charge of a Police Station.

Village Defence Organization: The Village Defence Organisation is a concept and organization unique to the state of Assam. It was established in the year 1949 when Late Harinarayan Baruah, the founder of the organization, set up a team of village youths to look after and safeguard their own village.

An Act was enacted known as the Village Defence Organisation Act in 1966, followed by the Assam Village Defence Rules in 1986, both of which govern the functioning of the organization. The Director General of Police is the head of the organization.

Government Railway Police (GRP) Assam: Established: 1905 with its Headquarters at Haflong. Later on it was shifted to Guwahati in 1980 with its HQ located at Old Railway Institute, Pandu belonging to Railways. Mr. E.C. Ryland was the first Superintendent of Railway Police of GRP Assam. The Government Railway Police is a separate branch of General Police force

Jurisdiction of GRP Assam:
Railway Division of NFR within Assam. That means it covers a part of Alipurduar Division, Rangiya Division, Tinsukia Division and a major part of Lumding Division.

Organization Structure:
1. GPR Headquarter.
2. Public Subdivision: Lumding, Badarpur, Rangia, New Bongaigaon.
3. Police Circles: Headed by Inspector of Railway Police at Chaparmukh, Bokajan, Mariani., Rangapara, Fakiragram.

Govt. Railway Police Stations: 12
GRP Out Posts: 18
GRP Investigation Centres: 03
GRP Patrol Posts: 10

Difference between Railway Protection Force (RPF) and Government Railway Police (GRP):

Railway Protection Force (RPF): It comes under the control of Government of India, Ministry of Railways. Everything is maintained by the Central Government.

Government Railway Police (GRP): This force is recruited by the respective state police for the Railways and that force receives its salary, half from the state and half from the Railways. There are different forces, but all do the same work with the same motive of providing a safe and secure journey to every passenger of the Indian Railways.

Criminal Investigation Department (CID):
Acts as an Intelligence Bureau for the Police Department. Initially it was formed during the British period and was headquartered at Shillong and divided into the following branches:
(i) The Investigation Branch.
(ii) The Intelligence Branch.
(iii) The Special Branch.
(iv) The Finger Print Bureau.

(However the exact date of starting of the CID is not definitely known but the first volume of the D.O. book has an entry dated 1.5.1922. signed either by the Special Superintendent of Police or by a senior Gazetted Officer or the P.A. of S.S.P)

After, the State of Meghalaya came into existence in 1972 and the capital of Assam shifted to Guwahati. Some of the locations of the C.I.D. were as follows :
1) Ganeshguri (Feb.,1973).
2) Lachitnagar (March, 1975).
3) Ulubari, behind Bora Service (December 1992).
4) Mathura Nagar (October,1994).
Finally the C.I.D. shifted to its own permanent building at Ulubari in January, 1998.
Jurisdiction

CID Police Station: A CID Police Station has started functioning from 1-11-1997 that enables CID to register important cases after preliminary enquiry has been made.

State finger Print Bureau: The State Finger Print Bureau functioning in the CID helps in investigation and in prosecution of cases.

Special Task Force: Established in 2008, with its office located at Panbazar, Guwahati.
Purpose: An elite force of Assam Police that will help in countering - investigation, murder, extortion, money laundering (hawala), drugs, narcotics, smuggling, FICN (Fake Indian Currency Notes), mafia groups, technical gadgets to perform exceptionally dangerous, high

risk, counter terrorism operations that fall outside of the abilities of the District Police.

Assam Police Border Organisation:
Established: 1962 under the P.I.P. (Prevention of Infiltration of Pakistani) Scheme.
Reason and Purpose: A special branch of Assam Police formed in order to prevent infiltration under the PIP (Prevention of Infiltration of Pakistani) Scheme and after the Bangladesh liberation in 1971, the P.I.P. Scheme was renamed as P.I.F. (Prevention of Infiltration of Foreigners) Scheme.

Objectives and Duties:
a) Monitoring entry and exit through ICPs (Immigration Check Post) in two bordering districts of Assam namely, Dhubri and Karimganj.
b) Prevention, Detection and deportation of illegal foreigners.
c) Acts as 2nd Line of Defence after BSF along the Indo-Bangla International Border.
d) Joint patrolling with BSF along the Indo-Bangla International Border.
e) Monitoring entry and exit along the 81 nos. of Inter-State Border.

Assam Police Battalion (APB):
Purpose: Assist the district police in maintaining Law and Order, guarding and other security duties.

List of Assam Police Battalions:
1st APBN is located at Ligiri Pukhuri in Sibsagar district.
2nd APBN is located at Makum in Tinsukia.
3rd APBN is located at Titabor in Jorhat district.
4th APBN is located at Kahilipara in Guwahati, district Kamrup.
5th APBN is located at Sontilla in NC Hills district.
6th APBN is located at Kathal in Cachar district.
7th APBN is located at Charaikhola in Kokrajhar district.
8th APBN is located at Abhayapuri in Bongaigaon district.
9th APBN is located at Berhampur in Nagaon district.
10th APBN is located at Kahilipara, Guwahati in Kamrup district.
11th APBN is located at Dergaon in Golaghat district.
12th APBN is located at Jamugurihat in Sonitpur district.
13th APBN is located at Lilabari in Lakhimpur district.
14th APBN is located at Daulasal in Nalbari district.

Assam Police Task Force:

1st Assam Police Task Force Battalion (APTF Bn) was raised on 2nd January 1984 with its headquarter at Dakurvita.

2nd Assam Police Task Force Battalion (APTF Bn) was raised on 12th March 1984 with its headquarter at Lumding.

3rd Assam Police Task Force Battalion (APTF Bn) was raised on 13th April 1984 with its headquarter at Khajuabeel.

4th Assam Police Task Force Battalion (APTF Bn) was raised on 4th March 1985 with its headquarter at Howly.

IRBN: In order to cope up with the increasing problem of Law and Order and emerging insurgency problem two I.R. Battalions were raised in Assam with the assistance of the Central Government. The Central Government however reserves the first right to call on these Battalions as and when required for deployment outside the state.

15th AP(IR)BN is located at Eraligool in Karimgunj district.
16th AP(IR)BN is located at Barmonipur in Morigaon district.

Assam Commando: It is the first commando unit of Assam Police. Established on 18th January 1996 with its first headquarters being temporarily set up at Kahilipara, in the 4th Assam Police Battalion campus. Presently the headquarter is located at Mandakata, North Guwahati.
Purpose: Raised as an elite force which will combat the growing insurgency problem in Assam.
The first commando unit was trained at the Commando Training Centre, P.R.T.C, Jahankhelam, Punjab Subsequently followed by training at National Security Guard Training Centre, Maneswar, Haryana.

Assam Police Radio Organisation (APRO):
Established: 12 March 1946.
Purpose: Connecting the then State HQ Shillong with the district HQs of Nagaon, Darrang, Goalpara, Lakhimpur, Sivasagar and Cachar as well as Tura and Haflong.

APRO Training School: Established in 1948 at Shillong, Presently located at Jalukbari, Guwahati since 1975.

Roles: Training in Wireless Communications, Electronics, Telecommunications, Information Technology and Amateur Radio Programmes or HAMs.

The Amateur Radio Operators or HAMs helps in communication support during natural disasters like earthquakes, floods, etc.

India's first female commando unit: Veerangana: India's first female commando unit to tackle rising crime against women has been set up by Assam Police. Established in 2012, it is India's first all-woman silent drill commando unit. This special platoon which has been raised to check violence against women was commissioned on January 26, 2013.

Now what led to the formation of this stealth force, well it was 2011 and the National Crime Records Bureau rated Assam as the second highest activity of crime against women in India also the molestation incident of a 21-year-old girl outside a pub on the G.S. Road in the capital region of Assam by a gang of rowdies for 40 minutes shook the entire nation.

The brain behind the formation of this special unit was then Assam Police Inspector General (Training and Armed Police) Bhaskar Jyoti Mahanta, now DGP Assam Police. The Veerangana Unit is presently under the command and control of the Commandant, 4th AP Bn, Kahilipara since January, 2015.

Reforms in Assam Police force: These reforms were uprightly initiated and adopted by CM Himanta Biswa Sarma, (Home Minister) in 2021.

A. Residential quarters would be built within premises of all police stations for an OC and 3 sub-inspectors.

B. CID will train OCs in preparing charge sheets.

The health department will conduct health check-ups every 15 days for police personnel.

C. All OCs will be provided one vehicle each for their police stations.

D. Motorcycles would be provided for police stations in difficult and inaccessible areas.

E. 3 computers would be provided to all police stations for streamlining FIR filing & other activities.

F. Filing of charge sheet within 6 months.

Completing police verification work within 7 days.
G. Every Police Station will receive 2.5 lacs annually as contingency fund.
H. One power generator for every police station.
I. Zero tolerance for crime against women.

For insurgency purpose:
Special Branch: The Special Branch came into existence in 1965. The branch deals with the collection, collation and dissemination of intelligence having security and law and order implications. It usually deals with sensitive matters like public agitation, subversive activities which carry potential and real danger to the security of the state and the nation. Security matters of the vulnerable persons, vital installations and key industries also fall within its purview.

The work of the Special Branch is carried out through two different setups:
1. Headquarters set-up
2. District Special Branch (DSB) setup in the districts.

There is a Special Operations Unit (SOU) to deal with activities of militant organizations and important cadres which has been notified as a Police Station. The S.P. of Special Operations Unit exercises the power of an Officer in Charge of a Police Station.

Achievements: In Nov, 2013, Suspension of Operation (SoO) agreement was signed with NDFB (RD) group. With this NDFB (RD) faction, total 13 nos of militant groups under SOU. These include -
(1) NDFB (P) (National Democratic Front of Bodoland (Progressive)
(2) ULFA (PT) (United Liberation Front of Assam) Pro-Talk)
(3) KLNLF (Karbi Longri N.C. Hills Liberation Front)
(4) NDFB (R) (National Democratic Front of Bodoland - Ranjan group)
(5) ACMA (Adivasi Cobra Milit`ary of Assam)
(6) BCF (Bircha Commando Force)
(7) KRA (Revolutionary Govt. of Kukigam (RGoK)/ Kuki Revolutionary Army)
(8) UKDA (United Kukigam Defence Army)
(9) KLO/ KLA (Kuki Liberation Organization/ Kuki Liberation Army)
(10) HPC (D) (Hmar People's Convention (Democratic)
(11) APA (Adivasi People's Army),

(12) AANLA (All Adivasi National Liberation Army and
(13) STF (Santhal Tiger Force).

The Adivasi militant outfit NSLA (National Saotal Liberation Army) and Reang militant outfit UDLF (B) have declared unilateral ceasefire w.e.f. 03/08/2012 and 20/02/2013 respectively under the coordination of SB HQRS. thus expressed their willingness to solve their demands through discussion.

In the Islamist militancy front, one module of the Jamat-ul-Mujahideen, Bangladesh (JMB) was successfully busted. In this regard, 14 persons were arrested till 20th Jan, 2015 (7 of them underwent training in Simulia and Mukimnagar Madrassa of West Bengal) and 10 bombs have been recovered.

5. Human Trafficking in Northeast India

"Trafficking" is defined by the United Nations as "any action that leads to the recruitment, transportation, harbouring, or receiving of individuals by the threat or use of force or a position of vulnerability." Human trafficking has been around for a long time. It is the world's third most lucrative criminal enterprise after the arms and drug trades. It was official and exchanged human beings on the open market from an early age, which was referred to as slave trade. Despite the fact that it is illegal at the moment, it is a worldwide sector that earns an estimated five to seven billion dollars every year. It is a problem that affects not just one state or country, but the entire world. Human trafficking poses a hazard to both human security and development. In recent years, millions of women and girls have been trafficked across borders and inside countries. According to a UNDP research, 300,000 to 450,000 persons are trafficked within Asia each year, with more than half taking place in South Asia. Women and children, particularly girls, are trafficked inside nations, across borders, and across regions and continents outside South Asia. Over the last decade, the rising problem of human trafficking in South Asia has been acknowledged and has become a significant concern. It may be described as a modernised version of the centuries-old slave trade.

Human trafficking is one of the most serious issues in Russia and the former Soviet republics, particularly among women and children. Following the fall of the Soviet Union, the trafficking of women and children from Eastern Europe has escalated. Human trafficking is a severe

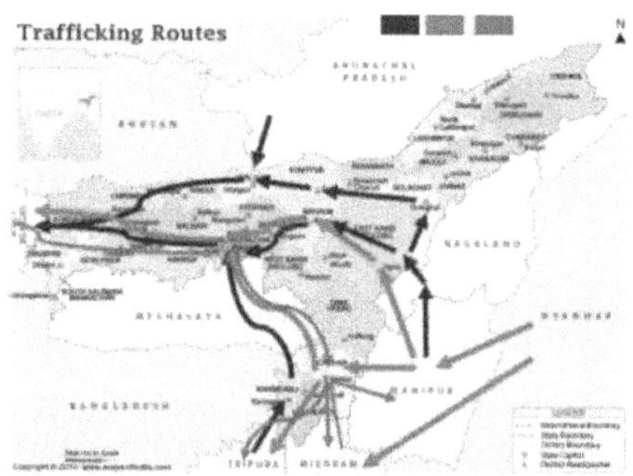

problem in Ukraine, although the nation's legislative statute introduced safety measures to combat the crime in 1998, making Ukraine the first country in Europe to explicitly declare human trafficking a criminal offence.

As we are studying about the human trafficking in the northeastern states therefore let's start with Guwahati (Assam) which is also known as the gateway to the North East. The seven sisters states share a crucial geographical location bordering autocratic China and militancy led coup governments of both Myanmar and Bangladesh. Among the seven states Assam has served as a source, transit, and destination for women and children trafficked for commercial sexual exploitation, forced labour, forced marriage, and domestic slavery, among other things. Despite its sixty-nine years of independence, India's economic progress has been lacklustre. The poorest people in India are still living in poverty, surviving on food, shelter, and clothing, all of which are fundamental human requirements. Women and children are more vulnerable to human trafficking when they are poor and hungry. Because of a lack of action, human trafficking continues to be a concern. Human trafficking occurs in the North Eastern area of India, both inside the states and over the borders of Myanmar, Bangladesh, and Nepal, due to poverty, unemployment, illiteracy, and traditional views of women. Assam, Meghalaya, Manipur, Nagaland, Tripura, Arunachal Pradesh, Mizoram, and Sikkim are the eight states that make up India's North Eastern region. This region has a geographical size of 2,62,185 square kilometres, accounting for roughly 8% of the country's overall geographical area. This area lies between 29 and 22 degrees north latitude and 89.46 and 97.5 degrees east longitude. The region has a total population of 3.9 crores, according to the 2001 census estimate. Despite having abundant natural resources like as biodiversity, hydro-potential, oil and coal deposits, and dense forest cover, the area nevertheless lags behind all of India's states economically. According to data from the Central Bureau of Investigation (CBI) in Ulubari, Assam, 42.03 percent of children were trafficked to the states of Haryana, Uttar Pradesh, Rajasthan, Maharashtra, and West Bengal between 2005 and 2010, with 31.88 percent going to metro cities like Delhi, Mumbai, and Kolkata, 14.49 percent going to unknown destinations, 7.25 percent going to the North Eastern region, and 4.35 percent going to other states. In the state, women and children are still at risk. In 2015, more than 20,000 cases of violence against women were reported. Similarly, through October 2015, around 1,386 minors, including females, were reported missing from across the state, compared to 1,577 juveniles who went missing the previous year. Human trafficking has become an insurmountable problem in North East India due to open national and international borders and a lack of security.

Year wise Rape cases registered in Assam for the year 2001 to 2023		
SL NO	YEAR	CASES REGISTERED
1	2001	817
2	2002	970
3	2003	1095
4	2004	1171
5	2005	1238
6	2006	1244
7	2007	1437
8	2008	1438
9	2009	1631
10	2010	1721
11	2011	1700
12	2012	1716
13	2013	1937
14	2014	1980
15	2015	1733
16	2016	1779
17	2017	3544
18	2018	3296
19	2019	3546
20	2020	1657
21	2021	1733
22	2022	1113
23	2023	989
24	2024 (UP TO July)	580

Causes of human trafficking:

1. Poverty, government corruption, economic instability, a lack of strict legal systems, and the easy money tendency or high financial gain in the trade are all factors that contribute to human trafficking. This is a problem that affects the whole globe today, regardless of caste or faith.

2. North East India is rapidly becoming a hotspot for human trafficking from all over the world. Because of the declining conventional societal value and high levels of corruption, human trafficking has lately arisen in India's North Eastern area. Many law enforcement officers are involved in the drug trafficking industry because of the widespread corruption.

3. When women and children are trafficked, they frequently have no other alternative. Young girls and women from North East India are abducted from their homes and transported to distant states in India or abroad for bonded labour and sex business.

4. According to government of India statistics, a child went missing every eight minutes in India in 2011, with the majority of them coming from West Bengal and North East India.

5. According to a First Post story, Delhi is the centre of India's human trafficking trade, with India housing half of the world's slaves. Illegal traders in Delhi sell girls and women from the North Eastern region, luring their parents with promises of a better life for their children.

6. Roti, kapra, and makan are in short supply in most of the North Eastern states. As a result, poverty is the leading source of illicit human flash business. Sexual exploitation, bonded labour, cross-border trafficking, and trafficking for human organs are all examples of human trafficking. It's become a well-organized industry across the country.

7. Around 80% of human trafficking occurs for sexual exploitation, with the remaining 20% being for bonded labour and other reasons. The need for commercial sex is one of the reasons of human trafficking in India, which is regarded as Asia's centre. Because of the strong demand for their

Mongolian appearance, the majority of the females in the North Eastern area are trafficked to Thailand, Singapore, and Japan as bonded labour or sex workers. Poverty and economic difficulties, along with drinking, has rendered most parents vulnerable to the offer of money in return for their daughters' children being sold into slavery over state lines.

Policies adopted by government for Anti human trafficking:
1. Throughout the nineteenth and twentieth century's, governments took steps to combat this threat on a global scale, including the International Anti-Slavery Convention, International Anti-Prostitution Convention, International Labour Law, International Human Rights Law, and the Rights to Children Act, among others. These are only a few of the many steps taken by governments throughout the world.
2. In India, the government has adopted a number of anti-trafficking steps to protect women and children from being exploited as a result of the threat of human trafficking. Article 23 (1) of the Indian Constitution states that "trafficking in human beings is forbidden, and any violation of this prohibition will be a crime and penalised." Article 39 (1) puts a duty on the state to orient its policies toward ensuring "that children are provided opportunity and facilities to develop in a healthy way, in a context of freedom and dignity, and that children and adolescents are safeguarded from exploitation..." The immoral Traffic Preventing Act of 1956 is the country's primary legislative tool for combating human trafficking. A National Plan of Action to address human trafficking and commercial sexual exploitation of women and children was adopted by the Indian Prime Minister in 1998.
3. Northeast various state government has made a number of initiatives to prevent human trafficking. If we talk about Assam then, the following are the important steps:

a) The Anti-Human Trafficking Cell has been established at CID headquarters, with the Nodal Officer being the IGP CID.

b) With the current manpower, 14 Anti-Human Trafficking Units have been established at district headquarters in accordance with Ministry of Human Affairs guidelines.

c) At the district headquarters, 26 Juvenile Justice Board Districts have been established.

d) In each district, a total of 26 child welfare committees have been established.

e) In Assam's 30 police districts, 30 Special Juvenile Police Units have been established.

f) In each district, three advisory boards have been established. IT(P) Act, Section 13(3)(b)

g) On the national level, as well as at the CID headquarters, a continuous process of training and sensitization on human trafficking is underway for officers and personnel.

h) Increased collaboration between the police and other government and non-government agencies

I) 7 Observation and Shelter Homes have already been built in districts.

k) District SPs are obliged to ensure the following in order to prevent the trafficking of women and girls:

l) At the PS/OP level, the investigation of crimes against women will be prioritised

m) Enhanced vigilance in areas where human trafficking is likely to occur, such as train stations and bus stops.

n) Prompt investigation/verification to distinguish cases of human trafficking from kidnapping, abduction, and missing entries.

o) Senior police officers will carry out successful raids with the help of anti-trafficking NGOs.

p) Organised rackets and its members must be recognised in order to face serious legal consequences.

q) Apart from that, immigration authorities and police officers from Assam's bordering districts have been notified to maintain a high level of vigilance in order to prevent trans-border trafficking.

1. There are also some Acts which aim to address the issues of human trafficking in India, such as, Prohibition of Child Marriage Acts, 2006, Young person (Harmful Publication) Acts, 1956, Bonded Labour System (Abolition) Acts, 1976,

Indecent Representation of Women (Prohibition) Acts, 1986, and the Transplantation of Human Organs Acts, 1994.

2. Article 23 of the constitution prohibits trafficking in human being and other similar forms of forced labour and pronounces that such acts are offences punishable in accordance with law. Article 24 of the constitution also provides that no child, below the age of 14 years, shall be employed to work in any factory or mine or engaged in any other hazardous employment.

3. The Directive Principles of State Policy contained in the part IV of the constitution of India, plays the major role in the formulation of state policy. The directive principles of state policy envisage the socio-economic rights of the citizens of India. Article 39 of the constitution directs the state to formulate suitable polices for protection and promotion of the health and strength of labours and workers, women and the tender age of children.

4. Section 366 of IPC provides that whoever induces any women to go from any place with intent that she may likely be or knowing that she will be forced or seduced to illicit intercourse with another person shall be punishable with imprisonment of either description for a term which may extend to ten years and shall also be liable to fine.

5. Further, section 372 of IPC, 1860 prohibits selling minor for the purpose of prostitution, and section 373 criminalizes the act of buying minor for the purpose of prostitution. Importation of any girl under the age of twenty-one years of age to India from outside India is also a penal offence under the Indian Penal Code.

6. The Immoral Traffic (Prevention) Act, 1956 is one of the main legislations enacted by the Parliament for preventing and combating trafficking in human beings in India.

S. No.	State/UT	Cases Reported			Mid-Year Projected Population (In Lakhs)	Rate of Cognizable Crimes (IPC)++	Chargesheeting Rate
		2019	2020	2021			
(1)	(2)	(3)	(4)	(5)	(6)	(7)	(8)
STATES:							
1	Andhra Pradesh	245	171	168	528.5	0.3	99.3
2	Arunachal Pradesh	0	2	3	15.4	0.2	0.0
3	Assam	201	124	203	351.6	0.6	56.2
4	Bihar	106	75	111	1237.0	0.1	88.0
5	Chhattisgarh	50	38	29	296.1	0.1	90.5
6	Goa	38	17	15	15.6	1.0	88.9
7	Gujarat	11	13	13	700.8	0.0	100.0
8	Haryana	15	14	37	296.0	0.1	84.8
9	Himachal Pradesh	11	4	5	74.1	0.1	100.0
10	Jharkhand	177	140	92	386.4	0.2	55.9
11	Karnataka	32	13	13	669.9	0.0	90.9
12	Kerala	180	166	201	355.4	0.6	86.9
13	Madhya Pradesh	73	80	89	848.6	0.1	98.8
14	Maharashtra	282	184	320	1247.6	0.3	99.6
15	Manipur	9	6	1	31.7	0.0	100.0
16	Meghalaya	22	1	1	33.0	0.0	4.3
17	Mizoram	7	0	0	12.2	0.0	-
18	Nagaland	3	0	0	22.0	0.0	-
19	Odisha	147	103	136	457.9	0.3	70.4
20	Punjab	19	17	15	304.0	0.0	81.3
21	Rajasthan	141	128	100	795.7	0.1	100.0
22	Sikkim	0	1	0	6.8	0.0	-
23	Tamil Nadu	16	11	3	764.8	0.0	100.0
24	Telangana	137	184	347	377.7	0.9	98.6
25	Tripura	1	1	1	40.8	0.0	-
26	Uttar Pradesh	48	90	103	2317.0	0.0	90.9
27	Uttarakhand	20	9	16	114.4	0.1	75.0
28	West Bengal	120	59	61	982.9	0.1	72.5
	TOTAL STATE(S)	2111	1651	2083	13284	0.2	84.8
UNION TERRITORIES							
29	A & N Islands	0	0	0	4.0	0.0	-
30	Chandigarh	2	2	2	12.1	0.2	100.0
31	DNH and Daman & Diu@	0+	2	0	11.1	0.0	-
32	Delhi UT	93	53	92	207.0	0.4	81.3
33	Jammu & Kashmir @	0*	2	4	134.4	0.0	50.0
34	Ladakh @	-	0	0	3.0	0.0	-
35	Lakshadweep	0	0	0	0.7	0.0	-
36	Puducherry	2	4	8	15.8	0.5	-
	TOTAL UT(S)	97	63	106	388.1	0.3	80.8
	TOTAL (ALL INDIA)	2208	1714	2189	13671.8	0.2	84.7

TABLE 14.1 - Page 1 of 1

Note: '+' combined data of erstwhile D & N Haveli and Daman & Diu UT

'++' Rate refers to Cases Reported per 1 lakh population

'*' data of unified Jammu & Kashmir State including Ladakh

'@' data of newly created Union Territory

• Population Source : Report of Technical group on Population Projections (July, 2020) National Commission on Population, MoHFW

Human Trafficking data published is based on annual data as provided by States/UTs from their Anti Human Trafficking Units

SPECIFICALLY WOMEN AND CHILDREN TRAFFICKING IN NORTHEAST INDIA

Human trafficking is a serious form of violation of human rights. It is also true that women and children are the most vulnerable section of the society and because of which they are prone to be the victims of trafficking for various reasons, including for sexual exploitation, prostitution, slavery and organ transplantation.

In order to combat and prevent women and child trafficking, the Immoral Traffic prevention Act, 1956 has been enacted by the parliament of India. The North Eastern States of India consisting of Assam, Arunachal Pradesh, Nagaland, Manipur, Meghalaya, Mizoram, Sikkim and Tripura has been one of the important sources of women and child trafficking as the region has been a fertile ground for trafficking because of various reason like, armed conflict, ethnic tension, lack of development and job opportunity and illiteracy. The government needs to take up appropriate legislative as well as administrative measures so as to combat the emerging issues of human trafficking in the region.

The UN Global Report on Trafficking in persons, 2012 shows that women and children are the two most frequently reported groups of trafficked persons. The UN conducted an assessment of trafficking in 2009 which also indicated that percentage of women among the total number of detected victims of trafficking globally is in the range of 60 percent.

Trafficking of girls accounts for about 15-20 percent of the total number of victims detected between 2007 and 2010, representing the second largest category of detected trafficking victims globally. Child accounts for a total of 27 percent of the victims. Among these, girls were more frequently detected than boys.

Trafficking in person report 2010, published by the United State, department of state carried the evidence of NGO report on duping of girls from North East India with promise to provide job and then forcing them into prostitution as well as forced marriage. It is also reported that brides are also in high demand in the state of Haryana and other Northern states of India due to the low sex ratio caused by sex selective abortion.

Assam is also on the top among the North Eastern States of India by registering a total of 165 cases of human trafficking. The department of Social Welfare, government of Manipur reported that a total of 379 children were rescued from different parts of the country during the year 2008 to 2012. It has also been reported in a local daily in Imphal that in yet another sensational rescue of trafficked children, altogether 76 children hailing from Manipur and Assam were rescued by the child welfare committee, Tamil Nadu from a children home in Magappair, Tamil Nadu. The National Commission for Protection of Child Rights acknowledged the case and recommended to provide proper residential educational rehabilitation of children from vulnerable families in the source area and to introduce effective monitoring mechanism at the block, sub- district, state and central level. It has also been reported in 'the Hindu', that the Guwahati Childline discovered that all the 24 trafficked minor boys were from the North Cachar Hills District, Assam.

6. Animal Trafficking in Northeast India

Humans have been reliant on wildlife for food and shelter throughout history. It could be said then that the use of wildlife both non-human animals and plants - is engrained within human cultures. This relationship with wildlife has led and is currently connected to the over exploitation of species. Today there is not an area of the world that is not touched by wildlife trade. Non-human animals and plants are traded by the hundreds of millions every year. Much of this is legal, but there is a persistent, pervasive illegal trade that is threatening many species. Trade is driven by human consumption; consumption of food and traditional medicines and ownership of rare pets, plants and decorative objects. All types of nonhuman animals and plants are victims of wildlife trafficking; cacti, orchids, pitcher plants, trees, amphibians, birds, insects, mammals and reptiles. Even a rare fungus in the Himalayas is overexploited. The trade in reptiles as pets, for consumption as food or use in traditional medicines poses an increasing threat to the conservation of many squamates native to the South-east Asian region.

Northeast India is highly vulnerable to wildlife crimes and serves as a major gateway for trafficking animals and their body parts. "Wildlife crimes are a threat to national security as sales and proceeds of wildlife trafficking is often used to fund terror, militancy and other related activities". "The Northeast is a mega biodiversity hotspot and with porous land borders with neighbouring countries, the region is both a source and a transit route for illegal wildlife trade". Director of Assam State Space Application Centre (ASSAC) P L N Raju pointed out how space technology, geospatial technology and even drone technology can aid conservation of wildlife and nature effectively and prevent wildlife crime.

The North-East region of India is rich in biodiversity. This region is a part of the nucleus of the South-East Asia for the global wildlife trade both as a source and as a consumer. Wildlife trade, for use in Traditional Medicine (TM), as pets and for food, poses a significant threat to the conservation of many species in the region.

In May 2022, kangaroos, rats, meerkats, white cockatoos and Burmese pythons, -- all exotic animals not indigenous to India were seized after they were smuggled from Myanmar. Few days later, a total of 468 endangered exotic animals, including 442 lizards, smuggled from Myanmar, were seized by the police and wildlife enforcement agencies in Mizoram's Champhai district and five people were arrested in this connection on May 25.

In a massive cross border smuggling bid, the Assam Police seized 40 rare and exotic animals, including 19 primates and two baby wallabies, from two West Bengal-bound Sports Utility Vehicles (SUVs) at Rangia in Kamrup district and arrested two people. The SUVs with the exotic animals had travelled more than 720 km through three northeastern states -- Mizoram, Meghalaya and Assam -- before being intercepted on National Highway-31 at Rangia.

In March, the Assam police found macaws, silvery marmosets, and golden-headed tamarin - all exotic animals from Brazil's Amazon - while conducting routine checks in Golaghat district. These animals were smuggled via Moreh, officials said.

Wildlife trafficking case study from NE. India

Gecko: A case of live trade: The North-East India is known for awesome natural bounty and amazing wildlife. While many have heard about endangered one horned Rhino and wildcat species found in these states, not many are aware about the rare reptile species. The truth is, in forest and hills of Northeast India, a number of rare and endangered reptiles are found Some of these are facing threat of extinction owing to trafficking and rampant killing by humans. One of these is the Tokay Gecko Lizard.

In recent years, the Tokay gecko is facing threat of extinction like never before. In states like Manipur and Nagaland, these lizards are being captured randomly and sold for reported medicinal properties. In Asian subcontinent, its body parts are sold at high rates owing to belief that its usage can heal killer diseases like cancer and AIDS. Some tribes also believe it can be used to cure diabetes. However, no feasible and scientific evidence exists that can corroborate such beliefs. In Tezpur of Assam and several other cities, illegal rackets of lizard trading have mushroomed in recent years. The Wildlife (Protection) Act, 1972 specifies trade of these lizards is illegal and killing them is not permitted either. However, more stringent laws need to be introduced and deployed to stop mass killing and trading of these lizards.

Rhinoceros: The horn of sorrow: Rhino poaching in NorthEast India especially in Assam is one of the major environmental issues in India which continues in the region of Kaziranga National Park, Manas National Park, Orang National Park and Pobitora Wildlife Sanctuary of Assam. The one horn rhino or Indian rhino is surviving in the North-East region of India, Assam account almost 95% of the total wild One horned rhino in the world. These rhinos are inhabited most of the floodplain of the Indo-Gangetic and Brahmaputra riverine tracts and the neighboring foothills.

Sport hunting became common in the late 1800s and early 1900s which results in abrupt decrease in rhino population in Assam. By 1908, the population in Kaziranga had decreased to around 12 individuals (Laurie, et al., 1983). In the early 1900s, the species had declined to near extinction. But, serious concern for conserving the One horned rhino since later part of 1900s is causing an increase in rhino population in the national park. However, due to increasing population the overexploitation of the wildlife is causing a serious effect on decreasing the number of the rhino population in the national park. A comparative assessment of the years between 1968 to 2017 shows that the highest number of poaching of rhinos go to 92 in Assam with maximum 45 (total 5.84%, 1986) in Kaziranga NP.

Table 1 Showing the year-wise poaching of One Horned Rhino in KNP, 1968-2017

Year	1968	1969	1970	1971	1972	1973	1974	1975	1976	1977
No. of Poaching	10	8	2	8	0	3	3	5	1	0
Year	1978	1979	1980	1981	1982	1983	1984	1985	1986	1987
No. of Poaching	3	2	11	24	25	37	28	44	45	23
Year	1988	1989	1990	1991	1992	1993	1994	1995	1996	1997
No. of Poaching	24	44	35	23	49	40	14	27	26	12
Year	1998	1999	2000	2001	2002	2003	2004	2005	2006	2007
No. of Poaching	8	4	4	8	4	3	4	7	5	16
Year	2008	2009	2010	2011	2012	2013	2014	2015	2016	2017
No. of Poaching	6	6	5	9	11	27	27	17	20	4

A Man's vision and Rhinos revival in Kaziranga: On sept 22, 2021, Assam CM Himanta Biswa Sarma send a strong message to the world that Assam only values the horns safely present on live rhinos not on the carcass and created history by burning 2,479 Rare Rhino Horns which were kept in six temporary furnaces by Hindu priests on the very World Rhino Day thus dismissing all the superficial belief of possessing medicinal properties in the horns that can cure ailments like hair loss, cancer, erectile dysfunction, and more. CM Himanta Biswa Sarma said Rhino horns are composed entirely of keratin, a protein found in fingernails and hair, which has been dismissed by several researchers as having any medicinal value. "I too have received the suggestion, 'Why not sell the horns to help the government build roads and schools?' But, this goes against our culture and constitution. Moreover, this will also encourage poachers and will send a message that Assam too subscribes to the superstition that rhino horns may have medicinal values." This exercise is done regularly and at a very large scale in many African countries, with the highest quantity burned being 105 tonnes of ivory and over a tonne of rhino horns in 2016. However, many rhino farmers have questioned the activity and suggested that the horn trade be legalised and regulated so that the countries can earn revenue by selling the horns -- specifically to countries like China and Vietnam where there is a traditional market for these materials, given the belief that rhino horns possess medicinal properties and can cure ailments like hair loss, cancer, erectile dysfunction, and more.

Conservation Strategies That Delivered Results: Since 2016, Kaziranga National Park has implemented several key conservation measures, contributing to the dramatic decline in rhino poaching:

Increased Protection: The government established new anti-poaching camps, boosting surveillance across the park. A special protection force was also created to specifically guard rhinos from poachers. The special task force, comprising members of the Assam police and the forest department, deserves much of the credit. These commandos, trained in the same vein as the National Security Guard or NSG and experts in counter insurgency operations in the state, are responsible for securing the park's fringe areas and carrying out strikes at known poacher launch pads. They even travel to other states to capture fleeing poachers.

Technology: The game-changer in the fight against poachers has been the use of technology. Electronic eyes, thermal sensors, camera traps, and night vision cameras are placed strategically throughout the park, and speed meters and high-resolution cameras monitor the national highway at the park's periphery. Drone surveillance and satellite phones for forest guards also play a role, with all data feeding into the command centre of the task force. Quick response teams are on standby to respond to every technical tip-off. The canine unit which has the famous Belgian Malinois dogs has also been a major help.

Kaziranga Model of Conservation: The park's globally recognized conservation model was further strengthened. Anti-poaching camps, set up every 5.82 square kilometers, now total 233 across the park, each staffed with dedicated personnel. These teams work tirelessly to deter poachers and protect the rhinos.

Expanded & Encroachment free Habitat: Efforts were made to expand the natural habitat for rhinos, ensuring they had more space to roam and thrive. This not only enhanced their safety but also supported the overall health of the park's ecosystem.

As per the April 2017 Indian Express report, Forest officials evicted 343 families and cleared about 2.35 sq km of area from the grip of encroachers in the Orang National Park. About 2.35 sq km on the eastern side of Orang National Park was cleared in a joint operation we launched with the help of the police and civil administration. Over 2,000 people who had been encroaching upon the National Park land for decades were evicted. The 78.8 sq km Orang National Park, which is also one among four tiger reserves in Assam, has been under tremendous pressure of encroachment and poaching, pointing out that poachers suspected to be from among the encroachers, had killed two rhinos in the current year. In 2016 poachers had killed one rhino there. While the Gauhati High Court had directed the forest department to evict the encroachers from Orang way back in 2014, it was only after the BJP-led government of Sarbananda Sonowal took over in May 2016 that eviction drives have been intensified. In September last year, the government had evicted over 330 families and cleared 24,00 bighas of land adjoining Kaziranga National Park. Orang, which was upgraded to a National Park in 1999 after it was declared as a wildlife sanctuary in 1985, had registered 100 rhinos during the last census carried out in 2012, while the last tiger census showed 24 tigers in 2013.

As per September 04, 2020, The Hindu reported, Assam Govt approved the Kaziranga National Park expansion by 3,053 hectares in two districts. The Assam government has approved the addition of 30.53 sq km to the 884 sq km Kaziranga National Park. The additional areas straddling two districts - Nagaon and Sonitpur — would make the larger Kaziranga National Park and Tiger Reserve (KNPTR) grow to 1085.53 sq km. And after the Post-Kaziranga expansion, Assam expects tiger surge as per The Sentinel report on 09 Apr 2023. Before 2015, Kaziranga had a lot of issues with the possession of land. A major portion of the park was encroached upon, and it had an adverse effect on the tiger population. Kaziranga now has 10 ranges, compared to its earlier four. At present, it has three divisions. Assam's two other tiger reserves, Nameri and Orang, are situated on two sides of Kaziranga. We have built connectivity with both of these tiger reserves. This has eased the movement of tigers among Kaziranga, Nameri, and Orang. Karbi Anglong forests are on another side of Kaziranga, which has hills. We have planned to build nine animal corridors that connect Kaziranga with the Karbi Anglong forests. This has facilitated the movements of animals during the floods.

As per reports published on G Plus News (Oct 04, 2024), Assam Expands Orang National Park to Kaziranga National Park thus Creating a 180-Km-Long Wildlife Corridor between the parks. Orang National Park now flows into Kaziranga National Park and the Burha-Chapori| Wildlife Sanctuary in such a manner as to create an uninterrupted 180-kilometer-long protected corridor for wildlife to roam about and thrive in. Assam has cleared 22,000 bighas of encroached land at Orang National Park and extended its protected area. Although several sections had protested the expansion of the national park, it was a giant step for the state towards biodiversity preservation.

Collaborating with International efforts: The international trade in rhino horn has been banned by CITES (Convention on International Trade in Endangered Species of Fauna and Flora) since 1977. It is also listed as a CITES Appendix I animal.

The World Wide Fund for Nature (WWF) is working with TRAFFIC on the Wildlife Crime Initiative to investigate, expose and crack down on poaching and the illegal trade in rhino horn – and reduce demand.

Efforts in India: The Indian rhinoceros is given the highest protection under Schedule I of the Wildlife Protection Act, of 1972. Union government is helping to expand protected areas, create new ones, connect isolated rhino habitats and increase security in these areas.

The Project Rhino platform ensures that efforts to protect white and black rhino populations are coherent and avoid duplication of work. It collaborates with anti-poaching and wildlife economy initiatives throughout southern Africa to share strategies and best practices.
The Kaziranga Model: Wildlife officials in Assam said the 'Kaziranga model' has become a template for conservation in many rhino-bearing areas across the globe because:
1. A commando-like special protection force has been deployed in the area.
2. A "zero-tolerance policy" has been adopted at the park towards poaching.
3. Surveillance camps in every 5.82 sq. km have been established. The Kaziranga National Park and Tiger Reserve has 233 anti-poaching camps, each manned by three to five personnel.

Gun surrendered campaigns: As per reports published on The Sentinel on 27 Sep 2021, Traditionally hunting with bamboo contraptions, including sharp spears and bow-and-arrows, to upgrading to modern guns and now to surrendering them, Arunachal Pradesh has come a full circle.

Since its launch in March 2021, more than 1,000 people have surrendered their air guns in Arunachal Pradesh as part of the 'Air Gun Surrender Campaign'. Till a century ago, Arunachal Pradesh remained cut off from other States, thanks to its deep forests and mighty rivers. The local communities - even they lived in silos in their respective territories - banked on wild meat mostly in absence of variety of food available in other parts and hunting was a tradition not just for variety of meat but also part of some religious rituals in almost all ethnic communities. Air guns do not require any license and scores of people hunt birds and smaller animals using these air guns across Arunachal Pradesh, unaware of the biodiversity loss. Much of the ownership of the land rests with the tribal communities and effectively very small area falls under Forest Department, rendering much of the wildlife related laws ineffective. The 'Airgun Surrender Abhiyan', a wildlife conservation initiative by the Arunachal Pradesh forest department, has received international recognition at the UNESCO's International Conference on Biosphere Reserves at Sabah in Malaysia. The initiative received a significant boost when it was featured in the 84th edition of the 'Mann Ki Baat' programme on December 26 the same year, with Prime Minister Narendra Modi personally acknowledging and appreciating these efforts. Earlier, the abhiyan had received acclaim from various national and international media outlets and was honoured at the sixth North East Green Summit of Forest Ministers of North East held at Silchar in Assam in 2021. Later on as published on Sentinel Digital on 21 Dec 2024, Air Gun Museum Inaugurated in Palin, Arunachal Pradesh, Dedicated to 116 Air Guns. Palin, located in the heart of the Kra Daadi district of Arunachal Pradesh, inaugurated a museum on dedicated to 116 air guns. And as published on Sentinel Digital on 05 Oct 2021, Jungpam village in West Kameng district of Arunachal Pradesh has been declared as the first 'Airgun-free village' of Arunachal Pradesh after all its inhabitants gave up their air rifles during the Airgun Surrender Abhiyan held at Rupa.

The trade of exotic species through Northeastern corridor.
According to Directorate of Revenue Intelligence (DRI) — the federal anti-smuggling intelligence agency traffickers have turned to exotic wildlife species as these are not protected in India, whereas there is a ban on trade in Indian species. These species mostly originate from countries like Africa, Australia, Southeast Asia, South America etc. There has been an exponential rise in the smuggling of exotic species and the main trafficking routes has been identified as the long and porous land border with Bangladesh and Myanmar in the Northeast region and by air. Once the species enter the country they are being transported to major cities like Chennai, Mumbai, Hyderabad, Kolkata, Cochin where the demand for exotic animals as pets are high. The animals are stuffed in small crates and containers and often they are camouflaged to escape security checks. This treatment often proves fatal.

"The wildlife trafficking routes remains uncontrolled whether it is from India through Nagaland, Manipur, Mizoram to Myanmar or vice versa. Initially, rhino horns, ivory, pangolin scale, tiger and leopard skin were mostly traded illegally which has a huge nexus in the Southeast Asia. In the recent past, heavy consignments of animal exotic in nature are being seized by enforcement officials. Exotic birds, reptiles, amphibians and mammalian species, including critically endangered ones are being traded. We do come across various kinds of colourful birds in stores and it obviously gives us the benefit of doubt that the pet market is flourishing. There is a high probability that such markets are being used as a cover for the smuggling of exotic species to India," said wildlife activist Mubina Akhtar.

A Guwahati-based official from the Directorate of Revenue Intelligence, said that the two main reasons for the booming exotic pet trade in India are - growing demand for exotic pets from the urban middle class especially from the metropolitan cities and stringent domestic Wildlife Protection Act which makes it difficult for having the luxury of Indian species as pets. Moreover, porous international land borders and proximity to Southeast Asian countries like Thailand, Vietnam, where captively-bred exotic birds and animals are easily available in designated pet markets, make northeast India an entry hub for this illegal trade.

IndiaSpend, a data analysis website revealed that more than 32,000 Indians, from 25 states and five union territories are in the possession of exotic animals. This came to light after the Ministry of Environment, Forest and Climate Change announced a voluntary disclosure scheme, asking people to declare their exotic pets.

The Guwahati-based official from the Directorate of Revenue Intelligence official further underlined that in accordance with India's Import Policy, legal import of live animals other than wild animals as defined under Wild Life Protection Act, is permitted against a licence to Zoos and Zoological parks, circus companies, private individuals. However, this permit is given on the recommendation of the Chief Wild Life Warden of a State Government subject to the provisions of the Convention on Inter-national Trade in Endangered Species of Wild Fauna and Flora (CITES). "This lengthy procedure coupled with the fact that most of the seized exotic wildlife don't satisfy the conditions of CITES make it smuggling prone," said the official.

The infamous route between India and Myanmar is not only a hotspot for illegal trade and smuggling of various highly addictive drugs, gold, arms and ammunition, but it has also turned into a smuggling hub of endangered and exotic animals. According to several reports, the smuggled items from Myanmar are supposedly ferried to West Bengal specifically the Alipurduar-Cooch Behar-Jalpaiguri-Siliguri belt through Manipur (India) and Myanmar border (Moreh) and then to other parts of the country. The diverse geography and difficult terrain are usually exploited by smuggling cartels with the help of the local populace. The usual modus operandi is carrying the contraband as head loads across the borders especially rivers to escape surveillance. Selecting the least inhabited locations along the IMB (Indo-Myanmar Border) line, the carriers usually trek through the dense jungles for hours together to reach their destination. Similarly, instances have been observed where the riverine border between India and Bangladesh along West Bengal Sector have been exploited by wildlife smugglers. Another factor that comes to light is Myanmar's unstable political crisis that has lured many people into smuggling activities. Private farms in Myanmar are selling off whatever they have to sustain themselves. May be they are not doing it for smuggling, but for livelihood, and the advantage is being taken by the illegal traders.

Professor Parthankar Choudhury, Dean of OP Odum School of Environment, Assam University, Silchar said, "This part of northeast India has become a happy heaven for smugglers to trade animals. Moreover, the rules as contained in the Indian Wildlife (Protection) Act, 1972 are strong enough to protect endangered Indian species, but are insufficient to impose punitive measures for illegal transit/trade of exotic animals. It is therefore imperative that necessary amendments be made in the WPA on urgent basis.

In one of the biggest seizures of the country, a total of 665 rare and exotic species of animals that could have fetched around 23 crore in the black market was seized by the DRI at Mumbai airport on Oct 2022. The consignment originated from Malaysia in the guise of aquarium fish. The animals were transported via air cargo by concealing them in boxes, while 548 animals survived, a total of 117 animals were found to have died during transit. Airports are also becoming a major conduit for trafficking wildlife contraband. As per a report, by a partner of the UN Environment Programme- Traffic, more than 70,000 native and exotic animals were trafficked through 18 Indian airports between 2011 and 2020.

Apart from the suffering the animals had to endure, the illegal trade poses significant biodiversity and disease transfer risks. It is considered to be the fourth largest illicit and organised transnational crime after drugs, arms and human trafficking. "There is a high degree of probability of Zoonotic diseases to spread through such animals. Micro organisms may even target human body in certain cases. It is therefore essential that detailed parasitological studies be conducted before housing them in Assam State Zoo cum Botanical Garden or similar such places.

With all the loopholes existing in the smuggling of exotic animals, all the experts have echoed similar concerns. Strict monitoring and vigilance needs to be installed at all important points, especially at inter-state border areas. Several agencies including the Wild Life Control Board, Zoo Authorities, concerned forest departments and even police have a big role to play and identify what is triggering the menace and take necessary steps. Moreover, they are hopeful that with the amendment of the wildlife act necessary actions will be initiated.

Some of the more significant issues created due to wildlife trafficking are:
Environmental impacts: Environmentally, wildlife trafficking threatens biodiversity through the extinction of the species that are trafficked; by the introduction of invasive species that can then out compete native species, disrupting ecosystems and again possibly leading to extinction; and through the introduction of diseases that might be transmitted to native wildlife, again causing ecosystem disruption and once again possibly leading to extinction.

Loss of biodiversity: Biodiversity loss is often associated with habitat destruction where plant and non-human animal species get squeezed out of their naturalranges because of human encroachment. A contributing factor to biodiversity loss, though acknowledged much less often, is the direct harvesting, collecting, hunting and poaching of wildlife for human use and consumption. This can destabilize the entire ecosystem as the food availability for many species is then out of balance (Shark Alliance, 2010). Biodiversity loss is the result of direct human consumption of wildlife. It also takes place because of the ecosystem disruption stemming from that consumption.

Disease transmission: Not only can invasive species brought by wildlife trafficking decrease biodiversity and destabilize ecosystems, but wildlife trafficking can also serve as a mechanism for carrying diseases. The international dimensions of both wildlife trade and markets where non-human animals from around the world are coming into contact with each other creates the conditions for naturally occurring diseases that were once isolated to certain species to be readily passed between non-human animals. This, coupled with the speed of modern transportation enables the spreading of disease in ways not witnessed before. There is also the possibility that the disease could endanger people, as it has been documented in recent years that some diseases do have the capacity to transfer to humans as well as non-human animals, such as Severe Acute Respiratory Syndrome (SARS), Covid-19 and the Ebola virus. The connection to industry leads to an exploration of economic impacts of the illegal trade of wildlife.

Economic impacts: The threats of wildlife trafficking may not be confined to impacting upon one aspect alone as mentioned above. Certain threats are in fact cross-cutting amongst the different aspects of society. That is the case with all of the above environmental impacts-loss of biodiversity, introduction of invasive species and disease transmission-all have the potential to induce economic impacts. This is because wildlife trafficking can threaten natural resources which a society might be reliant upon for income in the form of government tax revenue, business profits and personal livelihoods. Businesses can be threatened, such as within the agricultural industry when invasive species and diseases are introduced This can then damage the livelihoods of people in those sectors as well as decrease the profits of companies and the tax revenue for governments. Food scarcity and environmental insecurity also have economic impacts as they may force people to move to new locations. The financial burden of this may be at an individual level, but arguably, if it occurs on a large scale, this type of migration from environmental degradation may require to be supported by governments.

Business and industry: Many global industries and businesses depend upon a healthy environment to support their practices. In fact, the UNEP (2007) estimates that half of the world's jobs are linked to fisheries, forestry and agriculture, all of which are dependent upon ecosystem stability and health. As shown, loss of biodiversity, invasive species and disease can damage the health of the environment and in turn these industriesthat are reliant on it. The illegal wildlife trades, because it can and does cause these environmental threats, then has a connection to the economic well-being of industry, governments and individuals.

A prominent example comes from the poaching of the pangolin in N. E. India. The pangolin is an insectivore that is now one of the most trafficked non-human animals in Asia because of the demand for their exotic meat and traditional medicines made from pangolin scales (Pantel & Anak, 2010). One pangolin eats as many as 70 million ants and other insects annually, so is essential in balancing the ecosystem as well as controlling 'pests' within farming regions as per record of World Association of Zoos and Aquariums. With the loss of the pangolin throughout much of its range, it is predicted that pest levels will rise in the area and more crops will suffer damage, resulting in financial losses and the threat of food scarcity. Lack of food or damage to the environment that limits its ability to support life because of over exploitation of a species within that ecosystem is further proof of wildlife traffic king's link to environmental security issues. This raises concerns for businesses, governments and people.

Human impacts: As discussed above, there is the potential that wildlife trafficking can impact upon the revenue of businesses and governments. This of course has a personal impact upon individual people as well. So, human well-being can be damaged economically through the illegal wildlife trade. Additionally, though, from the environmental impacts, human well-being and security can also be physically threatened through the introduction of zoonotic diseases from unregulated wildlife, such as SARS from civet cats and Ebola from monkeys. Physical well-being and security can also be threatened by the violent nature of some of the black markets of wildlife.

Effect on livelihoods: When industries suffer because of an unhealthy environment, in this case from disease or invasive species introduced from the illegal wildlife trade, individual people are also negatively impacted. Since, as stated above, half of the world's jobs are linked to the environment (UNEP 2007), disease or degradation can have far-reaching negative consequences. The jobs referred to are within the fishery, forestry and agricultural industries, which are all susceptible to the dangers posed here. Large-scale damage to any of these sectors has the potential to negatively affect the security and the well-being of the people that are reliant on these products for food or as a means of employment.

Health: In addition to economic and subsistence livelihoods suffering from environmental degradation, which is tied to wildlife trafficking, individual human health can be threatened by the smuggling of wildlife. Trading of non-human animals can pose a risk to human health through the transmission of zoonotic diseases. Zoonosis is where a disease passes from a non-human animal host to a human. Spreading of such disease has been shown to correlate with unchecked wildlife trade (Naim, 2005). SARS and the Ebola virus, as mentioned, are two of the more well-known diseases of this kind. Yet, there are a myriad other that could threaten human well-being and are more prevalent than those mentioned.

National security impacts: The use of violence to gain and protect profits obtained from varying wildlife black markets uncovers the fact that the illegal wildlife trade should be and needs to be considered in traditional national security concerns. It can threaten national security because wildlife trafficking is carried out through corruption at various levels, organized crime and possibly terrorists and insurgents. All of these actors are known to challenge the rule of law and the sovereignty of various countries around the world. This can destabilize nations and regions and is therefore a national security issue. The concept of national security employed here is one that is broader than the traditional view of security that focuses on military security. Conceptualized here, national security encompasses larger territorial inviolability (Romm, 1994) in addition to economic and political interests that protect the values and stability of the state. Threats to national security occurs when actions or threats of actions impact upon the state's capability to ensure these interests and values. As is evident then, elements of wildlife trafficking can limit the state in these ways. Additionally, wildlife trafficking, as mentioned, creates environmental insecurity and this insecurity also limits the state's ability to protect economic and political interests as well as the values and stability of the nation. Environmental insecurity is therefore linked to national security and thus wildlife trafficking impacts upon national security in multiple ways.

Corruption: Official corruption is integral to much of the perpetration of the illegal wildlife trade. Much of the smuggling of non-human animals and plants that make up this black market would not occur were it not for corruption of the officials in origin, transit and destination countries as well as corruption of the employees of transportation agencies involved along the smuggling chain. Officials, who oversee the issuance of permits for procuring wildlife, and for importing and/or exporting, can be bribed to give permits that appear to make trading certain wildlife legal. Customs agents along the black-market routes are also subject to corruption and can ignore smuggling if bribed. Corruption can be beyond these individual people profiting from wildlife trafficking; it can be much more systemic in nature and occur at high levels of government. Those corrupt officials profiting from the black market may enable the trade to continue by not implementing the pertinent legislation. Additionally, there may be instances where enforcement of laws relating to wildlife trafficking are actively not enforced.

7. Drugs Trafficking in Northeast India

The drug menace in India's northeastern states has major implications for the country's external and internal security. India's northeastern states – the "Seven Sisters" as they are traditionally referred to – have historically been associated with the cross-border drug trade whose origins are linked to the "Golden Triangle" with Myanmar at the center of this international narcotics-fuelled economy. As a result, Indian police have been empowered to use government rules and legislations to hit hard against drug trafficking in the northeast. Heroin first made its entry into Manipur's Churachandpur district, which is located in the hills and borders the northwestern part of Myanmar, in 1983. Drug addiction picked up among young people (15-30 age group) before the menace spread to other states in the region. A 2019 Indian government report says that 22.1 percent opioids are used in Arunachal Pradesh (which also borders Myanmar), 25.67 percent in Mizoram, 25.22 percent in Nagaland, 14.22 percent in Manipur, and 2.9 percent in Assam. The government acknowledges that while drug consumption in Northeast India is a "serious problem," some new trends, such as drug syndicates and narcotic smugglers' "collusion" with Nigerian cartels, have added a new dimension to the problem that shows no signs of abating. There was a time when India's Northeast was associated with widespread drug addiction, HIV/AIDS infection, and insurgency. A 2016 report, however, re-emphasized that the region "is heading towards a much bigger problem to be tackled if not tightly noosed now." Around the same time, another study stated quite explicitly that the drug situation in the Northeast was "going beyond one's control." The drug-use problem was so pervasive in the region as far back as 2014 that reports indicated that in Manipur alone there were an estimated 45,000 to 50,000 drug addicts, of which nearly half used intravenous methods. A more recent study "revealed a diverse array of drugs being used" by young people in the state, with heroin (54.3 percent) being the most commonly abused, followed by opioids (47.1 percent) and methamphetamine (41.2 percent). The second category of drugs abused in Manipur constitute cannabis (32.8 percent), sedatives (27.5 percent), and inhalants (17.4 percent). This study reported an alarming 48.6 percent of respondents who used needles and syringes to "administer" injectable drugs.

Note: What are the Golden Triangle and Golden Crescent?
Ans: The Golden Triangle is located in the area where the borders of Thailand, Myanmar and Laos meet at the confluence of the Ruak and Mekong Rivers. Along with the Golden Crescent, it is regarded as one of the largest producers of opium in the world since the 1950s until it was overtaken by the Golden Crescent in the early 21st century.

Origin: Before the advent of the Golden Triangle and the **Golden Crescent**, China accounted for most of the world's opium production and trade following an unjust treaty imposed on it by Britain. The treaty was signed by the Chinese following their defeat at the hands of the British during the Opium Wars of the mid 19th century.

The situation began to change post-world war II however as the Chinese Communist Party gained power. They cracked down heavily on drug producers and consumers alike by forcing the consumers into compulsory rehab, having dealers arrested and executed, and opium-producing regions either burnt or planted with new crops. These measures forced the remaining opium producers to shift their operations to the south of the Chinese border. These areas would become the future Golden Triangle region.

The Kuomintang (KMT), a US-supported anti-communist resistance group, were the forbearers of the many private narcotics armies now operating in the Golden Triangle. Prior to the arrival of the KMT, the opium trade had already developed as a local economy under the colonial rule of the British.

Once the KMT arrived they forced the local villagers to become its recruits in exchange for food and money. In the name of protection, they even extracted a heavy tax on the opium farmers, forcing them to increase production to make ends meet. In the 1950s the annual production was close to 600 tons.

Production & trafficking: After Afghanistan, Myanmar has been a significant cog of the transnational drug trade as it is the second-largest producer of illicit opium. As per the data by the United Nations Office on Drugs and Crime (UNODC), a specialised **United Nations** Agency, it is estimated that there were 430 square kilometres (167 sq mi) of opium cultivation in Myanmar in 2005.

The opium and heroin base produced in northeastern Myanmar is transported by donkey and horse caravan to refineries along the Thailand-Burma border where they are converted to the final products. The finished products are then shipped across the border to towns in Northern Thailand and down to Bangkok for further distribution to international markets.

Heroin from the Golden Triangle is smuggled into the United States through couriers flying in through commercial airlines. The state of California is the focal point of entry for the Golden Triangle Heroin trade with the additional volume being trafficked into New York and Washington.

The Asian community of Southeast Asian descent had a monopoly on the drug trade on the Western seaboard of the United States, usually at street-level distribution. The monopoly was ended when law enforcement agencies cracked down on these traffickers during the 1970s.

This period of imprisonment led to the development of contacts between Asian and American prisoners. These contacts have allowed Southeast Asian traffickers access to gangs and organizations distributing heroin at the retail level.

India's geographical location between two major drug-producing regions, the Golden Crescent and the Golden Triangle, significantly exacerbates its vulnerability to drug trafficking and abuse. The Golden Crescent, comprising Afghanistan, Iran, and Pakistan, is a key global hub for opium production, directly impacting Indian states like Jammu and Kashmir, Punjab, Rajasthan, and Gujarat due to their proximity to the Indo-Pakistan border.

Similarly, the Golden Triangle, which includes parts of Laos, Myanmar, and Thailand, is notorious for the production and trafficking of heroin, with Myanmar alone accounting for 80% of the world's heroin supply. These regions not only serve as the source of illicit drugs but also use India as a transit route, posing serious challenges to the nation's internal security and public health.

India's Northeast is one of the routes for marketing of drugs produced in Myanmar's Wa and Shan states where drug overlords, insurgent outfits, and foreign collaborators work to operate poppy fields and laboratories. The response of the respective state governments in the Northeast has been at best patchy, while the central government's actions against drug trafficking has been more in the form of fits-and-starts. It is generally acknowledged

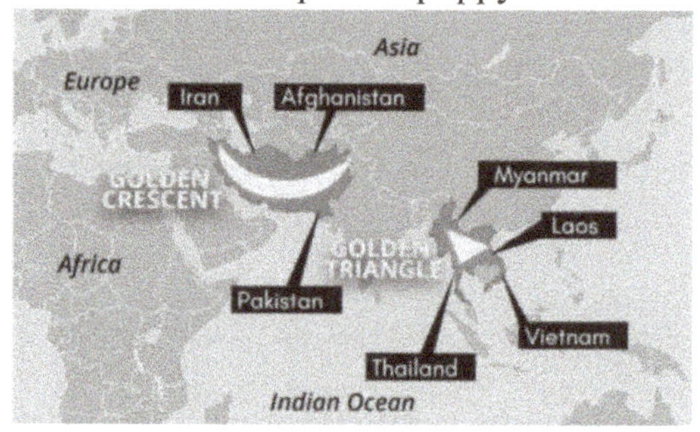

that the growth and production of drugs, including the deadly synthetic variants, in Myanmar "pose a serious challenge" to Indian security. Clearly, the current political instability in Myanmar, reflected in the civil war-like conditions in the strife-torn country, have produced a "conducive environment" for drug cartels operating in Wa and Shan states.

After the 2014, Modi led BJP Government came into power, efforts to battle drug trafficking became effective enough in terms of combating the menace across all northeastern states. The Narendra Modi government sought to crack down on cross-border narcotics trafficking and intensified its actions in a more concerted manner in 2022. Following a high-level meeting in Guwahati in Assam in October 2022, the Ministry of Home Affairs claimed that as part of its "Drug-free India" campaign, about 40,000 kg of narcotic substances were destroyed across northeast India. The government claimed that its anti-drug trafficking agencies ended up destroying about 150,000 kg of narcotic substances, which was twice the target set by the ministry.mThe government vowed to use drones, artificial intelligence and satellite mapping to identify and control areas where opium is grown. It also promised thorough investigation – from drug source to destination – and a crackdown on the "entire network." The government has announced a "zero tolerance policy" on drug trafficking as well as against the "dirty money" and "organized mafia," which could "damage the country's economy and national security."

Highlights of the high-level meet on Oct 2022; Union Home Minister Shri Amit Shah chaired a meeting with Chief Ministers, Chief Secretaries and Director Generals of Police of all North Eastern States on 'Drug Trafficking and National Security' in Guwahati, Assam. The meeting was also attended by the Union Home Secretary, Director General of Narcotics Control Bureau (NCB) and other senior officials. Shri Amit Shah said that the North Eastern region of the country shares international borders with four countries and the region is close to Myanmar which is the second largest producer of opium in the world after Afghanistan. He said that drug consumption in Northeast India is a serious problem. According to the Magnitude of Substance Report, 2019 published by the Ministry of Social Justice and Empowerment, the consumption of opium and ganja in seven northeastern states is at an alarming level, which is higher than the average of their consumption in the country. Therefore the government has taken many new initiatives for the North Eastern states such as:-

Regional Office of Narcotics Control Bureau (NCB) has been set up in Guwahati and in the coming years, NCB will work in four regions namely Assam, Manipur, Arunachal Pradesh and Tripura. Further proposals are being made to make New Regional Offices of NCB at Agartala in Tripura and Pasighat/Lower siang in Arunachal Pradesh. In addition, Zonal Offices are also being proposed at New Jalpaiguri for better coverage of the adjoining Sikkim areas.

Several measures have been taken against the illegal cultivation of ganja and opium poppy in the North Eastern region as well as in other parts of the country such as The Ministry of Home Affairs is setting up a study group to eradicate illegal farming in hilly and difficult areas using drones and latest technology on a large scale without causing any harm to the farmers. An inter-ministerial committee has been constituted on alternative livelihood arrangements for farmers engaged in cultivation of illegal crops. Simultaneously NCB is sharing satellite imagery to eradicate illegal opium poppy cultivation in the North Eastern region. All the North Eastern States have constituted the Anti-

Narcotics Task Force (ANTF) as a single nodal point for all issues related to Narcotics. The NCB has also conducted several special drives on enforcement activities across the country including in the North-East region, which include identification and detention of top 100 drug traffickers. Home Minister Amit Shah has urged the representatives of all the North Eastern states present in the meeting to make proper use of NCORD portal and NIDAN platforms for effective action against drug trafficking. He also asked to strengthen the Anti Narcotics Task Force constituted in the states so that decisive action can be taken in the war against drugs. Also various provisions of the NDPS Act should be strictly implemented. Establishment of fast-track courts may also be considered to ensure speedy trial. (The above data is available as per Press Information Bureau, Government of India, Ministry of Home Affairs, published on 08 OCT 2022).

Even as the Modi government sought to play up its achievements in its fight against drugs, it made sure to make a political statement as it compared seizures made during 2014-2022 and 2006-13 when the Congress-led United Progressive Alliance (UPA) regime was in power. Drug seizures is an indicator of the magnitude of the problem were few and far between. It sought to show that compared to 1,257 cases registered against drug traffickers during 2006-13, the Modi government lodged 3,172 cases between 2014 and 2022. Also, the total number of arrests during the same periods rose 260 percent from 1,362 to 4,888. On the seizure front, while 152,000 kg of drugs ($91,884,288) was seized during 2006-13, the anti-drug agencies and security forces confiscated and recovered 330,000 kg ($296,800,000) of narcotic substances in multiple raids. Detailed "vulnerability mapping" is carried out from time to time along the 1,642-kilometer border with Myanmar to deepen and widen surveillance by deploying electronic equipment. Long-range reconnaissance and observation and battlefield surveillance radars have also been deployed in some northeastern states. More recently, the government forbade the free cross-border movement of people. And then, on April 24, 2023; security forces seized heroin worth $418,000 from traffickers in a Manipur border district, which underscores the pervasiveness of the drug menace in India's Northeast. Most state governments of the region carry out intermittent operations against cross-border drug trade and announce massive seizure of various narcotics. This is, however, an indication that the menace is far from receding.

How is Arunachal Pradesh fighting against Drugs?

Ans: As per a report named " The war on drugs", published on 'The Arunachal Times' on July 26, 2021. On 16 July, the Arunachal Pradesh state cabinet approved the Policy on Psychoactive Substances 2021-26 to fight the drug menace in Arunachal. The policy, as informed, will base the fight on three pillars of 'supply reduction, demand reduction, and harm reduction.' The state police had been arresting drug peddlers and users across the state even before the policy or declaration of war against drug abuse was made. The announcement, however, has led to intensified efforts and an increase in the number of arrests, with some of the arrested being from the police force itself. As such, the state government said that stringent action would be taken against government employees who consume any narcotic drug or psychotropic substance, with one-time immunity from prosecution and disciplinary proceedings. Without clear details of the newly created policy, one cannot help but wonder whether it has been devised keeping in mind the two extremes of drug-control methods used in the Philippines and in Portugal, which are used as examples throughout the world. In 2001, Portugal decriminalized personal use and possession of all drugs after all methods failed in controlling its use and distribution. The Vice reports that, after the decriminalization, "Portugal in 2015 had the lowest drug-induced deaths in western Europe, which is 10 times lower than the United Kingdom and 50 times lower than the United States. The national health ministry estimates that the number of active heroin addicts has dropped from about 1,00,000 in 2001 to fewer than 25,000." On the other hand, Philippines President Rodrigo Duterte in 2016 declared a war on drugs. Duterte, in several of his speeches, has publicly indicated killing 'drug lords'. However, reports suggest that it is mostly the low-income level areas that are targeted, human rights activists, lawyers and journalists included. In fact, the International Criminal Court on 14 June sought a full investigation into crimes against humanity, torture and other inhumane acts. Also, in efforts to arrest as many drug users and distributors, a documentary showed how 5,000 men are cramped in a prison in Manila, Philippines, built for just 1,200 people, with only one guard for every 400 inmates. This raises questions on whether the jails and lockups in Arunachal are equipped to house the numerous drug peddlers and users that are being arrested almost every week throughout the state, apart from other criminals. In early June this year, the Arunachal Pradesh Police (APP) informed that 86 FIRs had been registered and 143 people arrested in connection with drug consumption and trafficking in 2021, which is nearly thrice the number of arrests than last year, when a total of 28 FIRs were registered and 56 people arrested from January to June 2020. As per officials, Arunachal currently has seven government-run drug de-addiction centres. These include the ones in Tezu, Pasighat, Khonsa, Lathao, Bordumsa, Hayuliang and Longding – all towards the east of Arunachal – infamous for drug activities. Approval for another drug de-addiction-cum-rehabilitation centre in Deomali has been recommended to the Centre by the SJETA special secretary. Though these centres, with their minimal resources, offer some respite to addicts and their families, military strategist Sun Tzu's quote comes to mind: "The supreme art of war is to subdue the enemy without fighting."

How is Tripura fighting against Drugs?
Ans: The Tripura Police established the Office of Superintendent of Police (Anti Narcotics) on November 12, 2018. This specialized unit is part of the Tripura Police Crime Branch and investigates cases related to the NDPS Act. Tripura is also earmarked the second state in North Eastern Region of India in terms of highest seizures and destructions, CM Dr Manik Saha added. Further CM Dr Saha said "Tripura was a hub of drugs before 2018. After we formed government, a war of destruction of cannabis plants have been declared. Cannabis were transported to Uttar Pradesh, Bihar and West Bengal while bulk quantity of narcotic substances were imported from Myanmar and one-third of the those are coming from neighbouring Assam and Mizoram. Tripura is being utilized as a corridor for exporting to neighbouring country Bangladesh. In the meetings of North Eastern Council and All Chief Ministers' meet in Haryana, discussion took place on combatting drugs menace. Our government is focusing on zero tolerance against drugs. Tripura bags the second highest position in seizures and destruction of narcotic substances."

As published on November 10, 2022: Northeast Today, Tripura CM Prof Dr Manik Saha claimed that the state government has adopted a 'zero tolerance policy' against narcotic substances further appealed everyone to come together in making Tripura a 'Drug-Free' state. The state government is working on the vision of union Home minister Amit Shah to call for the adoption of a zero tolerance policy against drugs. Again on, March 28, 2023: Tripura CM claimed that the State has become the hub of drugs before the arrival of BJP-led government in 2018, and the state government adopted 'Zero Tolerance' policy against narcotic substances. He advised to work in coordination between the concerned departments in making Tripura drug free. He laid special emphasis on increasing the use of Dog Squad and training them along with the need for scanners in CheckPoint areas. He also mentioned that necessary action should be taken against those who have amassed huge money and property in various ways by being associated with drug trade.

In the meeting, Chief Secretary JK Sinha said that Tripura's performance in the drug-free Tripura campaign was satisfactory. He said, there will be no compromise in the case of drugs. In this regard, he sought the assistance of the Narcotics Control Bureau. During the discussion, he also mentioned the remarkable work of the state's Forensic Science Laboratory. During the same meeting, Kolkata-based Narcotics Control Bureau Eastern Deputy Director General Monika Ashish Batra said that the central government has agreed to open a zonal office of the Narcotics Control Bureau in the state. Initiatives will be taken to start this zonal office soon.

Besides, in this day's meeting, Director General of Police Amitabh Ranjan discussed the role of defense administration in the anti-narcotics campaign. We are also using drone technology to find the plantation of cannabis in a move to destruction", said CM Dr. Manik Saha. The Chief Minister also directed all the OCs to be pro-people and said Tripura Police is maintaining the law and order properly. The Chief Minister has also said that the government has zero tolerance against the "mafia'. "Mafia word should be erased from Tripura. No mafia can stay in Tripura. Those who are involved in various anti-social activities including extortion, syndicates should be identified and immediate action should be taken against them. Police will take action against such illegal activities with a zero-tolerance policy. In this case, there will be no interference in police work", the Chief Minister added. Citing some of the measures, he said "A 10-bedded Drug De-Addiction Centre started at Modern Psychiatric Hospital, Narsingarh and Addiction Clinic OPD also started in this hospital where medicines were given free of cost. The government is considering to open such convenience in other districts. Awareness camps and Workshops for school and college students, and doctors, nurses and healthcare staff, respectively are being organized. State government has drawn the attention of the central government to set up a branch of Narcotics Control Bureau (NCB) in Agartala. Recently some NDPS (Narcotics Drugs & Psychotropic Substances) cases have been handed over to the Special Investigation Team (SIT) of the Tripura Police Crime Branch to trace the communication links between drug trafficking networks, financiers, major drug dealers, drug users and inter-state drug dealers through proper investigation. Proposal to purchase a Full Body Scanner is under consideration to scan vehicles carrying and identifying narcotic substances. 7 training courses have been conducted at the Police Training Academy (PTA) in collaboration with the National Institute of Social Defense (NISD) and Narcotics Control Bureau (NCB) in the last two years for the purpose of increasing the investigation skills of NDPS cases." CM Dr Saha also said that a total of 3,65,00,381 cannabis plants have been destroyed in the last three years as a result of regular operations for the destruction of cannabis plants. "In Dhalai district, Ganganagar police station staff during routine check 3.52 kilograms of heroin and 10,000 'Yaba' tablets were seized on February 09 last. Similarly, Kamalpur police station staff on March 18 last seized 2.977 kilograms of heroin."

How Assam is fighting against Drugs?
Ans: Here let's discuss the issue of drug trafficking in the state of Assam, from it's beginning till present. As published on Asom Barta on February 1, 2023, it was on June 21, 2021. A Assam Home Guard named Boring Bey and his team received an Intelligence report that a large consignment of the banned methamphetamine was being smuggled in a public bus in the district of Karbi Anglong, where he was eventually posted. He used all his experience and intelligence to unravel the drugs hidden in the bus where his other more experienced colleagues could not locate. Later It was rumoured that he was offered a lucrative deal to keep quiet but the policeman in Bey did not defy the call of conscience and reported the matter to his seniors. Not only drugs worth Rs.12 crore were seized but even those responsible were arrested. Further Bey was promoted as a constable by the state police force. However, neither the smugglers, peddlers, intruders nor the samaritan's didn't even thought that this was just the beginning of a massive crackdown on drugs by the Assam Police which probably Bey ignited.

As on 2023, The Assam Police in the last 18 months have managed to seize drugs worth Rs 1,066.29 crore and have arrested 7,659 peddlers in their mission to rid the State of drugs. The situation has come to such a state that neither a day or so has passed by without the news of a drugs haul reported by the State media, highlighting how galvanised the police has become in its quest to make Assam drugs free. Talking to Asom Barta, the then Assam DGP Bhaskar Jyoti Mahanta said that a sustained campaign against drugs was always on. "What has changed after a new Government under Dr Himanta Biswa Sarma has come to power is that the campaign has been intensified. The Assam Police has become ruthless in its quest to make the State drugs-free," Mahanta said, adding that the police has educated itself on the stringent laws governing peddling of drugs, while also taking advantage of technology.

A highlighting point is the app 'Drugs Free Assam' which encourages the people to post information on drugs on the app. Besides, the Narco Coordination Centre (NCORD) app of the Home Ministry is facilitating greater coordination between the State and various law enforcement agencies of the Centre in its fight against narcotics. "The matter came up during the Regional Conference on Drug Trafficking and National Security held in Guwahati. Union Home Minister Amit Shah while addressing Chief Ministers, Chief Secretaries and DGPs of the North Eastern States harped on the need for greater coordination among agencies while referring to the habit of drug consumption as one which can destroy generations," The Assam DGP told Asom Barta. The then Sanjib Kumar Saikia, Superintendent of Police, Karbi Anglong said police in his district are always on the alert since Karbi Anglong is the nodal centre of drugs trafficking in the region, especially consignment coming from Myanmar via Nagaland to other parts of Assam via the hill district.

In the year 2022, Assam police force confiscated 2833 kg of ganja, 20.36 kg of heroine, and 63,463 methamphetamine tablets, among others. Writer Jayant Madhav Bora, who has also penned a novel centring on drugs, was full of praise for the police initiative against drugs. It destroys not only one single body but a household and a society, he said, while exhorting writers, singers and poets to use the power of their art to raise awareness against drugs. In Guwahati city, drugs worth Rs 407 crore were confiscated in the calendar year 2022, including heroin, and cocaine. Assam Police maintain a close contact with our neighbouring States. Besides, the Assam Police works on forward and backward linkage to identify peddlers and consumers so that the problem can be tackled at the grassroots.

Some figures till 2023. Stern steps being taken to curb drug menace in the state and recoveries list under NDPS presented by Assam Government:

Recovery list under NDPS:

Head	10/05/2021-30/10/2023
Cases Registered	7,348
Person Arrested	12,229
Heroin (kg)	317
Ganja (kg)	90,637
Opium (kg)	336
Codeine Cough Syrup (bottles)	8,80,343
Tablets/ Capsule	1,13,19,235
Morphine (kg)	36
Crystal Methamphetamine (kg)	21
Cocaine (kg)	1
Cannabis plant (kg)	213
Tramadol (kg)	0.56
Raw opium bud (kg)	10
Mephadrone (kg)	2
Cash	4,90,50,994.00
Foreign currency	28,865.00
Poppy Straw	3,318
Cultivation destroyed (cannabis)	31 bigha, 3 katha, 12 lessa
Cultivation destroyed (opium)	658 bigha

Est market value: ₹1,794.05 crore

8. Armed Forces Special Power Act (AFSPA)

a. Enacted by the Parliament and approved by the President in 1958.

b. Grants extraordinary powers & immunity to the armed forces to bring back order in the "disturbed areas". An area can be disturbed due to differences or disputes b/w members of different religious, racial, language or regional groups or castes or communities.

c. Power to declare areas to be disturbed areas under Section 3 of the Act: Governor of that State or the Administrator of that Union territory or the Central Government, as the case may be, may, by notification in the Official Gazette, declare the whole or such part of such State or Union territory to be a disturbed area.

d. Special powers of the armed forces under Section 4: Any commissioned officer, warrant officer, non-commissioned officer or any other person of equivalent rank in the armed forces is given "special powers" under AFSPA, although they must be exercised with extreme caution.

Provisions:

Section 3: Empowers the Governor of the State/Union territory to declare the whole or part of the State or Union Territory as a disturbed area.

Section 4: Gives the powers to the Army to search premises and make arrests without warrants.

Section 6: Stipulates that arrested persons and the seized property are handed over to police.
Section 7: The prosecution is permitted only after the sanction of the Central Government.

Rationale behind its imposition:
a. Effective functioning of forces in counter-insurgency / terrorist operations.
b. Protection of members of Armed forces.
c. Maintaining Law & Order.
d. Security & sovereignty of the nation.

Criticisms:
a. Atrocities and human rights violations by security agencies.
b. Against democratic regime & threat to Fundamental Rights.
c. Ineffectiveness in countering insurgency.

Whether AFSPA is to be repealed?
a. Arguments in favour of Repealing AFSPA
1. Colonial-era law: AFSPA is compared to the Rowlatt Act, allowing arrests based on suspicion without due process.
2. Violations of Fundamental Rights: It violates citizens' fundamental rights under Articles 14, 19, 21, 22, and 25 of the Constitution.
3. Violates International Law: AFSPA, by its form and in its application, violates the Universal Declaration of Human Rights (UDHR), the International Covenant on Civil and Political Rights (ICCPR), the Convention against Torture.
4. Lack of Accountability: AFSPA grants sweeping powers to armed forces and immunity from prosecution without central government approval.
5. Militarisation of Governance: Critics argue that AFSPA contributes to the military ruling, undermining democratic principles and civilian authority in conflict-affected areas.
6. Centre-State conflicts: Law and order is a state subject, and concerned states are always in a better position to carry out direct assessment
on ground. However, AFSPA erodes states' autonomy even during peaceful times.

b. Arguments in favour of Repealing AFSPA.
1. Safeguard boundaries: AFSPA has enabled military forces to protect national borders effectively.
2. Constitutionality Valid: SC upheld the Act in the Naga People's Movement of Human Rights vs Union of India (1997) case, with guidelines to prevent abuse, such as consulting the state government before declaring a region as disturbed and there must a periodic review of the situation.
3. Effective counter-insurgency: AFSPA is essential for combating insurgent groups, particularly in Kashmir and the northeast.
4. National Security Imperative: AFSPA ensures a coordinated response to insurgency and terrorism, which individual states may lack.
5. Measures to curb misuse: In the Extra Judicial Execution Victim Families vs Union of India & Anr (2016) Case, SC ruled that AFSPA does not provide invincible immunity to armed forces from prosecution.

Present AFSPA situation:
a. By Central Government: On September 27, 2024, The Union Home Ministry on Thursday extended the Armed Forces (Special Powers) Act (AFSPA) in parts of Nagaland and Arunachal Pradesh for another six months from October 1. As per the latest notification, the AFSPA has been extended to all parts of eight districts and 21 police station limits in five other districts of Nagaland for another six months. The notification issued under Section 3 of the AFSPA for a period of six months with effect from October 1, "unless withdrawn earlier", will be effective in Dimapur, Niuland, Chumoukedima, Mon, Kiphire, Noklak, Phek and Peren districts and in Khuzama, Kohima North, Kohima South, Zubza and Kezocha police stations in Kohima district; Mangkolemba, Mokokchung-I, Longtho, Tuli, Longchem and Anaki 'C' police stations in Mokokchung district; Yanglok police station in Longleng district; Bhandari, Champang and Ralan police stations in Wokha district; and Ghatashi, Pughoboto, Satakha, Suruhuto, Zunheboto and Aghunato police stations in Zunheboto district. The last time the AFSPA was extended in these areas was on March 27.

In another notification, the Ministry extended the AFSPA in Tirap, Changlang and Longding districts in Arunachal Pradesh and the areas falling within the jurisdiction of Namsai, Mahadevpur and Chowkham police stations in Namsai district of the State along the Assam border for another six months.

b. By State Government:

Assam: Whereas, the Government of Assam in exercise of powers conferred under Section 3 of the Armed Forces (Special Powers) Act, 1958 (Act 28 of 1958) had declared the areas covering 4 (Four) districts viz. (1) Tinsukia (2) Dibrugarh (3) Charaideo (4) Sivasagar of the State of Assam as "Disturbed Area" vide notification No. HMA-19015/9/2019-Political(A)/Pt-1/93, dated 27/03/2024 with effect from 01/04/2024 for a period of 6 (six) months. Now, therefore, in exercise of the powers conferred under Section 3 of the Armed Forces (Special Powers) Act, 1958 and in sequel to the earlier Notification vide HMA-19015/9/2019-Political(A)/Pt-dis da vi 209mska,; a erugao eugen ha hale a de la ga oft sae of A am as "Disturbed Areas" for a further period of 6 (six months w.e.f. 01/10/2024, unless withdrawn earlier.

Manipur: the Governor of Manipur is of the opinion that the violent activities of various extremist/insurgent groups warrant the use of Armed Forces in aid of civil administration in the entire State of Manipur except the areas falling under the jurisdiction of the 19 (nineteen) Police Stations under i) Imphal ii) Lamphel (iii) City (iv) Singjamei (v) Sekmai (vi)Lamsang (vii) Patsoi (viii) Wangoiix) Porompat (x) Heingang (xi) Lamlai (xii) Irilbung (xiii) Leimakhong (xiv) Thoubal (xv) Bishnupur (xvi) Nambol (xvii) Moirang (xviii) Kakching and (xix) Jiribam. Further, the issue of declaration of "Disturbed area' status is very sensitive and may likely attract public criticism and resistance if proper care is not taken. Keeping in view of above and the overall law and order situation in the State and the capability of the State machineries, the State Government has decided to maintain status quo on the present disturbed area status in the State of Manipur excluding the areas falling under the 19 police stations as mentioned at Para 1 above, for a period of 6(six) months w.e.f., 01/10/2024.

Now, therefore, in exercise of the powers conferred by Section 3 of the Armed Forces (Special Powers) Act, 1958 (Act No.28 of 1958) as amended from time to time, the Governor of Manipur hereby accords approval to declare the entire State of Manipur excluding the areas falling under the jurisdiction of the 19 (nineteen) Police Stations listed below as "Disturbed Area" for a period of 6(six) months with effect from 1st October, 2024.

9. Defence corridor in northeast India.

As per reports published on business line (The Hindu) January 09, 2025 at 11:16 AM.
https://www.thehindubusinessline.com/news/national/after-up-and-tn-assam-seeks-defence-industrial-corridor/article69079399.ece#

After Uttar Pradesh and Tamil Nadu, Assam government has also reached out to the Central government requesting for a defence industrial corridor in their state to cater to large scale deployment of armed forces in the north-eastern states to secure borders with China, Bangladesh and Myanmar.

Assam Chief Minister Hemanta Biswa Sarma said at a function a day before that he was in talks with government of India to have third defence industrial corridor. He also expressed hope that the talks may materialise too.

"Maximum deployment of Army is either in Jammu and Kashmir or in Northeast. You take a tank to Northeast and it has to be brought to the mainland in ordinance factory for its repair. Assam can be a big defence corridor, the requirement is there, a big demand also. Supply should also be from there. I'm talking to government of India that after Uttar Pradesh and Tamil Nadu, the third corridor should be given to Assam. The talk is at fairly advanced stage and I hope it should happen also," CM Sarma said.

He also stated that if you look at Indian Army, half of their deployment is already in the northeast. "So, for the replacement and repair of arms and ammunition, they have to come all the way to UP and Rajasthan. Next defence establishments which are coming should be in Assam for effective supply chain. In case, if there is disturbance, arms and ammunition can be made available locally," he stated.

The CM also stated that having defence industrial corridor was part of thinking to bring investment into the state which did not exist earlier.

The Union government has set up two Defence Industrial Corridors (DICs) in order to attract total investment worth ₹20,000 crore by the year 2024-25 for defence industries, develop domestic supply chain and strengthen defence manufacturing ecosystem in the country.

In UP Defence Industrial Corridor (UPDIC), there are six nodes -- Aligarh, Agra, Jhansi, Kanpur, Chitrakoot and Lucknow. And Tamil Nadu Defence Industrial Corridor (TNDIC) has five nodes -- Chennai,

Hosur, Coimbatore, Salem and Tiruchirappalli. Uttar Pradesh Expressways Industrial Development Authority (UPEIDA) is the nodal agency for UPDIC and Tamil Nadu Industrial Development Corporation (TIDCO) is the nodal agency for TNDIC. Both the States have promulgated their respective aerospace and defence policy to attract investments in their respective DICs.

As per April, last year, 108 Memorandum of Understanding (MoU) were signed with industry and organisations in the UPDIC having potential investment of ₹12,191 crore. Investment of ₹2,445 crore has been already made and 1611 hectares of land has been acquired so far for development of UPDIC, the Ministry of Defence had said.

In Tamil Nadu, arrangements have been made through MoUs etc with 53 industries for potential investment of ₹11,794 crore. Investment worth ₹3,894 crore has been made and 910 hectares of land has been acquired so far for development of TNDIC, Defence Ministry had revealed.

10. Surrender of Insurgents (groups) and peace accords.

Bodo Accord: During the 1960s, the Bodos and other tribes of Assam called for a separate state of Udayachal. In the late 1980s, there was another demand for a separate state for Bodos – Bodoland, and for Assam to be divided "50-50". As a result of these continuous demands, there have been widespread incidents of violence over the years. To resolve the five-decade-old Bodo issue in Assam, the Bodo Accord was signed on January 27, 2020, resulting in the surrender of 1615 cadres with a huge cache of arms and ammunition at Guwahati.

Bru-Reang Agreement: Due to ethnic violence in the western part of Mizoram in October 1997, a large number of minority Bru (Reang) families migrated to North Tripura in 1997-1998. A landmark agreement was signed on January 16, 2020, to resolve the 23-year-old Bru-Reang refugee crisis by which more than 37,000 internally displaced people are being settled in Tripura.

National Liberation Front of Tripura (NLFT) Agreement: The National Liberation Front of Tripura (NLFT) formed in 1989 has been involved in violence, operating from their camps across international borders. After several years of negotiations with the Government of India and the Government of Assam, an agreement was signed with National Liberation Front of Tripura (SD) in August 2019 resulting in the surrender of 88 cadres with 44 weapons.

Karbi Anglong Agreement: The significance of militants' surrender in Assam, and history of Karbi insurgency. The insurgency by Karbi — a major ethnic community of Assam - groups, dotted by several factions and splinters, has had a long history in Assam, marked by killings, ethnic violence, abductions, and taxation since the late 1980s. The Karbis are a major ethnic group of Assam, whose history has been marked by killings, ethnic violence, abductions, and taxation since the late 1980s. To resolve the long-running dispute in the Karbi regions of Assam, the Karbi Anglong Agreement was signed on September 04, 2021, in which more than 1000 armed cadres renounced violence and joined the mainstream of society.

As of Feb 23, 2021:Five militant groups – PDCK (People's Democratic Council of Karbi Longri), KLNLF (Karbi Longri NC Hills Liberation Front), KPLT (Karbi People's Liberation Tiger), KLF (Kuki Liberation Front), and UPLA (United People's Liberation Army) joined the mainstream by ceremonially laying down arms. The groups were operating in the hill districts of Karbi Anglong and West Karbi Anglong. A total of 1,040 members belonging to the outfits laid down 338 weapons. Among the senior rebel leaders who joined the mainstream was Ingti Kathar Songbijit (IK Songbijit), chief of PDCK. He was earlier the self-styled C-in-C of the NDFB. But after Ranjan Daimary-led faction joined the 'Suspension of Operation' agreement, Songbijit, being a Karbi, was sidelined by the new leadership of the anti-talk faction, a police spokesman said.

Altogether 16 leaders from rebel groups and Adivasi civil societies signed the pact that includes the government's commitment to grant ST status to the Adivasi community, provision of an economic package of Rs 1,000 crore (Rs 500 crore from the State and Rs 500 crore from the Centre). Under the peace agreement, the land rights of the Adivasi community will remain intact as the protected class in tribal blocks and belts and also as per the Forest Rights Act, 2006. The pact also has a rehabilitation scheme for the former militants.

Tripura Peace Accord: Centre, Tripura sign a peace pact with Tripura insurgent groups. As of 4th Sep 2024, the insurgent groups National Liberation Front of Tripura (NLFT) and the All Tripura Tiger Force (ATTF) reaffirmed their commitment towards the development of Tripura by ending the 35-year-long conflict in the State. More than 300 armed cadres of two insurgent groups in Tripura have given up violence to join the mainstream and will "contribute not only in building a developed Tripura but also in building a developed India". Armed Forces Special Powers Act (AFSPA) was removed from Tripura in 2015.

ULFA Peace Accord: The ULFA's pro-talks faction signed a peace accord with the central and the Assam governments, agreeing to shun violence, surrender all arms, disband the organization, and join the democratic process. "Assam has suffered for a long due to the violence of the ULFA and 10,000 people have lost their lives in this violence since 1979,". The United Liberation Front of Asom (ULFA) - the oldest insurgent group of Assam - agreed to abjure violence, surrender arms, disband the organization, vacate their camps, and join the democratic process. A movement that started demanding the deportation of illegal migrants also witnessed the birth of the militant outfit the United Liberation Front of Assam (U.L.F.A.) in 1979. In Assam, at the beginning of the 1990s, two military operations, Operation Rhino and Bajrang, were launched against U.L.F.A. militants.

Peace Accord by Insurgent Groups of Assam: On 23 Jan 2020, More than 600 fighters belonging to eight different rebel groups surrendered to Indian authorities, responding to a government's peace initiative that will allow them to rejoin mainstream society. More than 300 belong to the National Liberation Front of Bengalis, an outfit formed around 2015 to protect Bengali-speaking people from rival armed groups in the state. The rest belong to the Adivasi Dragon Force, which represents the state's tea garden Adivasi community, and the United Liberation Front of Asom (ULFA), a faction headed by Paresh Baruah. Another faction of ULFA, headed by Arabinda Rajkhowa, is already in peace talks with the Indian government. Fifty of the remaining 344 militants were from the United Liberation Front of Asom (ULFA), eight from the National Democratic Front of Bodoland (NDFB), six from Kamatapur Liberation Organisation (KLO), 87 from National Santhal Liberation Army (NSLA), 13 from Rabha National Liberation Front (RNLF), 178 from Adivasi Dragon Fighter (ADF) and one from CPI

(Maoist). Earlier month, the National Democratic Front, a key Naga armed group headed by B Saoraigwra, signed a ceasefire agreement with Indian authorities in Assam state.

On November 16, 2021, 46 cadres of the Dimasa National Liberation Army (DNLA), along with Commander-in-Chief Mushrang, laid down arms in Assam's Dima Hasao district to join the mainstream. Dima Hasao was a hotbed of insurgency in 1994-95 and again in 2003-2009 but has been largely peaceful in the last decade. DNLA was the newest group to have taken up arms in Dima Hasao.

On April 27, 2023, An Assam-based insurgent group - Dimasa National Liberation Army (DNLA)/Dimasa People's Supreme Council (DPS) - which operates in the Dima Hasao district, signed a peace agreement with the State Government and the Centre in the presence of Union Home Minister Amit Shah and Chief Minister Himanta Biswa Sarma. **Know about DNLA?** - A relatively new insurgent group, the DNLA, operating in the Dima Hasao and Karbi Anglong districts, was formed in 2019. A release by the group at the time of formation said it was "committed to revamp the national struggle and fight for the liberation of a sovereign, independent Dimasa Nation". It aimed to "develop a sense of brotherhood among the Dimasa and also to rebuild the trust and faith among the Dimasa society for regaining the Dimasa Kingdom", The group had run on a model of 'extortion and taxation' and was believed to have drawn its support and sustenance from the NSCN(IM) of Nagaland.

On 12 December 2022, as published in the Deccan Herald, a total of 1,179 militants surrendered in Assam's Hailakandi district with weapons in another significant push for peace in the Northeast. The rebels, belonging to the Bru Revolutionary Army of Union (BRAU) and United Democratic Liberation Front (UDLF), deposited 335 weapons including 18 AK series rifles and large quantities of ammunition before Assam minister Pijush Hazarika. Of these, 634 belonged to UDLF and 545 to BRAU. The two groups were under ceasefire as peace talks began in 2017 but the groups refused to surrender earlier. The two groups were active in South Assam districts along the Assam-Mizoram border. The groups demand proper development of areas inhabited by the Reang community, including improvement of roads, schools, and hospitals. The two groups were involved in several abduction and extortion cases in the past.

Surrender of insurgents in Manipur: On 18 May 2024, At least 34 cadres, belonging to the Pambei faction of the United National Liberation Front (UNLF), surrendered before Assam Rifles after they tried to cross-infiltrate into Manipur from Myanmar following an 'intense gunfight' in the conflict-torn country. Sources said the militants from the Valley-based insurgent group surrendered several automatic weapons before the Assam Rifles at Nambil in Tengnoupal district. Assam Rifles guards the largely unfenced Indo-Myanmar border. The source said the UNLF had an intense gunfight' with the People's Defence Force (PDF), a rebel group in Myanmar over the past few days, following which the militants tried to sneak into Manipur for safety. The PDF has been fighting against the military regime for the restoration of democracy in Myanmar.

Assam Rifles Conducts Wreath-Laying Ceremony; Pays Tributes To The Bravehearts Of "Operation Hifazat" on August 18, 2022. As per North East Today, the Lunglei Battalion of 23 Sector Assam Rifles under the aegis of Inspector General Assam Rifles (East), conducted a wreath-laying ceremony to pay tribute to 18 bravehearts of this unit who sacrificed their lives in a gunfight with terrorists during "OP Hifazat" at Manipur on Aug 18, 1994. It was a special operation launched under Maj Sirohi with one JCO and 30 OR in the area Sangkhomei - Willong on August 18, 1994. The party moved from Shakhomei via the Yangkhullen jungle area. As the party reached Yangkhonou, where GHQ of NSCN (IM) was located in a dense forest, the party came under fire from NSCN (IM). Nk Harka Bahadur Thapa and 17 other ranks of this unit without concern for their safety, moved across in a flash and showing great determination dashed toward the firing terrorists.

Decline of insurgency in Northeast India: On 13 November 2022, as published in the Deccan Herald, Northeast witnessed an 80% reduction in militancy-related incidents where 6000 militants surrendered since 2014 when the Narendra Modi government came to power at the Centre. Also, the signing of an agreement between Assam and Meghalaya in March 2022, resolved disputes in 65% of areas of difference. A document released by the MHA said that security forces dismantled the "satellite camps" of insurgent groups operating from foreign soil following which at least four peace agreements have been signed with insurgent groups in Assam and Tripura (Bodo Accord, Karbi Accord, Bru-Reang Refugee settlement and NLFT).

As per MHA, "The year 2019 and 2020 witnessed the lowest number of insurgency incidents and casualties of civilians and security forces during the last two decades. In comparison to the year 2014, there has been a reduction of 80 per cent in the incidents of insurgency in the year 2020,".

As of 2022, The document said that due to significant improvement in the security scenario, the areas under the Armed Forces (Special Powers) Act (AFSPA), 1967 have been reduced. In Assam, 60 percent of areas are now free from AFSPA while 15 police stations in six districts have been taken out of the purview of the disturbed areas. In Nagaland, the AFSPA has been removed from areas under 15 police stations and only three districts and two police stations in another district in Arunachal Pradesh are under the AFSPA now. The act has been completely withdrawn from Meghalaya and Tripura.

On 28 May 2020, as published in The Indian Express, Anti-insurgency operations in the Northeast led to 2259 surrenders in 2020. There has been a decrease in insurgency incidents in the Northeast with reports of only 69 incidents taking place as of 2020 till now. Army's anti-insurgency operations in the northeastern states as of 2020 have achieved maximum surrenders with minimum collateral damage. Also, with the support of the Myanmar Army, key insurgent leaders have been repatriated from neighboring Myanmar. As per the data shared by security forces, while as many as 2259 insurgents have surrendered, 261 have been arrested so far. There has been a decrease in insurgency incidents with reports of only 69 incidents taking place this year till now. Sources added that the surrender of 382 arms as of 2020 is the largest in recent years.

The sources attributed the success of operations to the strengthening of ties with Myanmar. There were 223 insurgent incidents in 2019. Sources added that the good relationship with Myanmar has given a major boost to operations and building pressure on the insurgent groups.

As per sources, there are more than 40 camps of Indian Insurgent Groups (IIGs) in various clusters in Myanmar. Close cooperation between the Myanmar Army (MA) and the Indian Army resulted in

MA carrying out 'OPERATION SUNRISE' against IIGs in three phases - between January and May 2019 and in March 2020. During these operations, 26 cadres were apprehended and awarded two years of imprisonment in Myanmar. Further, Sustained efforts by ministries and various agencies concerned resulted in handing over 22 Indian-origin cadres to Indian authorities on May 15. This is also the first time that such a large number of insurgents have been repatriated to India.

Prominent leaders and cadres of NDFB(S), KLO, PLA, UNLF, PREPAK (Pro), and KYKL have been repatriated and are presently under quarantine at Imphal and Guwahati. They were interrogated followed by legal proceedings. Among those repatriated are some senior and long-wanted insurgent leaders viz SS Home Secretary of NDFB (S) Rajen Daimary, Capt Sanatomba Ningthoujam of UNLF, and Lt Pashuram Laishram of PREPAK(Pro).

This has provided much-required relief to the civil population from extortion and other illegal activities of these groups. Since 2015, a total of 1910 insurgent incidents have taken place leading to 3118 surrenders, 6096 arrests with 696 arms surrenders, and 2675 arms recoveries. During this time 177 civilians and 362 insurgents were killed.

To join the mainstream and give up violence, as many as eight militants of the Kuki Tribal Union (KTU) surrendered at 11 Assam Rifles camp based near Sarkari Bagan at Haflong in the presence of top officials of the paramilitary force. All surrendered cadres are breakaway members of the militant group Kuki Revolutionary Army (KRA), who later joined the KTU." The group mainly operates in Kuki-dominated areas of Nagaland, Dima Hasao, and Karbi Anglong in Assam and Manipur. The group had recently started collecting taxes in the Kuki areas of Jiribam and Tamenglong. " The group is affiliated to the NSCN (IM) and was receiving training from the outfit at Hebron camp in Nagaland. Their demand letters include both KTU and NSCN seals. It is said that KTU is the wing of NSCN (IM) since it is the only Kuki militant organization working closely with the NSCN (IM), It is to be mentioned that KTU /NSCN/GPRN was formed in the early 1960s as part of the NSCN-IM and is headquartered at Hebron in Nagaland.

Surrender of insurgents in Arunachal Pradesh: As of 12 March 2023, published in Deccan Herald, Arunachal Pradesh moved a step towards being an insurgency-free state with the surrender of 15 cadres belonging to Eastern Naga National Government (ENNG), a Naga rebel group and its president. The insurgents laid down their weapons before Arunachal Pradesh Chief Minister Pema Khandu and officers of police and Assam Rifles personnel at Itanagar. Arunachal CM Pema Khandu said although Arunachal Pradesh does not have a "homegrown" insurgent group, activities of ENNG kept the state's eastern region, comprising Tirap, Changlang, and Longding districts troubled for long. The surrender of the ENNG rebels will go a long way in making our state insurgency free too,". Activities by Naga insurgent groups, originating from neighboring Nagaland, have remained a concern in Tirap, Changlang, and Longding districts--popularly called the TCL region. However constant operations by the security forces led to the arrest of several militant leaders in the TCL region that shares a border with Myanmar. The state remains under peace more or less in history but the proximity of the state with Myanmar and Nagaland border is gradually afflicting insurgency in recent times.

The only case of indigenous insurgency movement in Arunachal Pradesh was the rise of the Arunachal Dragon Force (ADF), which was rechristened as East India Liberation Front (EALF) in 2001.

Surrender of insurgents in Mizoram: As of Apr 14, 2018, published in Hindustan Times, Over 100 militants of Hmar People's Convention-Democratic (HPC-D), Mizoram's last active rebel outfit, surrendered and laid down arms. The 'homecoming' ceremony of the rebels including its leaders and cadres at the Central Training Institute, Sesawng, 39 km from Aizawl, was attended by Mizoram chief minister Lal Thanhawla and several senior dignitaries. The surrender and laying down of arms, which follows the signing of a peace agreement on April 2 between HPC-D and the state government is expected to bring lasting peace to the northeastern state. "A total of 102 armed cadres of HPC-D and 12 civilian members of the outfit took part. The surrendered militants, clad in olive green outfits, also laid down 44 sophisticated weapons and thousands of rounds of ammunition. According to the peace deal, the Sinlung Hills Development Council (SHDC) in Mizoram would be renamed as Sinlung Hills Council by an Act of the state legislature. The new council would have administrative autonomy. The agreement stipulates the state government would grant amnesty to HPC-D cadres who have criminal cases pending against them and also take steps to provide relief and rehabilitation to surrendered militants.

The founder of the group - Lalhmingthanga Sanate - who heads another faction is in jail. Mizoram government says the faction isn't strong enough to disrupt peace. "Mizoram is a small state and can't afford the creation of another district as demanded by Lalhmingthang's faction. They are a small gang and isn't that significant," Mizoram home minister R Lalzirliana had said at the signing of the peace accord.
Dialogue with the Mizo National Front (M.N.F) remains the only example of the culmination of a successful peace process that ended militancy in Mizoram in 1986. Other peace deals such as the Shillong Accord in 1975 with the N.N.C. in Nagaland, the 1988 agreement with the Tripura National Volunteers in Tripura and The Bodoland Autonomous Council agreement of 1993 with the Bodo militants in Assam are also in effect, but with limited success.

Rehabilitation scheme by Central Government: Under the Revised Scheme for Surrender-Cum Rehabilitation of Militants in the North East States, 2018 of the Union Ministry of Home Affairs, rehabilitation benefits to be given to the surrendered cadres include a one-time financial grant of Rs 4 lakh to each surrendered cadre, which is to be kept in their respective bank accounts as a fixed deposit for three years, monthly stipends of Rs 6,000 per person and incentives for surrendered weapons.

11. International conspiracy on Northeast destabilisation.

Bangladesh, China, and Myanmar are the external factors of unrest in Northeast India and are somewhere backed by the USA and its policies as per reports.

China and its destabilizing strategies are: Abduction, Expansion, Land disputes, and Hydro war.

As of 5 Sept 2020, Chinese Army abducts 5 villagers from Arunachal Pradesh: The People's Liberation Army (PLA) of China has captured five people from the Nacho village of the Upper Subansiri district of Arunachal Pradesh along the Border. This kind of activity is carried out in the border areas very frequently due to its low demarcation, dangerous terrain, and climatic conditions. This helps the Chinese agency in spying activities in North-east India. Similar kinds of activities were carried by the PLA on 29th of March 2020, whereas the abducted man was released after a month through various meetings by the Indian counterparts.

China's policy of war-mongering and harassing the Indian government through their notorious tactics of disrupting the peace of the tribals living at the edge of the Indo-Chinese border continuously. Just like Ladakh and Doklam the PLAs are creating a nuisance while patrolling along the border, they try to enter the remote villages and try to create a problem so that the Indian Government lies at the bottom during the talks with Chinese counterparts. Arunachal Pradesh which is claimed by China as a part of the Tibet Autonomous Region is a very influential and tactical game plan to divert attention and open a new front besides Ladakh and Doklam.

The core problem with China's LAC is the improper demarcation of the border between two giant nuke nations. Starting from Ladakh to the remote parts of Arunachal Pradesh there are thousands of kilometers of demarcated border due to its heavy dangerous climatic conditions and terrain, which leads to a rise in tensions. In Arunachal itself there are hundreds of kilometers of unguarded land located in extremely remote, sometimes it takes more than 10 days to reach the demarcation line from the Military base of ITBP. Although the Indian Government is keeping an eye on these areas through proper surveillance, still the Government needs more infra development.

China's Thousand grains of sand strategy: This strategy or technique talks about the strong Chinese spying network across the globe through which they are able to collect the weak points of their foe nations by continuously keeping eyes on them. This name was given by a former China Analyst for FBI "Paul Moore". This kind of technique is very unique and different from the previous age old technique used by USA, USSR, Israel, India and other nations. Presently China is considered as to be the most potential threat for the USA rather than Russia. Although world media keeps more focus on Russia, how it infiltrated the 2016 US elections whereas China has opened a six front war against USA through their economy, diplomacy, infrastructure, education, technology and military by their daily cyberattacks. Paul Moore explains this strategy by means a sea beach. Suppose a beach is the target and countries are trying to collect information from the beach. What Russian will do? They will simply send a submarine, which will go near the beach and during the night the spyer will visit the shore a collect bucket full of sand, further which will be send to Russia for investigation. What US will do? They will launch many satellites through which they will be able to collect data. But what will the Chinese do? They will send a Thousand tourists and will assign them a task of collecting a grain of sand. After they return the Chinese would end up knowing more about the sand than anyone else without more investing and involving than Russia and USA. This strategy of China shows their infinite amount of patience in spying. They are willing to wait for decades to plant their spies in foes investigation agencies.

How they operate: By sending tourists, students through their Confucius Institute, which are spreaded in maximum number of countries, and further keeping a proper track on them. They collects small amount of data which will further lead to the bigger picture. Infiltration by Chinese nationals or students caught spying in India.

Palm and its five finger strategy of China: In the year 1949, People's Republic of China (PRC) was formed as a Communist country and Mao Zedong became its Supreme leader by overthrowing the Republic of China (Nationalist) presently known as Taiwan in a Civil War. This is the reason behind the One China policy, which is aggressively promoted by the Chinese Community Party (CCP) of the PRC through debt trap financing of its Belt and Road Initiative (BRI). One China policy is claiming the entire Taiwan as PRC. In the year 1950, the PRC annexed Tibet and made it an Autonomous Region by overthrowing the 14th Dalai Lama Government. After many disagreements and rebellions, the 14th Dalai Lama fled to Dharamsala, India in the year 1959 and formed a government in exile. After the annexation, Mao Zedong was heard saying informally that Tibet is a palm whereas Ladakh, Nepal, Sikkim, Bhutan, and Arunachal Pradesh are its five fingers and with due course of time China will go to any extent to gain its five fingers as its Territories. This strategy was neither said nor written formally by the CCP of the PRC but was used as propaganda material during the 1950s. During the 50s, it was written in various Chinese books and was a nationalistic discussion between the soldiers that were deployed in the region of Tibet. Now there is a reason why Mao Zedong wanted to annex Tibet and its fingers, and it was the Qing Dynasty that ruled China during the 16th century, which had a suzerine control of the Territories of Tibet, Nepal, NEFA (Present day Arunachal Pradesh), Myanmar and other South Asian nations and annexation of Tibet was the beginning of fulfilling the dream of having a greater China.

McMahon Line: This demarcation line was drawn between British India and the Tibetan government between the Indian state of Arunachal Pradesh then the North-east Frontier Agency (NEFA) and Tibet, which had suddenly changed to China. The annexation brought five new neighbors for the Chinese Communist government, where they had an earlier understanding with the Tibetan government in case of border issues but since the Chinese had an expansionist mentality therefore disputes were on their way.

Disputed Territory: Making it a disputed Territory by claiming its sovereignty by China will bring no investment for the state because no countries in the world are willing to invest in any disputed territory which will make the land dependable for investment in the country that controls it, and if the country fails to develop the state that will bring a major set back for the people residing there, also they will lose faith and get attracted towards its neighborhood.

In the year 1914, the demarcation of the border was done as per the Shimla convention between the British and the Tibetan government, which is the highest crest line of the Himalayas and named McMahon Line after British Secretary Henry McMahon. Adding the difference between the Line of Actual Control (LAC) and the McMahon Line is LAC is the border or demarcation line between Ladakh, Himachal Pradesh, Uttarakhand, and Tibet Autonomous Region of China which was coined by Chinese premier Zhou Enlai in 1959 note to Indian Prime Minister Jawaharlal Nehru and was accepted by both India and China in 1993 bilateral agreement after the 1962 Sino-Indian War.

Reasons: China claims Arunachal Pradesh is a part of South Tibet, and Tibet was always been a part of China and its Qing Dynasty. As Tibet was not a sovereign state therefore it didn't have the power to sign treaties as a result China doesn't accept the 1914 McMahon Line between British India and Tibet. Tawang is culturally connected to Tibet which was accepted by Dalai Lama till 2007 that Tawang was a part of Tibet.

China's Projected Dam on Brahmaputra River: China is going to build a super dam on the Brahmaputra River (Yangtze River) that will be more humongous than the world's largest hydro-powered three Gorges dam in Central China. The Dam will work as a trigger for the Chinese Communist government for both India and Bangladesh because it will give China an upper hand on the natural resources if they start storing the water in its reservoir, the river will face water shortage whereas if they release water suddenly it can cause massive damage.

India's countermeasures and development: India is looking forward to building a massive dam and a reservoir in Arunachal Pradesh, the dam will protect against the sudden release of water from Chinese territory, which can create heavy floods in the plains of Assam whereas the reservoir will help in storing water and releasing them during shortage. As per the study, the Brahmaputra also known as Siang in Arunachal Pradesh gets 90% of the water from its tributaries, all thanks to the beautiful monsoon of the North-east which clearly states that we aren't completely dependent on China. Moreover, the dam can create 10,000 MW of electricity which will the rural electrification in Arunachal Pradesh.

The bigger picture is related to fundraising because Arunachal Pradesh is a disputed Territory per China. After all, the Chinese have a claim on Arunachal Pradesh as a part of South Tibet which ceases all sorts of investment for the region because neither the World Bank nor Asian Development Bank or any Country funds any development work in any disputed territory and if they do, China block it. So India can approach USA or Japan and if they show their interest in investing that will be a big blow to China and a key development for the state of Arunachal.

Natural resources Vanadium, a rich metal in Arunachal is very near to possibility: As per the World's various top geologists and the Geological Survey of India, Arunachal Pradesh is very rich in minerals and resources, which makes our land more luring to the encroaching neighbors. As of Jan 2021, Vanadium has been found in the palaeo-proterozoic carbonaceous phyllite rocks in the Depo and Tamang areas of Arunachal Pradesh. This was the first report of a primary deposit of vanadium in India. The Exploration is being carried out by the Geological Survey of India (GSI). Vanadium is a High-value metal used to strengthen steel and titanium. Vanadium mineralization in Arunachal Pradesh is geologically similar to the "stone coal" vanadium deposits of China in carbonaceous shale. Vanadium steel is used in gears, bicycle frames, axles, and other critical components. 85% of the Vanadium produced in the world is used as a steel additive. India consumes 3,360 metric tonnes of vanadium annually. This is 4% of Vanadium consumed by the world. China produces 57% of the world's vanadium and consumes 44% of this metal. The largest deposits are in China, followed by Russia and South Africa.

<u>Myanmar</u>

Indian-insurgent involvement in Myanmar (then called Burma) began in the 1950s when the leader of the successionist Naga National Council, Angami Zapu Phizo, encouraged the Naga people of Burma to join the separatist revolt. In 1962, a misunderstanding occurred in India-Myanmar relations which led to Myanmar allowing Indian insurgents in its territory. In 1963, one of the largest Naga rebel columns, led by Dusoi Chakesang, traveled to East Pakistan through the Chin Hills. In January 1967, members of the Naga National Council traveled through Myanmar's Naga Hills To Yunnan to seek Chinese backing for their cause, which the Chinese would accept. In the later 1960s Indian Prime Minister Indira Gandhi began improving relations with Burmese dictator Ne Win, leading to the Tatmadaw Agreeing to crack down on Naga and Mizo rebels heading to China for training.

Starting in the late 1970s, several major insurgent groups -many of which are active in Myanmar- were founded. These include the:

People's Revolutionary Party of Kangleipak (1977)
People's Liberation Army of Manipur (1978)
United Liberation Front of Asom (1979)
National Socialist Council of Nagaland (1980)
Kangleipak Communist Party (1980)
National Democratic Front of Bodoland (1986)
National Liberation Front of Tripura (1989)
All Tripura Tiger Force(1990)

The ultimate round and-round story behind the story of the Northeastern insurgents led by Myanmar is the separation of Pro Democracy and Anti Democracy Military Junta government of Myanmar which led to the rise of many insurgent groups within the state of Myanmar where the Northeast insurgents backs or getting backed by either of the two or the Myanmar led insurgents. This makes the story more confusing and truly relies on international relations with the present government of Myanmar.

With the help of Myanmar many Indian-led operations, including Operation Golden Bird in 1995, Operation Hot Pursuit in 2015, or Operation Sunrise I and II in 2019, concluded in the areas where these insurgent groups are active and have scarcely experienced fighting. Amid the escalation of civil war in Myanmar in 2021, several sources claim that the majority of Indian ethnic armed organizations (IEAOs) are allied, or have some level of understanding, with the ruling military junta of Myanmar, which allows them to maintain bases inside mountainous areas of northern Myanmar, typically in return for the IEAOs attacking anti-junta resistance groups.

Conclusion

Only after Independence and re-organization of the States was a semblance of real Government, authority and administration brought into these far-flung areas. This was strongly resented by the newly educated elite of the tribal societies, who construed the efforts of the Government as an encroachment on their tribal way of life and freedom. Thus, based on racial, cultural, and religious differences from the majority stock of the plains, insurgency in NE India came into being.

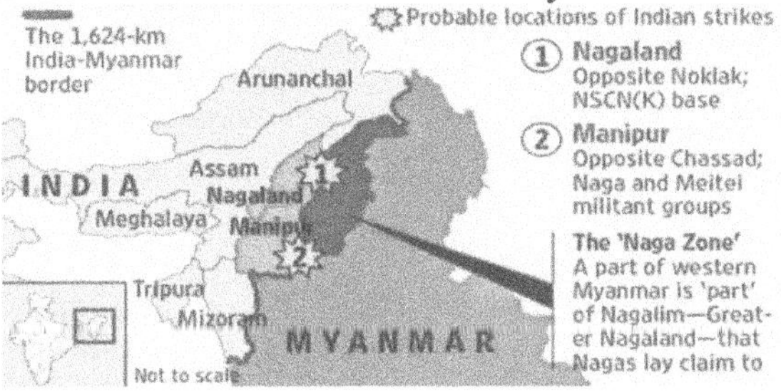

Issues of ideology are by and large irrelevant to the insurgency movements of the NE region. The single predominant factor that has withstood the test of time in this regard is either ethnic (such as in Assam and Tripura) or tribal as in Nagaland. It has also been seen that, within a particular State, insurgency by one set of tribals raises its head, finds roots spreads, and then dies with an agreement with the Government. Thereafter, in the same geographical area, another lesser tribe/sub-tribe undergoes the same cycle.

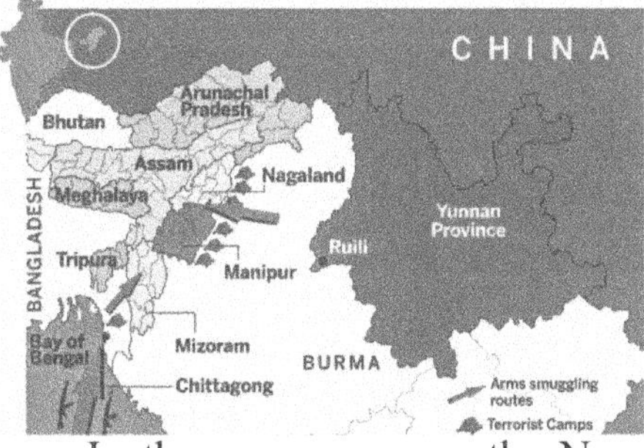

This is Mizoram, once the Lushai insurgency came to an end, we had the Hmars up in arms. In the same manner, the Naga insurgency once spearheaded by the Semas has now passed into the hands of the Konyaks in Northern Nagaland and the Tangkhuls in Southern Nagaland and NE Manipur with the once-dominant Semas and Angamis relegated largely to the sidelines. Similar to the Bodos, the Karbi Anglongs of Assam are showing all the signs of the itch to raise yet another movement. Thus it is evident that even if, at the point of origin ideology had any role to play, in the long run, it is the ethnic and tribal perceptions that truly matter.

The insurgency in our NE states first manifested itself in Nagaland and thereafter mushroomed to other areas. The insurgency in Nagaland has thus, in a sense, been an umbrella for all other insurgencies in the region. It is essential to know the historical context leading to these insurgencies.

The map of the NE has been altered with new lines drawn to recognise new political and administrative realities. The names of these entities have changed; the Naga Hills has become Nagaland, the Lushai Hills has changed to Mizoram and the North Eastern Frontier Agency, still known to many simply as NEFA, has become Arunachal Pradesh.

The jungles of SE Asia sweep down from Bhutan and Arunachal Pradesh across seven other nations – Bangladesh, Myanmar, Thailand, Laos, Kampuchea, Malaysia, and Vietnam-spanning political boundaries regardless of physical frontiers. Ethnic coalitions, oral traditions, and lifestyles based on respect for nature have mattered more in these regions than frontiers. Here men and women, with common origins but different nationalities, share a racial, historical, anthropological, and linguistic kinship that is more vital than their links with the mainstream political centers, especially at Delhi, Dhaka, Rangoon, or Yangon, as it is known today.

It is this affinity that has played a role in the unrest and insurgencies that have long troubled the NE of India. Affinity and Identity; these, more than any other factors, have represented the principal compulsions that triggered the Naga, Mizo, Meitei, Tripuri, and Assamese affirmation of separateness from the non-Mongolian communities that dominate the Indian subcontinent.

India's NE is a misshapen strip of land, linked to the rest of the country by a narrow corridor just 20 km wide at its slimmest, which is referred to as the "Siliguri Corridor". This region has been the battleground for generations of sub-national identities.

The anthropological composition of the inhabitants of North Eastern India presents a kaleidoscopic variety. Descendants of Aryan and Dravidian stocks co-mingle with the Indo-Burmese and Indo-Tibetan strains. Owing to its geographical isolation from the rest of India and the relative primitiveness of the tribal societies existing here, the region remained virtually cut off from the rest of India. From time immemorial till the near eclipse of the British Raj, and even to this day, this situation of isolation has continued in one form or the other.

To give a fair account of the feeling of non-"Indianness" of the tribal peoples, it is essential to understand that the phenomenon is more or less reciprocal with the rest of India being largely ignorant of the problems and privations of the peoples of NE India. One striking example of the psychological aloofness of the Indian people from this region is the massacre at Nellie in 1976. This incident in which over 3000 men, women, and children were slaughtered in one go, could engage Indian media attention for barely two weeks.

There is now a perceptible change in attitudes. The sheer scale and intensity of the ongoing political violence in Assam and the resultant continuous media coverage has brought about a situation where the rest of India is now aware of the existence of the region. Similarly, the opening of roads and related means of communication in the region has served, in conjunction with the spread of education, to bring about an awareness of the rest of India. The veritable flood of Hindi movies and their popularity in the region have also assisted in no small measure in this slow but sure process of absorption into the Indian mainstream.

Reference

https://indianarmy.nic.in/Site/FormTemplete/frmTempSimpleWithSixPara.aspx?MnId=dg9j7XZ5m4xV5cFEoHU0ew==&ParentID=wDlVgUql7PGl+AV+8hOGzg==
https://www.satp.org/backgrounder/india-insurgencynortheast-assam
https://www.iasgyan.in/daily-current-affairs/tribal-insurgencies-in-assam
https://www.idsa.in/publisher/issuebrief/bodo-karbi-and-dimasa-peace-agreements-in-assam-an-analysis/#:~:text=These%20Karbi%20insurgent%20groups%20are,%2DM%20(Mensing%20Kramsa)
https://www.satp.org/backgrounder/india-insurgencynortheast-nagaland
https://www.drishtiias.com/daily-updates/daily-news-analysis/naga-insurgency-1

https://en.m.wikipedia.org/wiki/Naga_Conflict

https://en.m.wikipedia.org/wiki/Insurgency_in_Tripura#:~:text=The%20insurgency%20in%20Tripura%20was,and%20was%20fueled%20by%20Tripuris.

How Tripura overcame insurgency: https://thg.page.link/AYaHw7wLRy5k6f6z8

https://tripurapolice.gov.in/PresentPhaseInsurgency

https://www.jstor.org/stable/4410771?seq=1

https://www.researchgate.net/publication/235558387_Ethnicity_and_Insurgency_in_Tripura

https://www.satp.org/satporgtp/publication/faultlines/volume14/Article6.htm

https://indianexpress.com/article/north-east-india/tripura/three-nlft-ultras-who-had-given-up-arms-arrested-for-working-with-outlawed-outfit-again-7179888/

https://indianexpress.com/article/north-east-india/tripura/tripura-extortion-notices-by-banned-insurgent-outfit-appear-in-border-village-6912709/

https://theprint.in/india/tripura-govt-will-deal-with-insurgents-with-a-firm-hand-says-chief-minister-biplab-kumar-deb/565795/

https://www.refworld.org/docid/469f389ac.html

https://m.economictimes.com/news/defence/militants-trying-to-reorganise-in-tripura-former-tripura-chief-minister-manik-sarkar/articleshow/77300018.cms

http://newsonair.com/News?title=Tripura%E2%80%99s-banned-insurgency-group-NLFT-(SD)-signs-agreement-with-centre-to-abjure-violence%2C-join-mainstream&id=369918

East-West Center Washington: Insurgencies in India'sNortheast: Conflict, Co-option & Change. No. 10, July 2007, by Subir Bhaumik. Subir Bhaumik is the Eastern India Correspondent for the BBC in Calcutta.

https://www.hindustantimes.com/india-news/80-reduction-in-insurgency-related-incidents-in-n-e-states-last-year-mha-data-101614676827488.html

https://www.jstor.org/stable/resrep06478?seq=1#metadata_info_tab_contents

https://usiofindia.org/publication/usi-journal/insurgency-in-north-east-india-genesis-and-prognosis/
https://thegeopolitics.com/the-origins-and-causes-of-insurgency-in-northeast-india/
https://www.drishtiias.com/to-the-points/paper3/north-east-insurgency
https://en.m.wikipedia.org/wiki/All_Tripura_Tiger_Force
https://en.m.wikipedia.org/wiki/Unlawful_Activities_(Prevention)_Act
https://en.m.wikipedia.org/wiki/Global_Terrorism_Database
https://en.m.wikipedia.org/wiki/Insurgency_in_Tripura
https://en.m.wikipedia.org/wiki/Tripuri_nationalism
https://www.google.com/search?safe=off&client=tablet-android-samsung-nf-rev1&sa=X&biw=800&bih=1334&sxsrf=ALeKk03Oi9B3B5jZfhdh-Z2An_U73Dc1xg:1621071573033&q=National+Liberation+Front+of+Tripura&stick=H4sIAAAAAAAAAONgFuLSz9U3MMkzLc8zV-IEsY2qivPStPic83Nz8_OCM1NSyxMrixexqvgllmTm5yXmKPhkJqUWgIkKbkX5eSUK-WkKIUWZBaVFiTtYGQGXWe_7UwAAAA&ved=2ahUKEwiQ-o-assvwAhXFQ3wKHUNgA0AQxA0wD3oECAoQBQ
https://en.m.wikipedia.org/wiki/Ranjit_Debbarma
https://en.m.wikipedia.org/wiki/All_Tripura_Tiger_Force
https://www.google.com/search?safe=off&client=tablet-android-samsung-nf-rev1&sxsrf=ALeKk02lIStuKD2Vy_Y-wIUQEHay36H2fg:1621071542299&q=Jamatia&stick=H4sIAAAAAAAAAONgVuLUz9U3SMuprKpaxMrulZibWJKZCAABOIhwFwAAAA&sa=X&ved=2ahUKEwjGnLyLssvwAhXTmuYKHerzD8wQmxMoAjASegQIDRAE&biw=800&bih=1334
https://www.google.com/search?safe=off&client=tablet-android-samsung-nf-rev1&sxsrf=ALeKk02lIStuKD2Vy_Y-wIUQEHay36H2fg:1621071542299&q=Biswamohan+Debbarma&stick=H4sIAAAAAAAAAONgVuLSz9U3MC2wMEiPX8Qq7JRZXJ6Ym5-RmKfgkpqUlFiUmwgAwSznAyQAAAA&sa=X&ved=2ahUKEwjGnLyLssvwAhXTmuYKHerzD8wQmxMoADASegQIDRAC&biw=800&bih=1334
https://en.m.wikipedia.org/wiki/Tripura

https://en.m.wikipedia.org/wiki/Government_of_Tripura
https://tripura.gov.in/
https://en.m.wikipedia.org/wiki/National_Liberation_Front_of_Tripura
D.N. Sahaya was Governor of Tripura from June 2003 and October 2009, and then of Chhattisgarh.)
https://www.satp.org/satporgtp/countries/india/states/tripura/terrorist_outfits/attf.htm
https://www.nextias.com/beyond-classroom/manipur-violence
http://cdpsindia.org/mizoram/insurgency-peace-process-overview/
B. Raman is Additional Secretary (retd), Cabinet Secretariat, Govt. of India, New Delhi, and, presently, Director, Institute For Topical Studies, Chennai
https://www.outlookindia.com/website/story/the-mizo-model/240401
https://theprint.in/defence/china-and-pak-supported-mizo-insurgency-reveals-mizo-national-front-leader-in-a-new-book/160979/

https://m.economictimes.com/opinion/et-commentary/air-attacks-in-mizoram-1966-our-dirty-little-secret/articleshow/18565883.cms?from=mdr
https://uca.edu/politicalscience/dadm-project/asiapacific-region/indiamizos-1960-present/
http://www.millenniumpost.in/mapping-the-states-of-india/insurgency-to-integration-458014?infinitescroll
https://indianexpress.com/article/opinion/columns/history-headline-when-mizoram-nearly-broke-away-insurgency-5484802/
https://www.skillsphere.org/tag/insurgency-in-mizoram/